South West Se

ISLE OF WIGHT TO THE SEVERN ESTUARY

Mark Rainsley

PESDA PRESS

WWW.PESDAPRESS.COM

First published in Great Britain 2008 by Pesda Press

Galeri 22, Doc Victoria
Caernarfon, Gwynedd
LL55 1SQ
Wales

Maps by Bute Cartographic.

Printed in Poland, produced by Polska Book.

Foreword

Having kayaked the entire coastline of the UK and Ireland I can say with some confidence that the South West offers the paddler some of the finest scenery to be found anywhere on our shores. The appeal goes beyond the physical beauty of this uniquely diverse section of coast. There is something spiritual about the experience; as if the myths and legends allow us to escape from the modern world, the distant horizons giving a sense of freedom and the movement of tide and wave provide an injection of youthful energy. Even though I now live thousands of miles away, the south-west of Britain is, and always will be, my home.

The magical Penwith peninsula of Cornwall is perhaps most famous as a world-class sea kayaking destination and whilst it has a very special place in my heart there are many other highlights. Dorset is a county of surprising contrast: the genteel serenity of Christchurch, the intriguing Jurassic coast and the wild expanse of Chesil Beach. Charming Lyme Regis was the venue for the start of my first kayak journey around the peninsula and is one of my favourite seaside towns. Devon's divided shoreline is characterized by the two moors that dominate the view inland. Dartmoor feeds the rivers that rush down its flanks before flowing more gracefully through the wooded hills of the South Hams and entering the English Channel via some of the most pristine estuaries you will find anywhere. The towering cliffs of the North Devon coast of Exmoor give way to the rolling hills and marshland of Somerset. But don't be fooled by the softer landscape. The grey waters of the Bristol Channel can be ferocious!

I have always been fascinated by islands, by the desire to circumnavigate. To start where you finish gives you a sense of completeness. The islands of the south-west of Britain may not be as prolific as those on the west coast of Scotland or Ireland but they are very special. If you could imagine your ideal sea kayaking destination: beautiful scenery, spectacular wildlife, great weather and lots of good pubs then the Isles of Scilly have it all in abundance. Lundy is a jewel, sparkling in the waters of the Celtic Sea, its charm irresistible but do check the weather as this island has a habit of welcoming you but being reluctant to let you leave.

South West Sea Kayaking is much more than a guide book. It is a monument to the author's yearning for discovery, his determination to complete a project and his generosity in wanting to share his knowledge with others. As well as being full of indispensable information to make your journey by kayak safer and more enjoyable this beautifully written book is resplendent with the finest images that together will inspire you to explore this incredible coastline for yourself.

Sean Morley

Contents

Contents

Coastal Access in South West England

Access to the outdoors in England is becoming increasingly encouraged (unless of course you wish to enjoy your fresh water river heritage by kayak, Heaven forbid) and the Countryside and Rights of Way Act (CRoW, 2000) has brought improved access to many areas of coastal land. Access problems are rarely encountered whilst sea kayaking. All of the routes in this book start and finish at beaches or harbours where public access to the foreshore is already established.

Areas of the coast between the high and low water mark are often described as 'foreshore' and most of this is owned by the Crown Estate. The Crown Estate does not normally restrict access to the foreshore. However, one unfortunate quirk of the South West is that the owners of several coastal islands attempt to deter or restrict landing by kayak, including some islands managed as public access nature reserves!

Access on the sea is restricted only in rare and extreme cases and information is given by the Coastguard during regular maritime safety information broadcasts. Access is frequently restricted in the vicinity of military firing ranges. These areas are usually patrolled by Ministry of Defence staff. Further information and firing times can always be obtained from the Coastguard.

At busy ports like Poole, Plymouth and Falmouth, advice should be sought from the harbour authority, either by VHF or mobile phone, before entering or crossing harbour entrances.

The south-west coast enjoys excellent public access due to a series of public footpaths. These include the 1,008km South West Coast Path National Trail extending between Poole and Minehead, the Isle of Wight Coastal Path, the West Somerset Coast Path and The Severn Way.

Further information can be obtained from www.countrysideaccess.gov.uk.

RESPECT THE INTERESTS OF OTHER PEOPLE

Acting with courtesy, consideration and awareness is essential. If you are exercising access rights, make sure that you respect the privacy, safety and livelihood of those living and working in the outdoors, and the needs of other people enjoying the outdoors. Maybe even jet skiers.

CARE FOR THE ENVIRONMENT

Sea kayakers are privileged to access remote places that others cannot. Many of these places have sensitive plant, animal and bird life. Be aware of and respect landing restrictions around nature reserves. Look after the places you visit, enjoy the land and leave it as you found it.

Natural England (www.naturalengland.org.uk) has created www.natureonthemap.org.uk, a source of incredibly detailed maps outlining protected habitats and sites. The Marine Conservation Society (www.mcsuk.org) offer advice on how to act appropriately around marine wildlife.

WILD CAMPING

This guide provides information on many commercial campsites. Although most are pleasant places, treat anything with 'Holiday Park' in the title with caution, if you value solitude and silence.

This author is happy to admit that he almost always camps 'wild' along the south-west coast, and has always been able to find an appropriate spot. Wild camping provides a special experience and forms an integral part of sea kayaking. There is no legally enshrined right to camp on the

English coast, and areas in the South West that *obviously* lend themselves to wild camping for sea kayakers are few and far between. Large groups requiring a roaring campfire and hearty sing-along are simply in the wrong region (and century?). There is however an established tradition of discreet wild camping being tolerated alongside the South West Coast Path for single tents and single nights, with permission sought from the farmer. The *Annual Guide* published by the SWCP Association (www.swcp.org.uk) offers useful advice in this respect.

If you decide to include a wild trip in your journey plans, choose a location away from dwellings and roads. Arrive late and do not pitch your tent until dusk. You should take down your tent early the following morning. *"Leave nothing but footprints and take nothing but photographs."*

Important Notice

As with many outdoor activities that take place in remote and potentially hostile environments, technical ability, understanding of the environment and good planning are essential. The sea is one of the most committing and unforgiving environments of all. With this considered, it should be treated with the constant respect that it deserves. This guide is designed to provide information that will inspire the sea kayaker to venture into this amazing environment; however it cannot provide the essential ingredients of ability, environmental awareness and good planning. Before venturing out on any of the trips described in this book, ensure that your knowledge and ability are appropriate to the seriousness of the trip. The book is purely a guide to provide information about sea kayaking trips. For the additional essential knowledge of safety at sea, personal paddling, environmental considerations and tidal planning, the author recommends gaining appropriate training and advice from experienced and qualified individuals.

WARNING

Sea kayaking is inherently a potentially dangerous sport. With this considered, users of this guide should take the appropriate precautions before undertaking any of the trips.

The information supplied in this book has been thoroughly researched; however the author can take no responsibility if tidal times differ or if the information supplied is not sufficient to negotiate the conditions experienced on the day. Conditions can change quickly and dramatically on the sea and there is no substitute for utilising personal experience and good judgement when kayaking or (arguably even more importantly) whilst planning a sea trip.

The guide is no substitute for personal ability, personal risk assessment and good judgement. Remember that the outdoors cannot be made risk free and that you should plan and act with care at all times for your own safety and that of others. The decision on whether to go out sea kayaking or not, and any consequences arising from that decision, remain yours and yours alone.

How to Use the Guide

To use the guide you will need an up-to-date tide timetable of the relevant area, the appropriate Ordnance Survey maps and the knowledge to use them. Unlike many inshore journeys in the UK, an Admiralty Tidal Stream Atlas is an important source of information for planning journeys around the south-west coast.

Each of the fifty trip chapters is set out into six sections:

Tidal & Route Information - This is designed as a quick reference for all the 'must know' information on which to plan the trip.

Introduction - This is designed to give the reader a brief overview of what to expect from the trip and whet the appetite.

Description - This provides further detail and information on the trip including the coastline, launching/landing points, the wildlife and environment, historical information and places of interest to visit.

Tide & Weather – Offering further tidal information and how best to plan the trip which takes the tides, weather and local knowledge into consideration.

Map of Route – This provides a visual outline of the route's start/finish points, landing places, points of interest and tidal information.

Additional Information – This section provides further information (including Admiralty Charts and other useful maps) that will complement the trip, or be of interest if in the local area.

Using the Tidal & Route Information

Each route begins with an overview of pertinent details beginning with the following information: grade of difficulty, trip name, route symbols, and trip number.

 Grade A | Relatively easy landings with escape routes easily available. Offering relative shelter from extreme conditions and ocean swell. Some tidal movement may be found, but easy to predict with no major tidal races or overfalls.

 Grade B | Some awkward landings and sections of coastline with no escape routes should be expected. Tidal movement, tidal races, overfalls, crossings, ocean swell and surf may be found on these trips. They will also be exposed to the weather and associated conditions.

 Grade C | These trips will have difficult landings and will have no escape routes for long sections of the trip. Fast tidal movement, tidal races, overfalls, extended crossings, ocean swell and surf will be found on all these trips. They will be very exposed to the weather and conditions, therefore require detailed planning and paddlers to be competent in rough water conditions. With this considered, the journey may require good conditions for the trip to be viable.

CIRCUMNAVIGATION   COASTAL PADDLING   SHELTERED   OPEN SEA CROSSING   NO LANDING ZONES   STRONG TIDAL EFFECTS   PORTAGE NECESSARY   VEHICLE SHUTTLE   FERRY SHUTTLE

ROUTE SYMBOLS

Distance	Total distance for the trip.
OS Sheet	Number of Ordnance Survey 1:50,000 Landranger map required.
Tidal Port	The port for which tide timetables will be required to work out the tidal streams.
Start	△ map symbol, name and six-figure grid reference of starting point.
Finish	◎ map symbol, name and six-figure grid reference of finishing point.
HW/LW	The high and/or low water time difference between local ports nearest to the trip and the tidal port.
Tidal Times	Location or area of tidal stream movement, the direction to which the tidal stream flows and the time it starts flowing in relation to the tidal port high water.
Max Rate Sp	The areas in which the tidal streams are fastest and the maximum speed in knots attained on the average spring tide.
Coastguard	Name of the relevant Coastguard Station.

MAP SYMBOLS

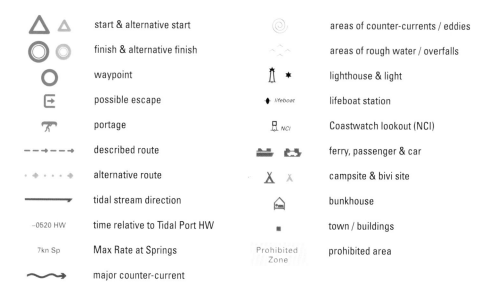

△ △ start & alternative start	◎ areas of counter-currents / eddies
◎ ◎ finish & alternative finish	‿‿‿ areas of rough water / overfalls
○ waypoint	🛆 ✳ lighthouse & light
⭲ possible escape	◆ lifeboat lifeboat station
ⵝ portage	🏛 NCI Coastwatch lookout (NCI)
– – ➔ – – ➔ described route	⛴ 🚗 ferry, passenger & car
· · ➔ · · ➔ alternative route	✕ ✕ campsite & bivi site
———➔ tidal stream direction	⌂ bunkhouse
–0520 HW time relative to Tidal Port HW	▪ town / buildings
7kn Sp Max Rate at Springs	Prohibited Zone prohibited area
∿➔ major counter-current	

About the Author
Mark Rainsley

Over 20 years ago, Mark was the only Scout in his troop to capsize and swim when they tried kayaking. Undismayed, he enrolled for an 'intro to whitewater' course run by Franco (of Pesda Press), who threw him upside-down in his kayak over a Welsh waterfall. Mark has since paddled whitewater in over twenty countries on six continents and made first descents. He also sits on the BCU Expeditions Committee and created the most popular UK paddling media, the UK Rivers and UK Sea Kayak websites. Unfortunately, the humiliating wipe-outs and swims continue.

Mark grew up near Britain's most inland point. For this reason, the sea has always retained a special allure for him, whilst retaining its air of mystery. After moving to the coast, Mark addressed this by buying a sea kayak and paddling solo around the South West. This 1997 paddle still ranks among his most cherished experiences. He has since sea paddled fanatically and has evangelically converted many other whitewater paddlers.

Acknowledgements

The author would like to express his thanks to all those who have assisted in the long process of bringing this book to fruition, not all of whom can be named here.

Special thanks to my lovely wife Heather, whose infinite patience and encouragement have been invaluable throughout.

Über-sea kayaker Sean Morley has been kind enough to share his love of the region with us in the foreword. AS Watersports in Exeter generously offered to host a launch party for the book. Numerous paddlers have offered their local knowledge and expertise to draft chapters, including Graham Beckram, Nick Benny, Eurion Brown, Owen Burson, Jonathan Crawford, Chris Dew, Liz Garnett, John Gilmour, Dillon Hughes, Chris Jones, Cailean Macleod, David Parker, Chris Peat and Richard Uren. Thanks also to those many folk who joined me on the water and politely endured endless detours and 'photo stops'.

Finally, thanks to Franco Ferrero (publisher) and Peter Wood (design) at Pesda Press, and Don Williams of Bute Cartogaphic (maps). Franco has been an inspiring and supportive editor, seemingly incapable of being fazed by anything at all.

Photographs

All photographs by Mark Rainsley, except where acknowledged in the captions.

The Isle of Wight

An introduction

Those living on the South Coast know it simply as 'The Island'. Despite being a very short distance offshore, the Isle of Wight is truly separate and distinct from the mainland. Its 150 square miles are often described as 'England in miniature' but a better description might be 'The 1950s in miniature' as there are unspoiled green rolling hills, quiet roads, chalk cliffs, 'kiss-me-quick' resorts, and sleepy villages.

It's possible that the Island is one of English sea kayaking's best kept secrets. The varied coastal scenery is a real gem, coupled with considerable historical and cultural interest. The north – Solent – coast is practically the world capital of sailing. The many forts attest to the Solent's continued strategic importance through the centuries. The busiest waterway in Britain, the Solent is not without natural beauty and quiet spots can be sought out. The south – Channel – coast is a total contrast, with little traffic and long sections of cliffs. The full circumnavigation of the Island comes highly recommended as a classic multi-day paddle. This mini-expedition should not be underestimated. In just 100km it slings pretty much everything at you; powerful tides, busy shipping, real exposure and commitment.

Environment

Over half of the Island is designated as an 'Area of Outstanding Natural Beauty', so you won't be surprised to learn that it's rather nice to look at. Two very different sections of the coast have been accorded special status; the 'Tennyson Heritage Coast' covers the entire south west coast and the 'Hamstead Heritage Coast' covers the north coast around the Newtown River.

About half of the eastern coast is within the AONB, although there are also some rather garish seaside towns.

Many of Wight's public campsites are loud and tacky. Thankfully, there are plenty of 'wild' camping spots to discover.

Tide and weather

Tide flows around the Island are very strong, but easy to grasp. The flood stream travelling up the English Channel simply parts at the Needles and forms parallel streams along the Solent and Channel coasts, rejoining off Foreland, the Eastern point. The ebb stream reverses the process, again with parallel streams.

Notable tide races form at the Needles and Saint Catherine's Point, with smaller races forming in Hurst narrows; 'The Trap'.

The Solent does of course offer sheltered waters, but the south-west segment of the Channel Coast regularly picks up the full Atlantic swell.

Background reading

Solent Cruising Companion, Derek Aslett, Nautical Data Ltd 2002, ISBN 190435811X

Solent Hazards, Peter Bruce, Boldre Marine 2001, ISBN 187168031X

Wight Hazards, Peter Bruce, Boldre Marine 2001, ISBN 1871680360

Solent Tides, Peter Bruce, Boldre Marine 1994, ISBN 1871680050

Diamond Coast - The Story of the Isle of Wight's Coast, Ian Williams, Dovecote Press 2004, ISBN 1904349153

Shell Channel Pilot, Tom Cunliffe, Imray 2006, ISBN 0-85288-894-5

Further information

www.wightaonb.org.uk – the Area of Outstanding Natural Beauty.

www.isleofwightweather.co.uk – tidal information and live weather.

The Needles

No. 1 | Grade B | 16km | OS Sheet 196 |

Tidal Port	Portsmouth
Start	△ Keyhaven (307 915)
Finish	○ Freshwater Bay (347 857)
HW/LW	HW Keyhaven is 1 hour and 15 minutes before HW Portsmouth at springs, and 5 minutes before HW Portsmouth at neaps. There is a 'long stand' due to the 'double HW' anomaly. LW is 30 minutes before LW Portsmouth.
Tidal Times	At Hurst Castle, the WSW going (ebb) stream starts 1 hour before HW Portsmouth. The ENE going (flood) stream starts 5 hours after HW Portsmouth.
Max Rate Sp	Between Hurst Castle and the IOW, 4.4 knots on the ebb and 3.9 knots on the flood.
Coastguard	Solent, tel. 02392 552100, routine VHF calls on Ch67 to avoid congestion, VHF weather 0130 UT

Introduction

The south coast's most famous landmark, and a centrepiece of Britain's maritime heritage! Paddling to the iconic red and white Needles lighthouse does not disappoint and an open crossing across tides and traffic adds a degree of commitment.

© Scratchell's Bay

Description

Keyhaven is a quiet backwater with several launching possibilities. At low water, only the slipway near the yacht club (tel. 01590 642165) is practical. Your first visible target is the lighthouse beside Hurst Castle; however there are no direct routes to it through Keyhaven Lake's tidal marshes. Follow a channel with boats moored, to avoid the many dead ends.

Curving Hurst Spit with its long squat castle (built for Henry VIII) guards the kilometre wide entrance to the Solent. A launch time in the last hours of the ebb will allow you to catch a tidal conveyor belt from the Spit, leading right to the Needles. Angle across to the Island or aim out direct for the Needles. A tidal race known as the 'Trap' forms off Hurst Castle on the ebb; nasty with wind from the south-west. The western end of the Solent is relatively quiet, but keep scanning for larger craft and pass around their sterns.

Paddling close in along the Island will slow the trip, as the ebb tide stream slackens in the successive bays. There are landing beaches all the way to Alum Bay, just short of the Needles themselves. Alum Bay's cliffs are famous for the multi-coloured strata of sand and clays.

It is only 1km from Alum Bay to the Needles. Even so, they feel exposed, with open water on three sides and 120m cliffs behind. The name derives from 'Lot's Wife', a 40m conical pillar which towered above the present stacks until being toppled by a 1764 gale.

As the tide floods back into the Solent, tide races form between and off the Needles. The first gap is treacherously shallow, and the reef has ripped keels off yachts during the annual Round the Island Race. The second gap was the location of Lot's Wife and even with small groundswell, waves disconcertingly break across it without warning. Regardless, you can't come this far and not visit the lighthouse.

The 33.25m perpendicular granite edifice was opened in 1859. James Walker designed it for Trinity House as the eighteenth-century lighthouse, located 60m up the chalk down, was ineffective in poor weather. The helipad was added in 1987 and the last keepers left in 1994. The light has red, green and white sectors. A night paddle will reveal that the different coloured beams form a nocturnal rainbow.

After exploring until the tide turns, you have a choice. You can ride the flood back to Hurst Spit, or you can 'turn the corner' and head 6km along the south coast to Freshwater Bay. Paddlers are dwarfed by epic cliffs reaching 130m at Tennyson Down. The only landing opportunity is the enclosed pebble beach of Scratchell's Bay, within sight of the Needles. Surf is common in Freshwater Bay.

VARIATIONS

The most likely reason for heading on to Freshwater is as part of the Island circumnavigation. One adventurous alternative is to trolley your boat 2km inland from Freshwater Bay to the Yar River, timing to arrive at local HW. It's then a pretty bimble downriver to Yarmouth harbour,

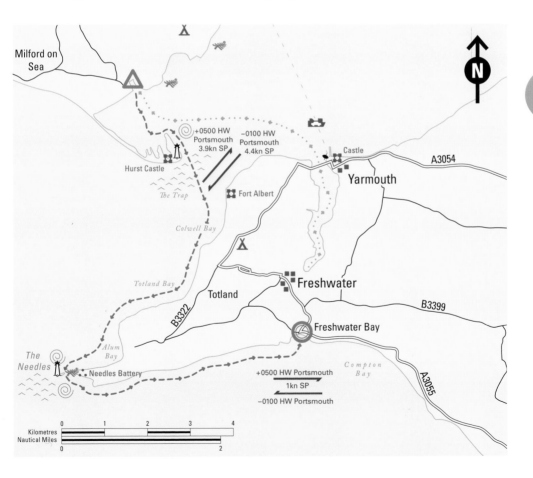

from whence you can paddle back to the mainland. A tide race forms west of Yarmouth on both the ebb and flood tides.

If crossing the Solent is too tame, and the Island too near to the mainland for your taste, then why not launch from Swanage? This 28km crossing links up the chalk strata between Old Harry Rocks and the Needles.

Tide and weather

The tide races at Hurst Point and the Needles break in south-west winds.

Groups have paddled to the Needles against the flood tide by hugging the Wight coast, assuming that the successive bays offer protection. They don't, there are no eddies. There is however little current in the bays during the ebb flow.

Solent CG make regular 'safety' broadcasts on Ch16 outlining traffic movements and giving amazingly detailed weather reports which break up the Island into four zones.

Additional information

Solent Coastguard is the UK's busiest station in terms of radio traffic, so communications work differently to the norm. If you call to outline your plans on VHF, they prefer initial contact to be made on Channel 67, rather than the standard Channel 16.

Hurst View campsite (317 936) is 2km from Keyhaven, tel. 01590 671648, www.hurstviewleisure.co.uk. Heathfield Farm (335 879) is 1km from Colwell Bay, tel. 01983 756756, www.heathfieldcamping.co.uk.

The Needles Battery

Consider the walk from Alum Bay up to the cliffs above the Needles. The National Trust manages the site, with its Victorian gun battery and tunnels through the cliffs. The 256lb guns mounted here had to be moved, as the cliffs began to disintegrate when they were fired! Bizarrely, the Needles are Britain's answer to Cape Canaveral. Perched on the cliffs are the remains of a space rocket testing facility which operated from 1956-71, developing the 'Black Knight' and 'Black Arrow' engines.

Wight Channel Coast ⊙⊟⊟⊠⊠⊖

2

No. 2 | Grade B | 44km | OS Sheet 96

Tidal Port	Portsmouth
Start	△ Freshwater Bay (347 857)
Finish	○ St Helens (637 895)
HW/LW	HW Bembridge Harbour is 20 minutes after HW Portsmouth at springs, and is at HW Portsmouth at neaps. LW is 1 hour after LW Portsmouth at springs, and 20 minutes after LW Portsmouth at neaps.
Tidal times	At Freshwater, the E going (flood) stream begins around 5 hours after HW Portsmouth. The W going (ebb) stream begins around 1 hour before HW Portsmouth.
	Between Saint Catherine's Point and Dunnose, the E going stream begins 5 hours after HW Portsmouth and the W going stream begins at HW Portsmouth.
	At Foreland, the tide starts to flow N into the Solent at about 2 hours before HW Portsmouth and ceases flowing N at about HW Portsmouth.
Max Rate Sp	Flows near Freshwater Bay are weak. They reach 5 knots close inshore near Saint Catherine's Point, but slacken offshore.
Coastguard	Solent, tel. 02392 552100, routine VHF calls on Ch67 to avoid congestion, VHF weather 0130 UT

Introduction

The south coast of the Isle of Wight is a big but achievable undertaking in one day, due to the powerful tidal streams. The highlight is the Island's southern tip at Saint Catherine's Point, a lovely location in itself and one of the south coast's biggest tide races. The latter half of this trip has some naff resorts to hurry past.

Description

Freshwater Bay is an appealing cove, a perfect launch spot if you just want to explore the nearby small stacks and caves. Victorian poet Tennyson spent four decades at Farringford House in Freshwater, trying to think of something to rhyme with *"... rode the Six Hundred"*.

The coast east of Freshwater is slightly monotonous, with low-lying red cliffs stretching to the horizon. These are unstable and you may spot dinosaur hunters rooting around among rock falls. They are a few million years too late for the real thing, but this is Europe's best spot for dinosaur fossil finds.

Local surfers take advantage of the reefs extending along this south-west coast, most notably the Brook Ledges, which begin 2.5km after Freshwater and extend for at least 4km along the shore, and the Atherfield Ledges which are found after about 12km. With groundswell, the breakers can extend a long way offshore.

This long quiet straight accumulates interest as you accelerate towards Saint Catherine's Point, a low plateau backed by cliffs and 200m hills. Impressive tide races extend around the Point, continuing for several kilometres and generating waves well over head-height at springs. Much of the race can often be avoided by staying close to shore, but be prepared to hit a series of eddy currents. If you stay far enough offshore to 'enjoy' the race, strong tidal streams flow long after the races have calmed. Ride this conveyor belt all the way past Ventnor to Dunnose and beyond.

As you enter the races, high above on St Catherine's Down is Saint Catherine's Oratory, known locally as the 'Pepperpot'. This is Britain's second oldest lighthouse, dating from around 1323. The currently operative lighthouse is 2km further on at the southern extremity. Trinity House erected the lighthouse after an 1836 hurricane dashed the 345 ton *Clarendon* into matchwood at Blackgang Chine, with the loss of most hands. One female victim eventually washed up in her father's garden at Southsea. The lighthouse is oddly truncated, subsequently having been shortened by 13 metres to avoid fog.

With the races cleared, you are better able to appreciate the Undercliff. This extends from Saint Catherine's Point past Ventnor, appearing from the water as a low-lying plateau backed by wooded cliffs. This attractive landscape actually results from numerous historical landslips, most recently in 2001.

Ventnor is a characteristically Victorian spa resort, offering the first easy landing since Freshwater Bay. It is most noted by paddlers for the seafront burger shop.

After Ventnor, the wooded vale of Luccombe Chine is quite beautiful. Shortly after, Shanklin Chine is similarly attractive but has been a tourist attraction since the nineteenth-century, with locked gates and 'fairytale' night-time illuminations! In 1944 the secret PLUTO (Pipeline Under The Ocean) ran through Shanklin Chine and thence underwater to Normandy, pumping 56,000 gallons of fuel a day to the D-Day forces.

The next 6km are dominated by the resorts of Shanklin and Sandown, with scenes plucked from a saucy '50s postcard. Steer your kayak amongst fat men on lilos, otherwise cross Sandown Bay direct to Culver Cliff. A Victorian holiday amusement was to be rowed out to take pot shots

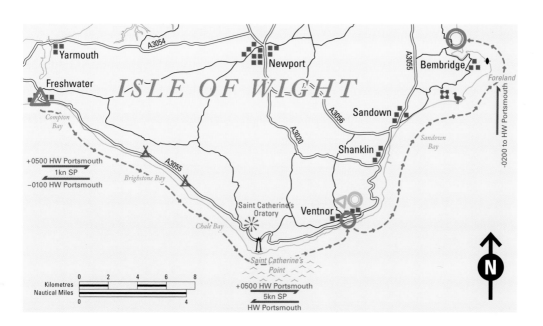

at the guillemots and fulmars nesting on the ledges. Culver Cliff suffered an enormous collapse in May 2007, a reminder that our coast is not a static environment. Just past Culver Cliff is Whitecliff Bay, where the beach café serves an impressive array of coffees and hot chocolates!

Foreland is the eastern tip of Wight, shielded by the Bembridge Ledges. During the last 2 hours of the flood tide, a strong stream flows north around Foreland and past Bembridge. Although Bembridge has parking just before the pier accessing the lifeboat station, it is worth using the tide to carry you 3km further to St Helens Beach daymark, just past Bembridge Harbour.

VARIATIONS

If you've come this far, you'll surely want to complete the paddle right around the island. For a shorter trip, consider starting or finishing at Ventnor (561 773).

Tide and weather

Atlantic groundswell generates surf along the reefs between Freshwater Bay and Saint Catherine's Point. Swell makes Saint Catherine's Point hair-raising.

Solent CG make regular 'safety' broadcasts on Ch16 outlining traffic movements and giving amazingly detailed weather reports which break up the island into four zones.

Additional information

Grange Farm (420 818) at Grange Chine, tel. 01983 740296, and Chine Farm (445 801) at Cowleaze Chine, tel. 01983 740228, www.chine-farm.co.uk, are both close to the beach.

© Sharing the water with 1,700 yachts during the Round-the-Island Race

Wight Solent Coast

No. 3 | Grade A | 37km | OS Sheet 196

Tidal Port	Portsmouth
Start	△ St Helens (637 895)
Finish	○ Yarmouth (353 898)
HW/LW	HW Bembridge Harbour is 20 minutes after HW Portsmouth at springs, and at HW Portsmouth at neaps. LW is 1 hour after LW Portsmouth at springs, and is 20 minutes after LW Portsmouth at neaps.
	HW Yarmouth is 1 hour and 5 minutes before HW Portsmouth at springs, and 5 minutes after HW Portsmouth at neaps. LW is 30 minutes before LW Portsmouth.
Tidal times	In the eastern half of the Solent, the WNW going (ebb) stream begins 1 hour and 30 minutes before HW Portsmouth. The ESE going (flood) stream begins 4 hours and 20 minutes after HW Portsmouth.
	In the central Solent, the W going stream begins 1 hour before HW Portsmouth. Around Cowes, a W going eddy forms an hour earlier.
	In the Medina River, the flood begins 5 hours and 30 minutes after HW Portsmouth and the ebb begins 15 minutes after HW Portsmouth.
Max Rate Sp	Streams reach 3.5 knots in the western half of the Solent and around Cowes, and maintain this rate close inshore. In the eastern half of the Solent, rates reach 2.5 knots. This rate

is maintained inshore from Ryde to Cowes for the first half of the ebb, but weakens as eddies form. Tides in the Solent are stronger on the ebb, subtract about half a knot for flood rates.

Coastguard   Solent, tel. 02392 552100, routine VHF calls Ch67 to avoid congestion, weather 0130 UT

Introduction

The Isle of Wight's Solent coast is a world away from the Channel coast. These are Britain's busiest waters, so keep an eye on the boats around you. Our top tip is to avoid the 40 knot 'Gin Palace' motor cruisers at all costs! Empty water is hard to find, but the traffic offers entertainment in itself and there are some beautiful spots to be explored.

Description

Outside Bembridge Harbour is The Duver, a beach allowing launching at HW. Park beside St Helens beach daymark, near a café. Offshore is St Helens Fort, the nearest of a defensive chain extending to Portsmouth. Portsmouth's Spinnaker Tower is a distinctive landmark for much of this trip.

The first obstacle is the resort of Ryde, defended by expanses of shallow sandbanks. Until the pier was completed in 1814, visitors to The Island were unceremoniously offloaded onto Ryde Sand, their luggage transferred 2km by mule to the shore. Ryde Sand can be frustrating to paddle across, with unexpected groundings common. Factor in the hovercraft ferries which scream across at regular intervals, and this isn't much fun. Simpler but more committing is to bypass it all by giving a wide berth offshore. Paddling out to the hulking No Man's Land Fort (639 937) lines you up for this.

After Ryde, sandy beaches and wooded shores lead to Wootton Creek, another ferry port. Shortly after, a stately boathouse and 'no landing' signs indicate that you are passing Queen Victoria's garden. Her opulent residence at Osbourne House overlooks the Solent across wide lawns. It is best viewed from a few hundred metres offshore, although a visit to the house proper is recommended on a spare day. The 2km to Old Castle Point passes wooded estate grounds backed by Norris Castle and fronted by a crumbling sea wall. Rounding Old Castle Point, you enter the daunting bustle of Cowes. On a summer's weekend, the traffic here resembles a motorway. The apparently straightforward crossing of the River Medina to the Royal Cowes Yacht Club might well be the most dangerous thing you ever do in a kayak.

A mere 3km past Cowes, the Solent changes character. The traffic eases and the coast is undeveloped. This is the Hamstead Heritage Coast, consisting of low-lying shores and marshy creeks around the Newtown River estuary. The estuary is a National Nature Reserve, home to innumerable terns and curlews. A paddle up to Shalfleet Quay for a walk to the New Inn (recipient of numerous Best Food awards) makes a civilised diversion.

The finish point is Yarmouth, perhaps the Island's prettiest harbour. To enter, you pass the pier and Yarmouth Castle, an unusually small and homely affair built in 1547 for Henry VIII.

Paddlers who have made the full circumnavigation will be looking onwards towards Keyhaven on the mainland, just a final 5km more across Hurst Narrows. A tide race forms just past Yarmouth.

VARIATIONS

The harbours and creeks of the Solent's north shore all have interest for paddlers, but are outside this book's remit.

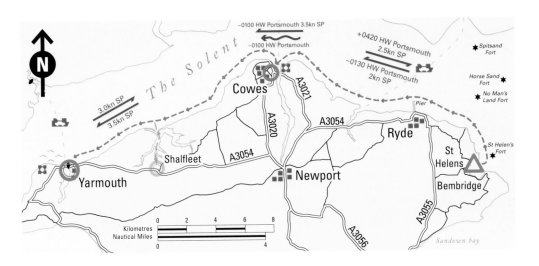

Lymington River

Tide and weather

This long trip literally whizzes past if the tide is fully utilised. The tide is strongest around Cowes and special care needs to be taken crossing the mouth of the Medina River, where holding back for ships entering or leaving Cowes can be challenging. The central Solent also sees massive ships being lead by pilot vessels into and out of Southampton Water. They have a vast turning circle; keep inshore.

Solent CG make regular 'safety' broadcasts on Ch16 outlining traffic movements (essential for this trip!) and giving amazingly detailed weather reports which break up the Island into four zones.

Additional information

Nodes Point Holiday Park (636 897) has good water access, tel. 0871 664 9758. Waverley Holiday Park (506 959) in East Cowes, tel. 01983 293452, www.waverley-park.co.uk, is 300m from the sea.

Dorset

An introduction

This region contains some of Britain's most stunning scenery and should feature on every paddler's wish list. It has inspired writers from Thomas Hardy to Enid Blyton! As a result of the region's complex geology, the variety of coastal landscapes is quite amazing.

The eastern edge of the Dorset coast is heavily developed, with the Bournemouth-Poole conurbation sprawling behind. The main thing to see here is sunburned flesh.

The remaining Dorset coast merits superlatives. Exploring the islands and creeks of Poole Harbour can offer surprising solitude and peace, despite being so close to 'civilisation'. The Isle of Purbeck showcases many impressive coastal landforms, some of which you'll recall from your geography lessons. Paddling 'around' the Isle is a classic overnight trip with major tide races and committing sections. A short open crossing can extend this trip to encompass the Isle of Portland and the infamous Portland Race.

Chesil Beach is another spectacular landform, although its 30km of monotonous pebbles is something of an acquired taste to paddle. The final reaches to the Devon border include the highest point on the south coast, Golden Cap, and the fossil haven of Lyme Regis.

Environment

Most of Dorset's coast is heavily managed and protected. The Purbeck and West Dorset Heritage Coasts encompass the majority of the county, and are themselves included in the 95 mile long Jurassic Coast World Heritage Site, which continues into Devon. The National Trust manages estates at Brownsea Island, Studland, Purbeck and Golden Cap. An unlikely environmental stakeholder is the Army, who maintain some of the finest parts of the Purbeck coast.

Tide and weather

Tidal flows along Dorset's coast are strong, with the exception of Weymouth Bay and Chesil Beach. The flood stream flows east and the ebb stream flows west, into and out of the English Channel. Several major tide races form along the coast, most notably off Portland Bill. Atlantic groundswell is uncommon this far up the channel, with any swell usually generated by relatively local storms.

Background reading

Inshore Along the Dorset Coast, Peter Bruce, Boldre Marine 2004, ISBN 1-871680-26-3

The Official Guide to the Jurassic Coast, Denys Brunden,
Coastal Publishing 2003, ISBN 0-9544845-0-9

The Jurassic Coast, Rodney Legg, Dorset Books 2002, ISBN 0-948699-77-9

Portland, Stuart Morris, Dovecote Press 1998, ISBN 1-874336-49-0

© Quarried cliffs near Dancing Ledge, Isle of Purbeck

Shipwrecks, Maureen Attwooll, Dovecote Press 1998, ISBN 1-874336-59-8

Tidal Streams between Portland Bill and St Albans Head, Peter Bruce, Boldre Marine 2003, ISBN 1-871680-16-6

Shell Channel Pilot, Tom Cunliffe, Imray 2006, ISBN 0-85288-894-5

West Country Cruising Companion, Mark Fishwick, Nautical Data Limited 2004, ISBN 1-90435-825-X

Further information

www.dorsetcoast.com – Dorset Coast forum.

www.jurassiccoast.com

www.theheritagecoast.co.uk – the World Heritage Site.

www.coastlink.org – local marine conservation.

Christchurch & Poole Bays

No. 4 | **Grade A** | **33km** | **OS Sheets 196 and 195**

Tidal Ports	Portsmouth, Poole and Dover
Start	△ Keyhaven (307 915)
Finish	◯ Sandbanks Beach (045 876)
HW/LW	HW Keyhaven at springs is 1 hour and 15 minutes before HW Portsmouth, and 5 minutes before HW Portsmouth at neaps. There is a 'long stand' due to the 'double HW' anomaly. LW is 30 minutes before LW Portsmouth.
	HW Christchurch Harbour is 2 hours and 10 minutes before HW Dover at Springs, and 1 hour and 40 minutes before HW Dover at neaps. There is a stand of 3 to 4 hours.
Tidal times	At Hurst Castle, the WSW going (ebb) stream starts 1 hour before HW Portsmouth. The ENE going (flood) stream starts 5 hours after HW Portsmouth.
	Along this coast, the W going stream begins 1 hour and 30 minutes before HW Portsmouth and the E going stream begins 4 hours and 45 minutes after HW Portsmouth.
Max Rate Sp	Between Hurst Castle and the IOW, the tidal stream reaches 4.4 knots on the ebb and 3.9 knots on the flood. In the Christchurch Harbour entrance ('The Run'), the flow can vary unpredictably from 3 to 7 knots. Inshore along Christchurch Bay and Bournemouth Bay, flows are weak and do not exceed 1 knot, except off Hengistbury Head.
Coastguard	Solent, tel. 02392 552100, routine VHF calls on Ch67, VHF weather 0130 UT. Portland, tel. 01305 760439, VHF weather 0130 UT

© Landing at Keyhaven, low tide

Introduction

This is the most developed coast in the South West and although it isn't going to win solitude awards, it's not an unpleasant day out. The buildings are mostly hidden beyond the cliffs, and Christchurch Harbour and Hengistbury Head are attractive enough.

Description

The quiet harbour of Keyhaven and surrounding Keyhaven Lake are described in route 1. Launch around local HW to speed you through the distance. Picking a route through the channels of Keyhaven Lake, you reach Hurst Castle and its lighthouse. On the ebb, 'The Trap' forms beside the castle, a tide race that will accelerate you out of the narrows across Christchurch Bay towards Hengistbury Head, a direct crossing of 9km with tidal assistance all the way. If you hug the coast, progress will be slower, but there is (slightly) more to hold your interest.

Shingle beach and groynes stretch past the unexciting towns of Milford on Sea (effectively a giant retirement home), Barton on Sea and Highcliffe. There are landmarks en route, such as the remains of the schooner *Lamorna* at Taddiford Gap (254 924), wrecked in the 1950s and visible at LW. The cliffs around Barton are eroding fast, with landslips, mudslides and (failed) defence works. The valley of Chewton Bunny denotes that you are crossing into Dorset (and also Portland Coastguard's territory) and then the grounds of nineteenth-century Highcliffe Castle are reached.

Christchurch Harbour entrance is known as The Run and generates strong flows on the ebb. Crossing The Run, you will encounter shifting sandbanks that can generate surf.

Hengistbury Head is the highest point on this coast. Archaeologists have established that this headland held a settlement from at least 10,000 BC, predating the English Channel! The Head's cliffs retreated considerably after ironstone rocks at the base were quarried in Victorian times. The groyne built to halt this erosion forms a tide race.

Three kilometres beyond Hengistbury Head, development encroaches once more. The beach, groynes and concrete esplanade stretch all 12km to Sandbanks, backed by the uninterrupted urban sprawl of Southbourne, Boscombe and Bournemouth. A typical summer's day will see the water crammed with up to 100,000 lobster-tanned bodies. All the paraphernalia which make up the classic British seaside holiday are here; deckchairs, funicular railways, ice cream stands, amusement arcades, fairground rides and, of course, the gaudy piers at Boscombe and Bournemouth, both dating from the 1880s. This now unfashionable 'kiss-me-quick' heritage has a certain charm.

The seafront at Bournemouth Pier is blighted by the vast and inappropriate IMAX cinema (voted the South's 'Most Hated Building' and closed in 2005). There is then a change of scenery as a series of 'Chines' are passed in the final leg to Sandbanks Beach. Chines are wooded valleys that interrupt the cliffs, the haunts of smugglers in the past. Now submerged beneath the sprawl of Bournemouth and Poole, they are the last hint that this developed coast was, until relatively recent times, a wild and unpopulated heathland. The railways have a lot to answer for.

VARIATIONS

A good place to divide this trip up is Avon Beach (188 921).

Exploring Christchurch Harbour is worthwhile. It is a shallow lagoon, making deviation from the buoyed channel unwise. Upstream where the Stour and Avon Rivers converge is Christchurch itself, with its imposing Norman Priory. The tidal River Avon splits into two arms that rejoin above the town, inviting an exploration of the 'Christchurch Loop'. Also consider following the River Stour to the tidal limit at Iford Bridge.

Tide and weather

Boscombe Pier was truncated in 2007 and work began on an artificial surfing reef. This project is breaking new territory and the effects of the reef upon the sea state and environment remain to be seen.

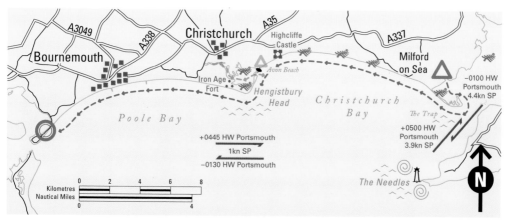

4

Additional information

Prior contact with the River Warden at Keyhaven, tel. 01590 645695, is a good idea if you have a large group.

Hurst View campsite (317 936) is two kilometres from Keyhaven, tel. 01590 671648 or visit www.hurstviewleisure.co.uk.

The 'Double High'

Tidal curves in Christchurch Bay, Poole Bay and Poole Harbour vary enormously between springs and neaps. Springs commonly feature a 'double high water' with a 'stand' in between. This disappears towards neaps when a more typical high/low pattern develops. HW times are very hard to predict and are affected by wind, atmospheric pressure and river flow levels. LW times are easier to predict, so these are the times usually supplied in tide tables.

Several interlinked factors cause the phenomenon, most notably the Solent's irregular shape and the funnelling of the English Channel's flow between Wight and Normandy's Cotentin Peninsula.

With thanks to John Gilmour, Swanage RNLI.

Poole Harbour
& Old Harry

No. 5 | **Grade B** | **26km** | **OS Sheet 195**

Tidal Ports	Poole Harbour, Portsmouth and Dover
Start	△ Wareham (924 872)
Finish	○ Swanage (035 787)
HW/LW	As for Poole Harbour. Local HW should be considered approximate, with tide tables only able to confirm times for LW! This is a consequence of the 'double high water' (see Route 4).
	HW at Swanage is 2 hours and 35 minutes before HW Dover at springs, and 1 hour and 20 minutes after HW Dover at neaps.
Tidal times	In Poole Harbour the flood stream runs for around 5 hours. The ebb stream runs in two segments totalling about 7 hours 30 minutes, with a short period of slack (or even mild flood) in between.
	At Poole Harbour entrance, the out-going (ebb) stream begins 1 hour and 20 minutes before, but does not become strong until 2 hours and 25 minutes after, HW Portsmouth. The in-going (flood) stream begins 5 hours and 50 minutes after HW Portsmouth.
Max Rate Sp	At Poole Harbour entrance, the flood rate reaches 3 knots and the ebb rate 4.7 knots.
Coastguard	Portland, tel. 01305 760439, VHF weather 0130 UT

Introduction

This journey involves travelling down through one of Europe's largest inland harbours and out to sea, taking in a wide variety of environments along the way. Despite never being far from a city of 140,000 people, you will find surprisingly peaceful and unspoilt locations.

Description

RIVER FROME

There is always enough water to paddle from Wareham Quay, but the best time for launching to complete this trip is local HW. Note the Saturday market that fills the Quayside car park. The twists of the River Frome double the distance to the harbour. Alternative launch spots are found at Redcliffe Farm (932 867) 1km downstream and also Ridge Wharf Marina (938 872) after 2km, with prior permission, tel. 01929 552650.

POOLE HARBOUR

Poole Harbour opens out as you pass marshy Gigger's Island. Sunken posts mark deep water channels. The harbour has an average depth of 48cm, so expect to run aground in silt or clay if you stray outside the marked channels. The solitude in the upper harbour can be impressive. The south shore is the little-visited Arne peninsula, an RSPB reserve. However, this shore is also the harbour's water-ski area, so expect loud and fast company at weekends.

The harbour narrows to 1km wide and development encroaches in the form of the garish caravans of Rockley Park; henceforth the north shore is always developed. Lake Pier (983 905) is another possible launch point, and home to Poole Harbour Canoe Club. Just past Lake Pier, beached landing craft denote *RM Poole*, the home of the Special Boat Service (SBS). Paddlers have encountered heavily armed SBS units on the harbour at night, also in kayaks. Don't upset them.

From Patchins Point, you have a choice of routes to the harbour entrance. The first option is to paddle along the busy north shores of the harbour, taking in Poole Quay with perhaps a quick diversion to the RNLI National Headquarters in Holes Bay. This route then passes through the kite-surf area at Whitley Lake and past the gardens of Sandbanks, the unlikely location of the world's fourth most expensive housing. The second and shortest route is to make the 2km crossing direct to Brownsea Island and pass it to the north or south. The third route from Patchins Point is the longest but quietest and most scenic, heading south to explore the creeks and islands along the southern rim of the harbour. There is a reclusive seal colony in this area, as well as the last bastion of our native red squirrel. The islands along the south side of the harbour are all privately owned. Long Island is the only uninhabited island and camping is possible with prior permission.

Whichever route you choose, all converge just inside the harbour entrance at Brownsea Road. If sea conditions outside do not suit, the trip can be finished by landing near South Haven Point (033 862).

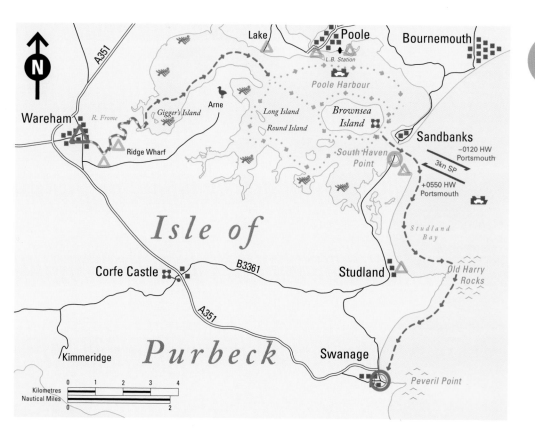

Poole Harbour & Old Harry

© Long Island landing

Approach the harbour entrance carefully. It is advisable to cross to the southern side of the channel early and hug the shore as you make your exit. A chain ferry criss-crosses the entrance every 20 minutes in daytime, traffic is constant and tide flows can be strong. Don't try to share the entrance with the 24,534 tonne ferry MV *Bretagne*!

OLD HARRY ROCKS

Paddle out past sandy Shell Bay and then after 1km you will spy Old Harry Rocks, 4km distant. You can either follow the line of markers towards Old Harry along the shallow 'training bank' delineating the inshore side of the shipping channel or choose to paddle inshore along Studland Bay. Studland is partly a naturist beach, be warned!

The wonderful eroded chalk stacks and caves of Old Harry Rocks reward close exploration and it is possible to land. The stacks point out from Handfast Point towards the Needles on the Isle of Wight, 28km across Bournemouth Bay. 'Old Harry' is an archaic name for Satan, and is generally used to describe the stack at the seaward end. In the nineteenth-century Harry had a wife, but he was widowed in 1896 when this accompanying stack collapsed into the sea.

A tide race forms off the outer edge of the rocks, an interesting place for playing (or being played with) when a swell is running. When leaving Old Harry, remaining inshore and out of the race is recommended, otherwise you miss the spectacular chalk spires and caves that follow. The cliffs stretch progressively higher, but fall away anticlimactically when you enter Swanage Bay.

A good spot to land is Monkey Beach (035 787) to the right of the pier on the southern side of the bay. There is a car park a hundred metres uphill.

VARIATIONS

The obvious variation on this trip is to shorten the journey by starting or finishing at Poole Harbour's entrance. Launch just inside the harbour after a short walk across dunes from the

Poole Harbour & Old Harry

road at South Haven Point (033 862). This is also a good spot from which to circumnavigate Brownsea Island, as is Baiter Park in Poole (019 902).

For something different, paddle the 'Wareham Loop' down the River Frome and up the River Piddle(!) back into town.

To explore Old Harry Rocks in isolation, park at the Bankes Arms in Studland village and carry several hundred metres down to the beach (041 825).

Tide and weather

Timed right, tidal flow will assist you all along this trip.

Poole Harbour offers a degree of shelter and this section of the trip can often be attempted when seas are foaming outside the entrance.

The tide race at Old Harry deserves respect, especially in swell. A sea kayak race in February 2007 saw the safety RIB being capsized, necessitating lifeboat and helicopter assistance.

Whilst exploring Old Harry, one very real hazard is the wake of Brittany Ferries approaching Poole Harbour. This causes a series of steep waves to break dramatically on the beaches and shallow reefs around the stacks, and the caves are not a good place to be at such times.

Additional information

Poole Harbour's rules and regulations can be found at www.phc.co.uk.

Permission for camping on Long Island was previously sought via Rempstone Estate Office, Cow Lane, Wareham, Dorset BH20 4RD. However, the island was up for sale in late 2007 (asking price £1 million!).

Brownsea Island

The largest of Poole Harbour's islands has been owned by the National Trust since 1963. Prior to this, Brownsea had a series of eccentric owners, latterly Mrs Bonham Christie who allowed the island to revert to wilderness and employed *'a blonde and powerful female Scandinavian PT instructor to throw visitors off the island'*. There is still a degree of privacy. The NT only permit landing at the visitors' pier near Branksea Castle (032 877) upon payment of a landing fee. Additionally, the island is closed to visitors between November and February. Unusually, landing between the high and low tide range is forbidden on Brownsea. All that noted, should you find yourself inadvertently forced ashore on Brownsea (say, by adverse weather?) then there are some points of interest near the beaches. The village of Maryland (011 882) was built for pottery workers in the nineteenth-century, but was torched in an attempt to divert Luftwaffe bombers from Poole town centre. The ruins are now overgrown. Brownsea is of course most famous for being the site of the first Scout Camp. A stone commemorates the spot (016 877) where, in 1907, Baden-Powell commenced Scouting for Boys.

© Purbeck Cave

The Isle of Purbeck ▰▰▰▰ ⬤ 6

No. 6 | Grade B | 19km | OS Sheet 195

Tidal Port	Dover
Start	△ Swanage (035 787)
Finish	◯ Kimmeridge (909 789)
HW/LW	HW Swanage is 2 hours and 35 minutes before HW Dover at springs, and 1 hour and 20 minutes after HW Dover at neaps.
Tidal times	At Peveril Point, the NNE going (flood) stream starts 5 hours after HW Dover. The SSW going (ebb) stream begins 2 hours and 15 minutes before HW Dover.
	At Durlston Head, the NE going stream starts 5 hours and 30 minutes after HW Dover. The SW going stream begins 30 minutes before HW Dover.
	At St Alban's Head, the E going stream begins around 5 hours and 45 minutes after HW Dover. The W going stream begins 15 minutes before HW Dover.
Max Rate Sp	At Peveril Point, the race reaches 3 knots when SSW going and 1.5 knots when NNE going. At Durlston Head, flows reach 3 knots in either direction. At St Alban's Head, flows can reach 4.7 knots in either direction.
Coastguard	Portland, tel. 01305 760439, VHF weather 0130 UT

Introduction

The Isle of Purbeck inspired that literary giant, Enid Blyton. She holidayed at Swanage thrice yearly for two decades. The smuggler's tunnels, cliffs and castle where the 'Famous Five' adventured are all hereabouts. This is a committing trip, with big tide races and few opportunities to land. This also happens to be the author's local (and favourite) paddle.

Description

Swanage is a lively seaside town with limited seafront parking. Best option is to drop your kayaks at Monkey Beach beside the pier and then drive to the car park just uphill.

Swanage pier is used for scuba training, watch where you stick your paddle! Passing the lifeboat station you begin to feel the gravitational pull of Peveril Point's tide race.

The Peveril ledges lead out to sea from the southern edge of Swanage Bay, forming an overfall that operates for the majority of the tidal cycle. With its easy access and inshore eddy, this is an ideal rough water training spot. Directly overlooking the ledges is a Coastwatch lookout station, inform them first if you are about to try anything dramatic.

Across Durlston Bay to the south, Durlston Head is recognisable by its overhanging cliffs and mock castle on top. Dolphins have been encountered here, but you'll be preoccupied with negotiating the Durlston race and its accompanying back eddy. As the race eases, you reach a major guillemot colony. Look out for the fixed camera that monitors the birds. As you pass Tilly Whim Caves and then the lighthouse of Anvil Point 45m above, the view that opens up is of 50m cliffs stretching almost unbroken to St Albans Head, 7km away.

You can paddle direct to St Alban's Head and utilise the tide flow, but exploring inshore comes recommended. You will see plenty of climbers at first, and pass the Ragged Rocks where the *Alexandranova* was wrecked with the loss of all hands in 1882. More recently, a brand new 40 foot yacht was destroyed here in May 2006. This story made the tabloids as the (recently divorced) owner jumped from the rocks onto the inshore lifeboat, abandoning his terrified girlfriend. Well, she had steered his yacht into the cliffs.

The cliffs form strange ledges, overhangs and caves. Whilst some of this is natural, much is due to extensive quarrying in the nineteenth and twentieth centuries. A series of large caves are encountered after Anvil Point, Long Hole and Blacker's Hole being the most notable.

Three platforms have been hewn at water level by quarrymen. You will successively encounter Dancing Ledge, Seacombe and Winspit. Landing on them is difficult, spare a thought for the quarrymen who manhandled vast blocks of granite onto ships here. Dancing Ledge with its shallow sloping reef is perhaps the easiest landing for kayaks. Explore the cliffs between the ledges closely; there are hidden caves and a tiny colony of puffins to discover, nestling among the many guillemots, razorbills and kittiwakes. Halfway between Seacombe and Winspit, a distinctive slab of rock angles up from the water. This is Halsewell Rock, close to where the East Indiaman *Halsewell* was driven whole into a cave during a 1786 snowstorm. Of the 240 souls on board, only 82 survived until dawn, when crew members scrambled up the rock to seek help.

St Alban's Head is named after Saint Aldheim, and features a beautiful twelfth-century chapel atop the cliffs, alongside a Coastwatch lookout. The headland accelerates towards you as the tide flow focuses around it, and the race can often be heard from miles away. You'll know you're entering the race when you spy the distinctive Anvil Rock on the cliffs above. The tide race can be massive on springs, with large waves stretching over 1km. With wind against tide, the waves break. The biggest waves can be avoided by staying very close to shore, but you will hit a sudden and powerful back eddy.

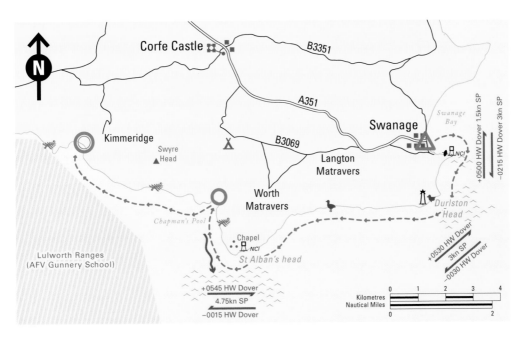

Swimming pool cut from Dancing Ledge

The Isle of Purbeck

6

From St Alban's Head, you can utilise the tide stream direct across open water towards Kimmeridge, or you can hug the coast. If the latter option is taken, after 1km you reach the rocky beach of Pier Bottom. A path rises from here directly up to the Chapel at St Alban's Head but landing is awkward. It is another kilometre to Chapman's Pool, the first good landing of the trip. Those who camp at this lovely secluded cove will spot the fisherman who thrashes his truck down a dirt track to the little breakwater and slipway early each morning, to check his lobsterpots.

Leaving Chapman's Pool, you pass Egmont Point, the scene of the SS *Treveal* tragedy.

The cliffs now completely change in character to the sombre greys and blacks of Kimmeridge shale. For the remaining 6km to Kimmeridge Bay, these cliffs form a slightly gloomy backdrop which is improved by heading offshore until you see the green curves of 203m Swyre Head behind. Another reason to stay offshore is the Kimmeridge Ledges. These shallow reefs stretch out for up to a kilometre, churning up world class surf when there is clean groundswell in the English Channel. On such days, stay out back! If there is no swell, paddle across the ledges and relish the clear water below. Spider crabs and lobsters scuttle about in full view.

Kimmeridge Bay is marked by the famous Black Tower on the cliffs. This nineteenth-century folly is currently being moved back from the crumbling cliffs and rebuilt, at epic expense. If there is surf, stay out back past the tower until you can see the clear route into the bay. Kimmeridge Bay has several slipways and car parks to choose from. The road to the bay is private. The Smedmore Estate may charge you for the pleasure, but note that they don't get up very early.

VARIATIONS

This could be combined with route 7 for a superlative weekend's paddling or overnight venture.

Tide and weather

A launch around HW Dover will allow a leisurely exploration of the coast as the races build up, whilst launching 2 hours after HW Dover at springs makes a turbo-charged 2 hour trip feasible.

The tide races are more pronounced during the ebb flow. Naturally, winds from the south and west make them more so. All of the races form pronounced eddies on the ebb, most notably at St Alban's Head where the counter-current extends back to Chapman's Pool.

Along the Kimmeridge Ledges, tide flows become much less discernable.

The Wreck of the Treveal

In January 1920, the 5,200 ton steamship SS *Treveal* left Portland in a sleet storm. Seeing her course, a Lloyd's officer laid a bet that she would hit the Kimmeridge Ledges. Within an hour she was indeed aground, at Egmont Point outside Chapman's Pool. After twelve hours of pounding by heavy seas, the ship had broken in two but was firmly grounded on the Kimmeridge Ledges and unable to sink. With waves breaking over the ship, the captain gave the order to abandon ship. The two ship's lifeboats turned side-on to the breaking waves and capsized. Despite heroism by local men and women who waded out to the drowning sailors, only seven of the forty-three strong crew came ashore alive. Cruelly, this might have been avoided; the *Treveal* survived the storm well enough for the galley fires to still be burning when it was eventually boarded by salvage teams. The bodies that were recovered are buried at nearby Worth Matravers.

Camping near Chapman's Pool

Additional information

Woody Hyde campsite (977 801) is inland at Corfe Castle, but central for the shuttle, tel. 01929 480274, www.woodyhyde.co.uk.

© Worbarrow Bay

Lulworth Cove ▨▨▨

No. 7 | Grade A | 26km | OS Sheets 194, 195

Tidal Ports	Portland and Dover
Start	△ Kimmeridge (909 789)
Finish	⬡ Weymouth (677 790)
HW/LW	HW between Kimmeridge and Weymouth occurs 4 hours and 45 minutes before HW Dover.
	HW Weymouth is at the same time as HW Portland.
Tidal times	The E going inshore flood stream begins 3 hours before HW Portland. The W flowing inshore ebb stream begins 3 hours after HW Portland.
Max Rate Sp	Flows reach up to 1.1 knots on the flood and 1.4 knots on the ebb.
Coastguard	Portland, tel. 01305 760439, VHF weather 0130 UT

Introduction

The western part of the Isle of Purbeck includes some of Britain's most unique and stunning coastal scenery. The dazzling white arches, coves and stacks feel out of place in gloomy Britain and seem more suited to the Mediterranean.

43

Description

Kimmeridge Bay is part of the Smedmore Estate, so you will have to pay a toll to drive down to the bay and use the car park. Kimmeridge is the home of the Purbeck Marine Wildlife Reserve, with underwater trails set up on the bedrock reef for snorkellers and divers. It's worth wandering into the Marine Centre building beside the slipway, to find out about their work.

The Army's Gunnery School begins at Broad Bench, the reef that forms the western end of Kimmeridge Bay. Give the Bench a wide berth unless you relish fast shallow surfing onto bedrock. On the far side, paddle beneath the daunting and unusual Gad Cliff, with its enormous overhanging blocks of limestone suspended far overhead. Peregrine falcons nest here. The shoreline is composed of smashed remnants of the cliffs above.

4km out of Kimmeridge, you reach Worbarrow Bay. The view that opens before you is surely a contender for England's prettiest scenery? The eastern entrance to the bay is guarded by Worbarrow Tout, a sliver of rock disconcertingly marked by a giant luminous target facing inland. Landing behind the Tout for a walk is recommended; follow the permitted range path for 1.5km inland to the ghost village of Tyneham. This was forcibly evacuated for military use during WWII. The Army subsequently reneged on their promise to return the village and today it remains empty and crumbling; 'The Village that died for England'.

Further around Worbarrow Bay is Arish Mell beach, with caves and a long tunnel hidden nearby. Beyond the beach you'll spy Lulworth Castle on the far edge of the military land. The blown up tanks here are nothing new, for this is where the very first tanks were trialled during

WWI. This new invention was so secret that local farmers were instructed to stand behind wicker screens whenever the tanks drove past.

Past Arish Mell, the bay becomes known as 'Mupe Bay', hemmed in by the Mupe Rocks, with an authentic smugglers' cave on the shore. For the final 2km to Lulworth, you leave the bay and follow vertical cliffs. This can be quite awkward in swell, as the waves bounce off erratically. Some fencing and a hut on the cliffs mark the point where the military land ends.

Lulworth Cove (824 799) is among the UK's most popular scenic attractions, and needs little introduction. Wave action has broken a gap through the limestone cliffs to erode a perfectly sculpted arc out of the softer rock behind. If you wish to break up this trip, this is the most convenient place to land or launch between Kimmeridge and Weymouth. You will however have to contend with real crowds in summer. The expensive car park is probably big enough to be visible from space, but is awkwardly located several hundred metres from the water. Driving a vehicle down to the water's edge to off-load is permitted early morning and during the winter months. Otherwise, you need to lug your boats from the car park, whilst negotiating the tourist slalom.

If conditions are stormy and the sea outside is boiling, just paddling within the Cove itself is pleasant enough. If you land on the eastern side of the Cove, it is just a short walk up to see the fossilised forest where 140 million year old tree trunks are preserved in the limestone pavement.

Outside Lulworth Cove is Stair Hole, a cluster of archways and caves, with more fossilised tree trunks. There is always a crowd of hard-hatted Geology students here, deciphering the erratic folds of the rock strata.

The cliffs soar higher heading west, with the next landmark being Man o'War Rocks then just after, the fabulous Durdle Door. This is a huge but slender limestone arch that from certain angles resembles the form of a Brontosaurus. Paddling underneath can be surprisingly lively in swell, a peculiar whirlpool forms!

Bat Hole follows, a tiny tunnel through the monolithic headland of Bat's Head. Through this you will spot the curved shape of White Nothe, the final white cliffs of the Purbeck coast.

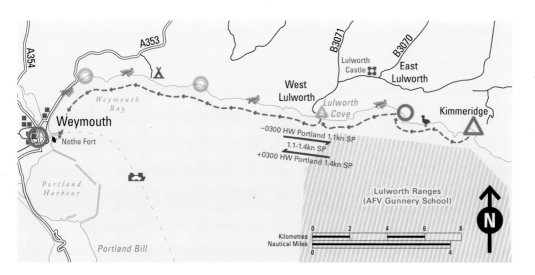

© Lulworth Cove fisherman

The 'Burning Cliff' beach (763 814) in Ringstead Bay is a good lunch spot. Paddlers often turn around here and head back to Lulworth, but the coast to Weymouth is not without interest. Ending the trip at Ringstead village (751 813) is a possibility, as there is a car park and (more crucially) a tea shop. A series of bedrock ledges past Ringstead and Osmington Mills villages often form surf, and look out for the remains of the coal barge *Minx* that ran aground here in 1927. When you reach the long beach of Weymouth Bay, you can either finish the trip right away at the grim holiday resort in Bowleaze Cove (703 819), or continue for another 4km to enter Weymouth Harbour; paddle upriver to land at the Council slipway and car park on Commercial Road (677 790).

VARIATIONS

A shorter trip starting or finishing at Lulworth Cove (825 799) will still be very worthwhile.

Those heading further along the coast may wish to bypass Weymouth Bay by making the 10km open crossing from White Nothe to the Isle of Portland, carrying on into route 8.

Tide and weather

This trip is largely tide-flow free and sheltered from much of the Channel swell by Portland Bill. The deep water around Lulworth Cove itself can generate lots of clapotis close to the cliffs.

The geology of Lulworth Cove by Heather Rainsley

Lulworth Cove's perfect horseshoe curve is a geologist's delight. Passing in through the narrow gap of its entrance, you will be paddling through a wall of near vertical beds of tough Portland and Purbeck limestone. These were deposited horizontally about 210 to 150 million years ago, in the warm tropical seas of the late Jurassic period and later forced into their current upright position by the same earth movements that formed the Alps. Once through the narrow entrance, you are paddling forwards in time another 50 million years through the Cretaceous period, over and past Wealden Beds, greensand and finally, at the back of the Cove; chalk.

Like a shield, the durable vertical Portland and Purbeck limestone has thus far largely withstood the erosive power of the sea, having been only narrowly breached, perhaps at the end of the last Ice Age, as the Lulworth Stream carried away melt water. Once the softer Wealden beds behind were exposed to the sea, they were scoured away at a much faster rate than the harder limestone. The greensands and chalk at the rear of the cove are harder than the Wealden beds and so are eroding more slowly, contributing to the cove's unique outline. To the west, Stair Hole gives an idea of how Lulworth Cove might have looked 10,000 years ago, at the onset of its formation. Further west again, Man o'War Cove and Rocks hint to the future of Lulworth Cove, once the Purbeck and Portland beds finally succumb to the sea. Durdle Door is also formed from the same band of vertical limestone.

© Bat Hole

Additional information

The British Army's AFV (Armoured Fighting Vehicle) Gunnery School stretches from the western edge of Kimmeridge Bay nearly all the way to Lulworth Cove. The firing ranges extend out to sea covering a buoyed area, so access is often restricted. Phone or check online beforehand to find out if your planned trip will be rudely aborted by incoming ordnance. Whilst paddling through, you are allowed to land on the inter-tidal zone, but don't venture inland. The burned out tanks should persuade you of this, in any case. If the ranges are closed, the paddle from Lulworth Cove to Weymouth is still excellent. The Coastguard may be able to advise of firing dates, otherwise the AFV Gunnery School Range Office is contactable at tel. 01929 404819 (further details from www.atra.mod.uk/atra/armourcentre).

Osmington Mills campsite (737 820) is 500m from the water, tel. 01305 264091, www.osmingtoncampsite.co.uk.

Portland Bill ⊙⬛⬛⬛⬛⬛⬛

No. 8 | Grade C | 28/46km | OS Sheets 193, 194

Tidal Ports	Plymouth and Dover
Start	△ Weymouth (677 790)
Finish	○ Chesil Cove (683 733) or West Bay (462 904)
HW/LW	HW in Portland Harbour is approximately 4 hours and 30 minutes before HW Dover.
	HW at West Bay is 5 hours before HW Dover.
Tidal times	At Portland Bill, the east going (flood) stream begins about 1 hour before HW Plymouth. The west going (ebb) stream begins about 5 hours and 30 minutes after HW Plymouth.
	Along Chesil Beach, the SE going stream begins around 2 hours before HW Plymouth. The NW flowing stream begins around 5 hours after HW Plymouth.
Max Rate Sp	Off Portland Bill, rates reach 6-7 knots although flows of 10 knots(!) have been recorded close to The Race. Tidal streams along the eastern side of the Isle of Portland reach 5.1 knots when going SSW. During the brief period when they flow NNE, rates reach 1.6 knots. South going streams along the western side of the Isle of Portland reach 3.5 knots. During the brief period when they flow north, rates reach 0.9 knots. Inshore along Chesil Beach rates do not normally exceed 1 knot.
Coastguard	Portland, tel. 01305 760439, VHF weather 0130 UT

Introduction

The Isle of Portland will challenge your planning skills, with complex and powerful tidal streams and limited landing opportunities. The reward is a constantly interesting trip with harbours, cliffs, historical and industrial remains and a classic lighthouse. Paddlers extending their journey along Chesil Beach get to experience this unique geological feature close up, but will require a high boredom threshold.

Description

Weymouth Harbour is guarded by the guns of the 1860 Nothe Fort, although a more probable risk is being run down by the SeaCat ferry. Outside the harbour, you get an imposing view of the Isle, rising 140m behind Portland Harbour's grim walls. These immense breakwaters were constructed between 1849 and 1906, a testament to Victorian engineering and imperial confidence. Constructing the 4km wide harbour involved scaffolding piers carrying five railway lines, whilst thousands of convicts quarried six million tons of Portland stone.

Diverting through the Harbour is recommended, although note that all three entrances become rough when the tide ebbs out against the wind. The breakwaters are adorned with buildings of WWII or older heritage (landing forbidden). On 5th June 1944, the US 1st Division departed Portland for the carnage of Omaha Beach. The two huge concrete barges (687 747) near Portland Castle are 'Phoenix' floating breakwaters. Such breakwaters were towed to Normandy and sunk to form 'Mulberry Harbours' for the D-Day forces. The Navy closed HMS *Osprey* in 1999, but development for the 2012 Olympic sailing event is reinvigorating the harbour.

Only small craft can negotiate the South Ship Channel, since HMS *Hood* was scuttled in WWI to block submarines. Once outside, the trip is committing with landing only possible in calm seas, on the eastern side of the Isle. Portland's east coast is characterised by a mix of cliffs and scree-like quarry spoil. You will spot the remains of stone jetties and 'derricks', wooden cranes for loading stone onto barges.

Church Ope Cove is the best landing hope, but is awkward due to large stones. Behind, Pennsylvania Castle was built in 1800 for Portland's last governor, John Penn, whilst the ruined castle topping a cliff is the thirteenth-century Rufus Castle. Below are the remains of the church that gives the bay its name. The nearby Portland Museum is worth visiting.

The succeeding cliffs are low but undercut with numerous interesting caves, reefs and storm beaches extending 2km to Dorset's most southerly point, Portland Bill. One of the largest caves, Cave Hole (687 691) has a grille-covered opening in its rear roof.

Around the Bill there are two discontinued lighthouses, the Old Lower Light and Old Higher Light. The current lighthouse is unmistakeable with its 41m tapering form and red stripe. It was

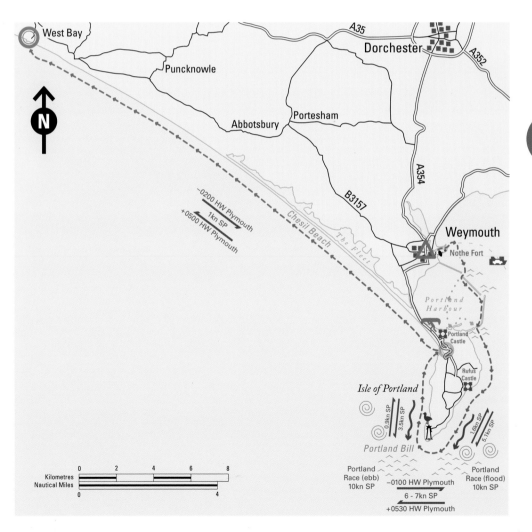

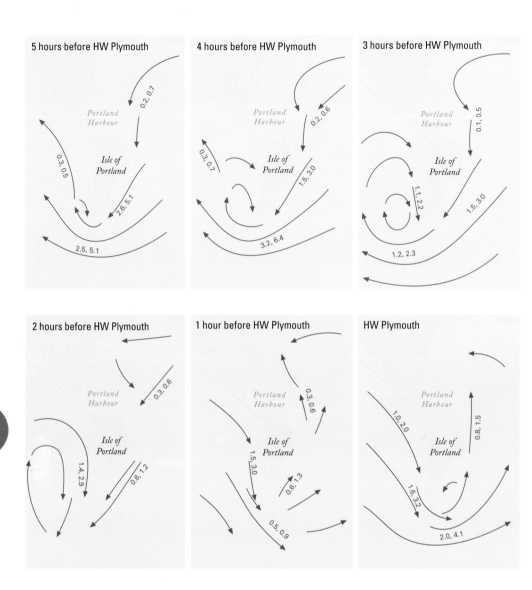

5 hours before HW Plymouth

Portland Harbour

Isle of Portland

0.2, 0.7
0.3, 0.5
2.6, 5.1
2.5, 5.1

4 hours before HW Plymouth

Portland Harbour

Isle of Portland

0.2, 0.6
0.3, 0.7
1.5, 3.0
3.2, 6.4

3 hours before HW Plymouth

Portland Harbour

Isle of Portland

0.1, 0.5
1.1, 2.2
1.5, 3.0
1.2, 2.3

2 hours before HW Plymouth

Portland Harbour

Isle of Portland

0.3, 0.6
1.4, 2.9
0.6, 1.2

1 hour before HW Plymouth

Portland Harbour

Isle of Portland

0.3, 0.6
1.5, 3.0
0.6, 1.3
0.5, 0.9

HW Plymouth

Portland Harbour

Isle of Portland

1.0, 2.0
0.8, 1.5
1.6, 3.2
2.0, 4.1

opened in 1906 after a 1901 storm destroyed 14 ships. South of the lighthouse beside the water is a 7m white obelisk, inscribed 'TH 1844'. Trinity House erected this to warn of the shallow ledge you are paddling over! Shortly after, the 'Red Crane' is a derrick that was used for launching fishing boats. Tourists will be watching from metres away, but you are exposed with no easy landing, tide races and a confused eddy awaiting as you turn north at Pulpit Rock (known as the 'White Arch' before quarrying reduced it).

Tall cliffs stretch down Portland's west coast. Shortly after the Bill, you'll encounter caves and a guillemot colony. These cliffs are known as 'Whitehall', a clue to their quarrying use. An inlet forms a spectacular blowhole (675 688) at its apex, albeit in conditions where you might not want to be paddling! The cliffs fall back after passing beneath a Coastwatch station, with jumbled blocks at the water's edge.

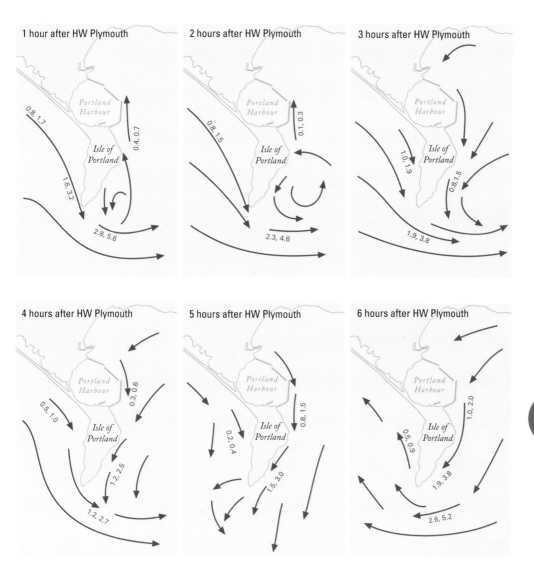

1 hour after HW Plymouth

Portland Harbour
Isle of Portland
0.8, 1.7
0.4, 0.7
1.6, 3.2
2.8, 5.6

2 hours after HW Plymouth

Portland Harbour
Isle of Portland
0.8, 1.5
0.1, 0.3
2.3, 4.6

3 hours after HW Plymouth

Portland Harbour
Isle of Portland
1.0, 1.9
0.8, 1.5
1.9, 3.8

4 hours after HW Plymouth

Portland Harbour
Isle of Portland
0.5, 1.0
0.3, 0.6
1.2, 2.5
1.2, 2.7

5 hours after HW Plymouth

Portland Harbour
Isle of Portland
0.2, 0.4
0.8, 1.5
1.5, 3.0

6 hours after HW Plymouth

Portland Harbour
Isle of Portland
0.5, 0.9
1.0, 2.0
1.9, 3.8
2.6, 5.2

The Looters of Chesil Beach

In 1749 the Amsterdam vessel *Hope* was driven ashore. After rumours circulated that she was carrying gold, the army dispersed a crowd of 10,000. In 1795 six ships from Rear Admiral Hugh Cloberry Christian's fleet were driven ashore. Three hundred bodies were interred in a mass beach grave, but not before locals had stolen their clothing. Following the 1872 wreck of the *Royal Adelaide*, thousands of looters descended on the cargo of rum. Nearly as many revellers died of alcohol and exposure as drowned in the shipwreck!

Should you also find yourself wrecked ashore here, avoid the locals.

Most will finish at Chesil Cove. On the calm day needed for this trip, it's hard to visualise the weather that Chiswell sometimes experiences. In major storms, the sea overtops Chesil Beach. The Great Gale of 1824 killed 27 and destroyed 80 homes. In 1853 a fishing boat wound up on a hotel roof!

Fancy Chesil Beach? It is featureless for the entire length, and high enough to obscure the landscape behind. After the beach reconnects with the land near Abbotsbury, it gradually lowers and shelves less. The first guaranteed landing is inside the harbour of West Bay, making for a potential 28km of commitment.

VARIATIONS

If you are concerned about landing at Chesil Cove, consider paddling around the Isle anti-clockwise. You can shuttle or trolley 1.5km from Sandsfoot Beach (687 744) to launch at Chesil Cove. A shorter paddle (15km) is possible between these two locations.

Tide and weather

Complicated!

The barrier of the Isle of Portland disrupts the tidal flow along the English Channel. Four hundred metres off Portland Bill, a violent extended tide race forms when the tide stream passes over a ledge. The Race forms east of the Bill during the flood, and to the west during the ebb. Kayakers can take advantage of the 'inside passage' close to the Bill to avoid the worst of The Race.

Portland Harbour old military buildings

When the east going (flood) tide squeezes past the Bill, it forms an enormous eddy curving anti-clockwise back towards the Bill, encompassing all of Weymouth Bay. Therefore although the tide off Portland Bill is flowing east, there is a stream flowing strongly SSW along the east side of the Isle towards the Bill, with attendant smaller tide races (known locally as 'shaffles'). During the west going (ebb) tide, the effect is reversed (albeit with weaker flows), with a vast eddy curving clockwise along Chesil Beach and south along the west side of the Isle.

These eddies mean that for ten out of twelve hours in the tidal cycle, paddlers will round the Bill to find the tide against them. The chink in this daunting armour is that for a short period around slack water, the tide bends around the Bill and continues flowing down the coast on the other side.

It is worth re-emphasising that any swell makes landing dangerous between Portland Bill and West Bay, forming one of Britain's longest no-landing zones.

A final thought; try not to be inside any of Portland's caves when the SeaCat goes past!

Additional information

Portland Harbour Radio operates on Channel 74. A (rarely enforced) tariff of several pounds per boat is payable for paddling within Portland Harbour, see www.portland-port.co.uk.

Freshwater Beach (898 479) at Burton Bradstock, tel. 01308 897317, www.freshwaterbeach. co.uk, is the only campsite with sea access.

8

Portland Bill

© *Approaching Pulpit Rock*

Portland Stone

Portland's 140 million year old limestone has sustained a quarrying industry for at least a thousand years. Large sections of Portland's surface are simply gone, leaving a sparse landscape of quarry pits, hewn plateaus and waste. Much of this is observable from the water, but is arguably interesting rather than ugly. Much of Portland's stone now adorns London's public buildings. After the 1666 Great Fire, Sir Christopher Wren utilised 6,000,000 tons to rebuild St Paul's and 50 other churches. The nineteenth-century saw Portland stone used for constructing the breakwaters. Whilst the industry peaked when 100,000 tons were quarried in 1904, Portland stone is still employed for significant projects such as the United Nations building in New York and the Commonwealth War Graves Commission's headstones and memorials.

Golden Cap

East Lyme Bay ▨▨▨

No. 9 | Grade A | 23km | OS Sheet 193

Tidal Port	Dover
Start	△ West Bay (462 904)
Finish	○ Seaton (246 898)
HW/LW	HW West Bay is 5 hours before HW Dover.
	HW Lyme Regis is 4 hours and 55 minutes before HW Dover.
	HW Seaton and Axmouth is 4 hours and 33 minutes before HW Dover.
Tidal times	The W going (ebb) stream begins at HW Dover. The E going (flood) stream begins around 6 hours after HW Dover.
Max Rate Sp	Inshore streams are weak with a maximum rate of less than 1 knot.
Coastguard	Portland, tel. 01305 760439, VHF weather 0130 UT

Introduction

This coast served as the dramatic backdrop for John Fowles' novel *The French Lieutenant's Woman*, and is a Mecca for enthusiasts of geology and palaeontology. The striated cliffs display fossilised

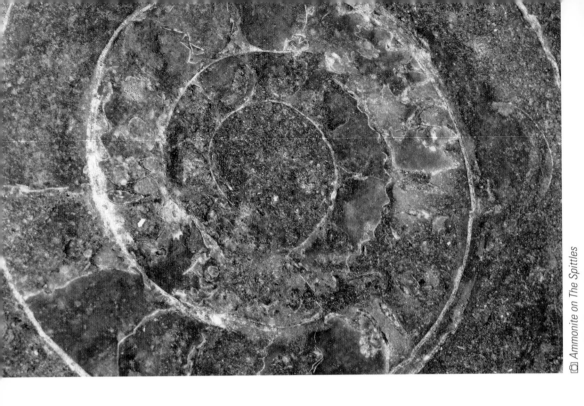

creatures that inhabited warm shallow seas here 200 million years ago. More recent enormous earth movements created the wild Undercliff.

Description

Park beside the slippery slipway in West Bay Harbour. Maritime soap opera *Harbour Lights* was filmed here. West Bay has put this atrocity behind it, with waterfront redevelopment and a new breakwater.

West, successive tall hills are interspersed with valleys plunging to sea level. The first valley is Eype's Mouth (448 910), divided by Thorncombe Beacon and Doghouse Hill from Seatown (419 917), 3km further. Both offer parking and launching.

Golden Cap (191m), highest point on England's south coast, dominates the skyline. The name describes the lighter Cretaceous sand atop the Jurassic cliffs. Boulders extend from the base of Golden Cap, augmented by frequent rockfalls.

Between the valley of St Gabriel's Mouth and Charmouth, the cliffs are visibly crumbling. This is the famous Blue Lias limestone, laid down 195 million years ago on the bed of a warm shallow Jurassic sea. Enlightened Victorians perceived that its fossils implied a world predating 4004 BC, the generally accepted date of Creation. If you can't find an ammonite here, you never will!

Charmouth Heritage Coast Centre (www.charmouth.org) on Charmouth beach offers advice on fossil hunting. This beach owes much of its material to a 1979 flash flood that deposited a pebble delta (and caravans) at the River Char's mouth.

The Princess of Palaeontology

Mary Anning (1799-1847) of Lyme Regis gained the accolade of being, *'the greatest fossilist the world ever knew'*.

Anning first sold her remarkable finds to curious tourists, but witnessed fossil collecting develop into serious science. Anning earned an international reputation for her finds, including the first ichthyosaurus and the first complete plesiosaur. Scientists visiting her were surprised to discover that Anning (a woman!) was not just a 'fossil finder', but was better conversant with the underpinning science than almost anyone else. Anning's finds contributed to the development of the theories of extinction and evolution. Sadly, many of her finds were attributed to others and her significance was largely unacknowledged within her lifetime by the (entirely male) scientific community.

Between Charmouth and Lyme Regis, the cliffs of Black Ven and the The Spittles offer further evidence of this coast's dynamism. In the 1930s, tourists came to view a 'mud glacier'! At least seven massive terraces rise staircase-like from the sea. Each terrace is subsiding, the most recent major landslide being in 2000. The Spittles is another fossil hunting spot, with large sea-polished ammonites on the shore.

The central focus of the spa town of Lyme Regis is of course the 200m Cobb, Britain's oldest working breakwater. This thirteenth-century barrier appears indestructible, but has been repeatedly rebuilt. In rough weather, stand on The Cobb and re-create *The French Lieutenant's Woman*! West of the Cobb there is parking (337 916) behind Monmouth Beach. Here in June 1685, the Duke of Monmouth landed and proclaimed himself King. That September, a dozen of his supporters were hanged and dismembered on the beach.

You now cross into Devon. The remaining 10km traverse the Landslip National Nature Reserve. As the name implies, this entire coast is in flux. The greatest landslip came on Christmas Eve

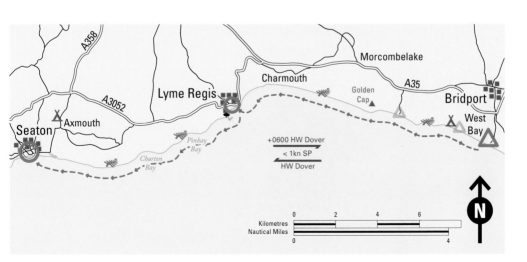

1839. A vast chasm opened in the Undercliff, the 'No Man's Land' between sea and clifftop. The shore shifted 500m seawards and offshore, a 1.5km reef arose. This was discussed in Parliament as a potential naval base, however it soon eroded away. The Undercliff has evolved into a densely overgrown wilderness ecosystem, making these upheavals difficult to visualise. However, major slippages occurred as recently as 2001.

The Undercliff ends at the River Axe. A car park is located a block behind Seaton beach (246 898) on Harbour Road.

Tide and weather

These are some of the South West's weakest tide flows.

If fossil hunting, be alert to the very real danger of landslips or rock falls, especially after wet weather.

Additional information

Highlands End campsite (425 919) is beside Eype Mouth beach, tel. 01308 422139, www. wdlh.co.uk. Axe Farm (256 913) is 1km inland beside the River Axe, accessible at HW, tel. 01297 24707, www.axefarm.co.uk.

The Lyme Bay tragedy

Our sport changed forever on 22nd March 1993. At 10.05, a group from a local outdoor centre launched from Lyme Regis to paddle to Charmouth. The group comprised two instructors, one teacher and eight Sixth Form students. The instructors were inadequately trained and the students did not have spraydecks.

Offshore winds separated the group and pushed them offshore. The kayaks swamped and most of the group wound up swimming. There was no means of summoning help. The group were due back at 12.00, but the emergency services weren't summoned until 15.30.

The final group member was rescued by helicopter at 18.44. Four teenagers died in this tragedy, which as the Devon County Council report stated, *'quite simply, should not have happened.'*

A positive legacy was the creation of the Adventure Activities Licensing Authority, which regulates outdoor activity provision for young people. A less tangible outcome is that outdoor activity is now often viewed with suspicion. As a result, young people arguably now have fewer opportunities to enjoy the outdoors.

East & South Devon

An Introduction

Arriving at Plymouth having paddled all the way from Seaton, it's hard to conceive that the shores encountered en route were all in one county. There is more diversity and variation along Devon's English Channel coast than in any other region of the (diverse and varied) South West. Between the ancient sandstone stacks of East Devon and the fabulous wave-cut platforms of South Devon, paddlers have plenty of choice. The conurbation of resorts known as the 'English Riviera' is sadly overdeveloped but not without scenic interest. Offshore, there is the exposed Eddystone Lighthouse to visit. Leading inland are numerous estuaries and rias, each offering engaging paddling in the transitional zone between freshwater and ocean.

One close association with this coast is the business of 'free trading' (smuggling) of goods between England and France. This generated one of Devon's chief incomes through the eighteenth and nineteenth centuries. East Devon's illicit trading was considered particularly notorious and impervious to the law, with all sections and strata of society shamelessly profiting.

More gloriously, Devon is also closely associated with our Navy, past and present. Elizabethans such as Drake, Raleigh and Hawkins ventured forth from South Devon's harbours and estuaries to discover new territories and plunder Spanish shipping. Modern South Devon is home to numerous Royal Naval bases, from the Britannia Royal Naval College at Dartmouth to the vast Devonport base in Plymouth.

Environment

The East and South Devon Heritage Coasts encompass most of the region's shores, as do the East and South Devon Area of Outstanding Natural Beauty (AONBs). The 'English Riviera' is conspicuously omitted from both, but received UNESCO Geopark status in 2007. About a third of the Jurassic Coast World Heritage Site is within East Devon, and the Tamar valley is part of the Cornwall and West Devon Mining Landscape World Heritage Site.

The National Trust owns and manages long tracts of wild coast and there is a Voluntary Marine Conservation Area (VMCA) around Wembury.

The Royal Navy of course manage substantial estates around Plymouth, not always reassuringly; in 2007 it was revealed that Devonport base had suffered 200 'radiological incidents' in the previous five years.

Tide and weather

Paddlers in South Devon can find a trip to suit any weather. The Lyme Bay coast as far as Start Bay is often sheltered from prevailing south-west winds, with relatively weak tides. Conversely, the South Hams peninsula is fully exposed to the weather and Atlantic groundswell with strong tidal flows and large races. Bigbury Bay has weak tides but is known for its regular surf. The estuaries and rivers of course offer a high degree of shelter from wind and swell, but all generate strong tidal flows and should not be underestimated. In 2007 alone, South Devon's estuarine mud flats caused more than one paddling group to require extrication by emergency services.

Background reading

The Official Guide to the Jurassic Coast, Denys Brunden, Coastal Publishing 2003,
ISBN 0-9544845-0-9

The Jurassic Coast, Rodney Legg, Dorset Books 2002, ISBN 0-948699-77-9

Exploring the Undercliffs, Donald Campbell, Coastal Publishing 2006, ISBN 0-9544845-2-5

Tidal Stream Atlas of the South Devon Coast, Mike Fennessey, Moorprint,
Coastal Research 1997, ISBN 0-9530656-0-X

Shipwrecks of South Devon, Richard and Bridget Larn,
Bossiney Books 2005, ISBN 1-899383-35-2

Secret Nature of Devon, Andrew Cooper, Green Books 2005, ISBN 1-903998-50-6

Devon Smugglers, Robert Hesketh, Bossiney Books 2007, ISBN 978-189938393-1

West Country Cruising Companion, Mark Fishwick, Nautical Data Ltd 2004,
ISBN 1-904358-25-X

Shell Channel Pilot, Tom Cunliffe, Imray 2006, ISBN 0-85288-894-5

Further information

www.jurassiccoast.com

www.cornish-mining.org.uk – The World Heritage Sites

www.englishrivierageopark.org.uk – The English Riviera Geopark

www.southdevonaonb.org.uk – South Devon Area of Outstanding Natural Beauty

www.eastdevonaonb.org.uk – East Devon Area of Outstanding Natural Beauty

www.devonwildlifetrust.org – Devon Wildlife Trust

© Near Ladram Bay

West Lyme Bay

No. 10 | Grade A | 30km | OS Sheet 192

Tidal Port	Dover
Start	△ Seaton (246 898)
Finish	○ Exmouth (998 805)
HW/LW	HW Seaton is 4 hours and 33 minutes before HW Dover.
	HW Exmouth Dock is 4 hours and 55 minutes before HW Dover.
Tidal times	Off Beer Head, the west going (ebb) stream begins at HW Dover. The east going (flood) stream begins approximately 6 hours after HW Dover.
Max Rate Sp	Inshore streams between Seaton and Straight Point are weak with a maximum rate of less than 1 knot. Straight Point forms a small tide race. Tide rates in the entrance to the Exe Estuary can attain 5 knots on the ebb.
Coastguard	Portland, tel. 01305 760439, VHF weather 0130 UT

Introduction

The Jurassic Coast World Heritage Site is a bit of a con at its western extremity, as the cliffs and rocks span right from the Cretaceous period through the Jurassic to the Triassic. In other words,

paddlers get to time-travel backwards, from around 70 million to 250 million years ago. The result is a startlingly varied paddle among unique and compelling chalk and sandstone cliffs.

Description

Seaton isn't the south coast's most riveting town, but offers easy launching, with a car park located one street back from the beach (246 898) on Harbour Road.

Directly west is Beer, an attractive village nestled between chalk cliffs. The local fishing fleet is often pulled up on the beach.

The paddle around Beer Head traverses the south's most westerly chalk cliffs. Past the Head, the cliffs are topped by tottering chalk spires, a legacy of the Hooken landslip of 1790. The village of Branscombe inadvertently received international media attention in January 2007, when the MSC *Napoli* was beached 1km offshore. Check with the Coastguard to see whether any navigational restrictions remain in the wreck area.

At Branscombe, the cliffs change dramatically to a dark shade of red. This 200-250 million year old Triassic sandstone was created by layers of sand and grit being laid down successively on a desert floor, the red colouring due to iron minerals oxidising under hot sun. Look for wavy patterns reflecting dune formation, water deposition and wind erosion. This sandstone extends to Exmouth, although sometimes topped by contrasting chalk.

Weston Mouth and Salcombe Mouth are passed en route to Sidmouth, similar roadless valleys making for good rest spots. Sidmouth is an unusually 'untacky' resort, boasting fine Regency architecture along the seafront. A number of sea defences need negotiating before you pass bemused tourists on the promenade around Chit Rocks. Chit Rocks used to be Chit Rock, an imposing stack destroyed in an 1824 hurricane.

Two kilometres further, the coast lays on a treat. The eroded stack of Big Picket Rock is dwarfed beneath 157m High Peak and seven more sandstone stacks follow as you paddle around to Ladram Bay. Some of these stacks have coral encrusted bases, and all are inhabited by seagulls nesting upon carefully sculpted mounds of guano! Best avoid LW, to allow paddling around the stacks. The exceptional scenery hardly diminishes after Ladram Bay. Cliffs rise sheer from the water with intricate strata to decipher and shallow reefs to rockhop through. One mystery is a man-made tunnel emerging into Chiselbury Bay; answers on a postcard!

The mouth of the River Otter heralds arrival at Budleigh Salterton, famous for possessing Britain's highest proportion of OAPS. The hard quartzite beach pebbles are 440 million year old rocks from Brittany. They were transported north by river, a relatively recent 240 million years ago. Makes the locals seem positively youthful.

The cliffs to Littleham Cove and Straight Point are a new twist on the sandstone theme, being pocked with wind eroded carvings. Straight Point is the home of a Royal Marines rifle range, firing eastwards (i.e. at you). More appealingly, the Point has a small tide race on the ebb and the west side is home to a colony of kittiwakes, each with their own white guano-nest stuck to the red sandstone.

Orcombe Point predates the dinosaurs. A ladder allows tourists to study the strata but you don't need this, as you've been privileged to view the Triassic coast by the best possible means. Orcombe Point is topped by the 'Geoneedle', celebrating the World Heritage Site. Less aesthetically, the *actual* end of the Site is the first groyne encountered soon after. Park and land at The Maer (004 802) or, past the Coastwatch station, at Exmouth Beach (999 805). Tide flows are strong in and out of the Exe Estuary.

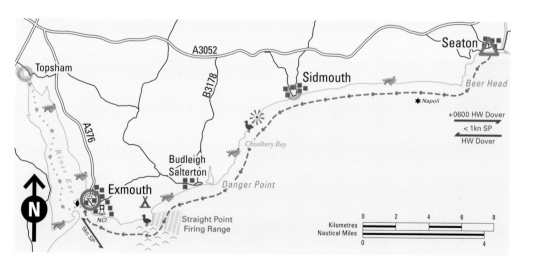

© Containers from the Napoli at Beer Head

VARIATIONS

For a shorter paddle, Sidmouth conveniently breaks up this trip with beachfront parking (125 872).

The Exe Estuary is worth exploring. It is 9.5km to Topsham, alternatively portage onto Exeter Canal and paddle to Haven Bank Quay in central Exeter. Of course, avoid LW.

Tide and weather

These are some of the South West's weakest tide flows, but gain some strength close to Exmouth.

Many of the landings are steep pebble beaches, which dump in a swell.

Additional information

Straight Point Firing Range operates on weekdays between March and October. Buoys denote the danger zone and red flags flying on the cliffs denote firing. If firing is taking place, a range launch will also be patrolling. The Coastguard should be able to advise on firing times and the range can also be contacted by VHF on Channel 8, call up 'Straight Point Range'.

Axe Farm campsite (256 913) is 1km inland beside the River Axe, accessible at HW, tel. 01297 24707, www.axefarm.co.uk. Devon Cliffs (038 800) is pleasantly located behind the MOD firing range and adjoins Sandy Bay, tel. 01395 226226.

10

Smuggling at Beer

Beer was infamous for its involvement in cross-channel smuggling, with beacons lit on the local cliffs to guide illicit vessels in. It was home to Jack Rattenbury, whose celebrated *'Memoirs of a Smuggler'* (1837) offer an entertaining (and not entirely reliable) insight into this murky profession, with tall tales of evading and outwitting customs men, soldiers, press gangs and the French.

Smuggling wasn't always funny and harmless. An epitaph in nearby Branscombe churchyard reads:

"Here lieth John Hurley, Custom Officer ... he was endeavouring to extinguish some Fire made between Beer and Seaton as a Signal to a Smuggling boat then off at Sea He fell by some means or other from the Top of the Cliff to the Bottom ... He was an active and Diligent Officer and very inoffensive in his life and Conversation."

MSC Napoli

Quiet East Devon was thrust into the media spotlight in January 2007. 'Disaster at Sea' proclaimed the *Sunday Times*, 'Looters Swarm over Ship Booty' declared the *Daily Telegraph* and 'Environmental Disaster Feared' foreboded the *Independent*.

On January 18, the 62,000 tonne container ship MSC *Napoli's* hull fractured in massive waves and storm force winds, 80km south of The Lizard. The 26 crew abandoned ship and were rescued from their life raft within hours, a helicopter breaking two winch lines in this dangerous operation. Unexpectedly, the *Napoli* didn't sink.

Whilst under tow towards Portland Harbour, it became apparent that the *Napoli* would not survive the voyage. Controversially, the decision was taken to beach it offshore of the Jurassic Coast World Heritage Site.

No one foresaw what came next. Containers washed ashore from the wreck burst open to reveal such riches as new BMW motorcycles. Thousands of scavengers descended on Branscombe beach, spiriting away everything portable and generating an enormous mess. This chaos probably hindered efforts to pump oil from the *Napoli* and belatedly, the police closed the beach.

A few days later, we paddled to see for ourselves; rubbernecking with an environmental conscience. Listing precariously with over 2,000 containers perched atop, the *Napoli* was certainly a sight. The removal of 3,500 tonnes of oil had gone well and oil spills were stabilised by booms. We saw hardly any oil on the water and coast. On Branscombe Beach, cranes had commenced removal of the beached containers, smeared along several miles of coast with discarded junk everywhere. A policeman told us that he was having a boring, but well-paid day. The only visitors now were, "... *morons who think that there will still be new motorbikes lying around*".

Shortly after we'd concluded that the environmental damage was negligible, we encountered oiled guillemots flapping their wings pathetically, trying to fly; a distressing sight. A local canoe club were using open canoes to collect these contaminated birds, just several of over 1,000 birds that received treatment.

It's hard to see how the *Napoli's* wreck could have been better handled. Within a week, the impact had been minimalised, the clean-up had begun and far worse scenarios averted. By May, all containers had been removed from the wreck and attempts were made to refloat her. These were unsuccessful, so the wreck was blown up into manageable sections.

 Torquay

The English Riviera ▦▨▢

11

No. 11 | Grade A | 31km | OS Sheets 192 and 202

Tidal Ports   Plymouth and Dover

Start   △ Dawlish Warren (982 787)

Finish   ○ Brixham (924 566)

HW/LW   HW Teignmouth is 4 hours and 50 minutes before HW Dover.

HW Brixham is 5 hours and 5 minutes before HW Dover. HW Torquay/Paignton is 5 minutes later.

Tidal times   Near Teignmouth, the SSW going (ebb) stream begins 5 hours and 10 minutes after HW Plymouth. The NNE going (flood) stream begins 1 hour and 35 minutes before HW Plymouth.

At the mouth of the River Teign, the in-going stream begins 5 hours and 35 minutes before HW Plymouth. The out-going stream begins 40 minutes after HW Plymouth.

Max Rate Sp   Streams between Dawlish Warren and Torquay reach less than 1 knot. Around Hope's Nose tides reach 2 knots. Tidal streams within Tor Bay are very weak. The ingoing and outgoing streams at the mouth of the River Teign can reach 5 knots.

Coastguard   Brixham, tel. 01803 882704, VHF weather 0110 UT

The English Riviera

69

Introduction

This paddle includes some attractive scenery, but also large resorts. We have the Victorians to thank for the term 'Riviera', as they convinced themselves that Tor Bay reminded them of Mediterranean France. Although the climate is mild and the occasional palm tree can be spotted, nowadays only the tourist board maintain the charade. The resorts look jaded, and the coast bears the scars of thoughtless development. There is much to enjoy here however, and who can resist paddling past the Gleneagles Hotel, inspiration for *Fawlty Towers*?

Description

Pass the railway in Dawlish Warren (980 787) and park at the end of the car park, reducing the carry/trolley to the beach. The 7,000 year old dune system of Dawlish Warren National Nature Reserve gives sanctuary to 20,000 wading birds between August and March. There are 600 different flowering plants to avoid treading upon whilst launching.

Langstone Rock is a lone outcrop of Permian sandstone forming a natural arch. The arch is partly blocked by a wall, setting the tone for much of this coast; too much man-made intrusion. Behind is the South Devon Railway, an engineering feat accomplished by Brunel in 1846. It follows the coast to Teignmouth, darting in and out of cliff tunnels.

Dawlish railway station (965 767) is another possible start point. With its amusement arcades and illuminated gardens, Dawlish is *the jewel in the crown of South Devon* according to the Tourist Board … hmm. A series of cliff-backed coves leading out of Dawlish display fossilised sand dunes, but also spray-canned graffiti. Things improve around the Parson and Clerk formation, where a stack has separated from the cliffs but still leans lazily against the headland. The narrow tunnel between can be squeezed through. Smugglers cut contraband caves into these cliffs, later obliterated by railway construction.

A long strand of pebbles backed by concrete defences leads into Teignmouth. If this scene feels familiar, it's because newspapers regularly carry photographs of storm waves breaking across passing trains.

There is a Coastwatch station north of Teignmouth's rusting pier. On completion in 1865, the pier maintained propriety by segregating male and female bathers. The harbour is located just inside the estuary and is the most interesting part of town, with the fishing fleet drawn up on Back Beach. Reaching this spot is awkward, as the river mouth channels strong tidal flows, felt up to 1km offshore. Across the river mouth is Shaldon beach, covered at HW. Wednesdays ('1785 Days') are somewhat disturbing in Shaldon, as the locals dress up in costumes to commemorate a French attack.

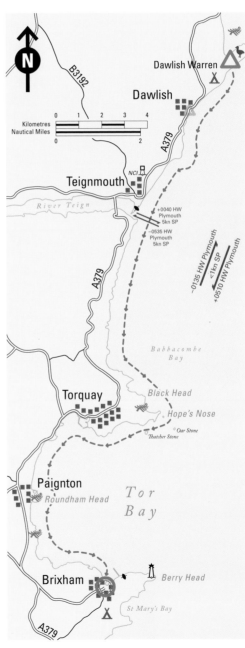

Rejoice, for the scenery improves dramatically! Overgrown sandstone cliffs are an appealing backdrop for the 10km to Hope's Nose, with a multi-entranced tunnel and caves to be found. Passing Torquay, there are several small coves with cafés and suchlike, but this sprawling resort is hidden from view. Oddicombe beach with its cliff railway has an odd claim to fame. In 1884, local girl Emma Keys was murdered in a beach hut. John 'Babbacombe' Lee, her murderer, is remembered as 'the man they couldn't hang' after three attempts inexplicably failed.

Hope's Nose marks the entrance to Tor Bay, and a disheartening vista of built-up coast opens up. The promontory itself is attractive, with raised stone beaches and isolated stacks surrounding. The temptation is to paddle 6km direct across Tor Bay from Thatcher Rock to Brixham; not the worst plan ever.

If you choose to persist, the coast has its moments. The garish hotels on the north side of the bay are interrupted by the cliffs around a natural arch known as London Bridge. The waters

around Torquay Harbour are cursed by jetskis but the cafés inside on Beacon Quay are pleasant. The net structure is 'Living Coasts', a sea life centre and home to Torquay's penguin population.

Livermead's cliffs boasted fine caves, but they've been bricked up. Madness! Another local form of insanity is the propensity for painting hotel and location names in large letters on the shore. Paignton follows Torquay, only being distinguishable by its colourful beach huts. The sad thing is that although Tor Bay clearly possesses natural charms, they have been neglected and submerged. Console yourself by imagining how it appeared to Napoleon, two centuries ago. En route to St Helena, he spent seven weeks anchored here in HMS *Bellerophon*, never touching English soil.

The last 3km offer respite, with woodland and sandy coves. Just inside Brixham Harbour is a car park and slipway (924 566).

Tide and weather

Much of this coast is sheltered from the prevailing wind. Outside Teignmouth, eddies and over-falls form over 'The Bar' on the ebb tide.

Additional information

www.theenglishriviera.co.uk is the Tourist Office website. Tor Bay is a Geopark, a UNESCO designation for areas of unique geological interest. See www.englishrivierageopark.org.uk.

Leadstone Camping (974 782) in Dawlish is 800m from the beach, tel. 01626 864411, www.leadstonecamping.co.uk. Upton Manor Farm (926 549) is 500m from St Mary's Bay in Brixham, tel. 01548 580538, www.uptonmanorfarm.co.uk.

© Boat Envy, Dittisham

 # The River Dart ⊙⊿🛶⛴

No. 12 | **Grade A** | **16 km** | **OS Sheet 202**

Tidal Ports	Plymouth and Dover
Start	△ Totnes (806 600)
Finish	○ Dartmouth (879 514)
HW/LW	HW Dartmouth is 5 hours and 10 minutes before HW Dover.
Tidal times	At Dartmouth, the outgoing stream begins 25 minutes after HW Plymouth and ends 5 hours and 50 minutes before HW Plymouth. The duration of the outgoing stream increases progressively upriver. During neap tides and after rainfall on Dartmoor, Totnes can have no ingoing stream at all.
Max Rate Sp	At Dartmouth, flows can attain 3 knots.
Coastguard	Brixham, tel. 01803 882704, VHF weather 0110

Introduction

The River Dart needs no introduction to paddlers, being one of Britain's best whitewater rivers. The salt water reaches of the Dart are less frequented by paddlers, but the journey from Totnes out to where the Dart joins the open sea at Dartmouth is recommended as a beautiful and relatively sheltered trip.

© Kingswear

Description

This trip follows the ebbing tide downstream, so aim to depart within two hours of local HW. Totnes is a bustling market town which for some reason is heavily populated by new age hippy types, perfect if you happen to be shopping for energy crystals or alternative therapists. Driving through Totnes, follow signs for Steamer Quay which is on river left just below the bridge, with a large car park. Launching at HW springs is easy as the water will almost reach the car park. Otherwise, make use of the various steps and ramps hereabouts.

'Completists' may wish to paddle 2km upstream to the tidal limit at Totnes weir. Otherwise, the first 2km downstream (the 'Home Reach') are straight and will be almost fresh water if the Dart is flowing well. Mind out for rowers. The buildings of the Baltic Wharf on river right are soon left behind and the scenery changes to the steep wooded hills and tidal mud flats that characterise this trip. The trees often reach right down to trail in the water, idyllic! There is plenty of birdlife thriving along the water's edge, Canada geese and egrets being particularly visible.

Around the first left bend, the sorry remains of the *Kingswear Castle* bask in the mud. This 1904 paddle steamer ferried tourists along the Dart and served as a hospital ship in its later years, being burned in 1924 to prevent contagion.

The Dart now winds through a series of tight bends flowing past the vineyards of Sharpham House and then the small salmon fishing hamlet of Duncannon. Bow Creek opens up on the right and offers a potential diversion of 2km to Tuckenhay if the tide hasn't run too far out. Improbably, in 1806 a Mr Abraham Tucker attempted – and failed – to convert tiny Tuckenhay into a major port. He did however succeed in making it the first place in Britain to be gas-lit.

The next 4km is known as the Lake of the Dart, being up to a kilometre wide. The village of Stoke Gabriel is tucked away beside a tidal pond on the left bank. If you call in for a pint here, be aware that the pond is dammed and that your kayaks may become trapped as the tide falls!

The Lake of the Dart ends at the Dittisham ferry narrows. This is perhaps the best pub stop, with the Ferry Inn directly to hand on the right. Just visible up the left bank is Greenway House, which belonged to Agatha Christie. It is also the birthplace of Elizabethan explorer Humphrey Gilbert who founded the colony of Newfoundland. Gilbert also inspired John Davis to seek the fabled North West Passage. Davis was born 2km upriver at Sandridge and launched his three expeditions from Dartmouth.

Leaving Dittisham, the river squeezes around the Anchor Stone, forming strong eddy lines. In the trees on the left is the Paignton and Dartmouth Steam railway, and you just might have your paddle interrupted by the *Flying Scotsman* itself.

You now enter Dartmouth port, and for the final kilometre you will dodge numerous jetties, small ferries, and pleasure craft. The harbour is a lovely sight, with the steep valley sides, colourful buildings, bustling harbour traffic and just beyond ... the sea. First, you pass Old Mill Creek on your right and in front of this is a buoyed area. This is the training ground of the Royal Navy's

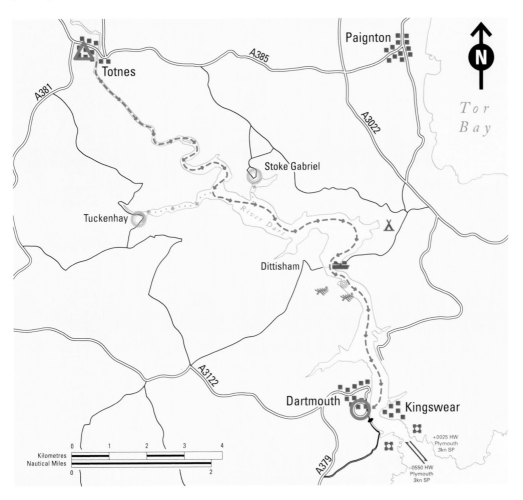

officer school. Britannia Royal Naval College was opened in 1905 and sprawls impressively on the hill behind. You will paddle past our future Nelsons and Collingwoods as they learn how to drive and steer small craft. At the quay, HMS *Hindostan* is permanently moored to give cadets experience of a larger ship.

The left bank is Kingswear, worth a paddle across to see and the best place for viewing the Britannia College. Your destination however is the harbour at Dartmouth. You have the choice of paddling under the road into this small enclosure ('the boat float') or of using the public pontoons just outside. Roadside parking is available close to hand, as are fish and chips; perfect.

Tide and weather

A number of large upstream-flowing eddies will be encountered along the river, reaching 2 knots. This is an ideal trip for poor weather, as the river is often sheltered from the wind and there are few spots where the water is open enough to whip up waves.

Additional information

Buses leave hourly from beside the harbour for the 40 minute journey back to Totnes. Another possibility is to catch the ferry back upstream to Totnes (www.riverlink.co.uk). This takes 90 minutes and includes a running commentary, which you may or may not relish.

A tour of Britannia R N College makes an interesting end to this trip, www.britannia.ac.uk.

Galmpton campsite (884558) overlooks the estuary, tel. 01803 842066, www.galmptontouringpark. co.uk.

Slapton Sands, near Start

Berry Head

No. 13 | Grade B | 25km | OS Sheets 192, 202

Tidal Ports	Plymouth and Dover
Start	△ Brixham (924 566)
Finish	○ Torcross (824 423)
HW/LW	HW Brixham is 5 hours and 5 minutes before HW Dover.
	HW Dartmouth is 5 hours and 10 minutes before HW Dover.
Tidal times	Between Berry Head and Combe Point, the SW going (ebb) stream begins 4 hours and 40 minutes after HW Plymouth. The NE going (flood) stream begins 1 hour and 5 minutes before HW Plymouth. The outgoing stream from the River Dart begins 25 minutes after HW Plymouth and ends 5 hours and 50 minutes before HW Plymouth.
Max Rate Sp	Reach 1.5 knots.
Coastguard	Brixham, tel. 01803 882704, VHF weather 0110 UT

Introduction

Tucked between Tor Bay and Start Bay is a delightful stretch of coast. A 1906 guidebook noted, *"Rocks succeed sands, and sands follow rocks; headlands alternating with bays … Not a soul will you see,*

not a house, save the coastguards and their station and cottages at Man Sands. And this in overcrowded England!" A century on, little has changed.

Description

Kayakers who have sampled the dubious delights of Torquay and Paignton will be glad to find that Tor Bay's third resort is more appealing. Brixham Harbour is constantly busy with fishing boats coming and going. At the rear of the harbour, Brixham Coastguards co-ordinate the chaos, not far from a full-size replica of Drake's *Golden Hind* (www.goldenhind.co.uk). Uphill on Fore Street is Brixham's Heritage Museum (www.brixhamheritage.org.uk), whose maritime exhibits offer a bad weather alternative. Best place to launch is a car park and slipway (924 566) on the south-west side of the harbour. Another possibility is Breakwater Beach (932 567) outside the harbour.

Rounding the harbour breakwater you'll spy Berry Head, 2km east. This side of the Head has been almost entirely quarried away, leaving a peculiar landscape of raised platforms and isolated limestone spires, interspersed with remnants of Napoleonic fortifications. The platforms are usually crammed with fishermen, and experience has suggested that they can be unfriendly.

Things improve dramatically at the Head itself. The 59m cliffs are an amalgam of limestone and mudstone, the latter having an engaging 'mushed up' appearance. The 1906 lighthouse up on top is easily missed, being an underwhelming 5m tall. Tucked at the base of the cliffs are caves, proving to be surprisingly extensive when explored; take a headtorch. The coast between Berry Head and Sharkham Point is a National Nature Reserve, hosting the largest breeding colony of cormorants on the south coast. A thousand cormorants make a lot of noise (and guano), even before you factor in a additional thousand guillemots and significant numbers of gulls, kittiwakes and fulmar. In early summer, this is a raucous place!

The 8km from Sharkham Point to the River Dart are worth prolonging with a lunchstop on one of the empty sand beaches encountered. The approaches to the Dart are guarded by the jagged bastions of the Mew Stone. If you pass this offshore, you'll glimpse the Coastwatch station and the 24m hexagonal stone daymark above Froward Point, built in 1864 to welcome Royal Mail ships returning from the colonies.

The River Dart's entrance has accumulated numerous fortifications down the centuries, most notably Dartmouth and Kingswear Castles. Built in the 1480s to keep out Frenchmen, they were also utilised to bar Cornishmen from landing fishing catches. A short trip option is to struggle upriver to Kingswear and finish there.

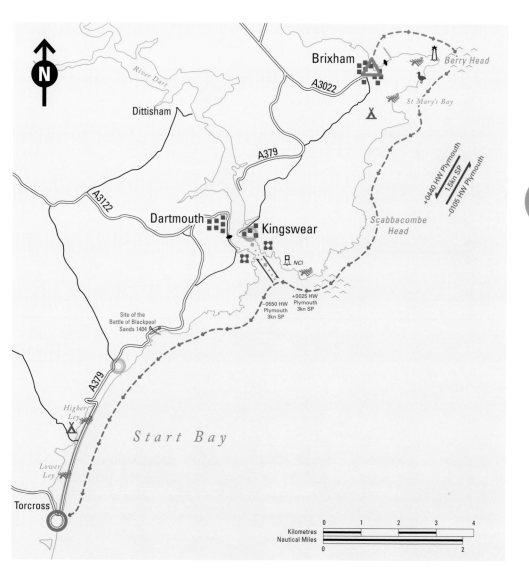

The 6km to Start Bay remain attractive, with miniature coves and the pretty rockscape of the 'Dancing Beggars' to discover. A highlight is the perfect strand of Blackpool Sands. The improbably titled Battle of Blackpool Sands took place here in 1404, when local militia massacred 200 marauding 'Frenchies'. Unfortunately, this is a fee-charging 'private' beach and the degree to which sea kayakers are welcome remains unclear.

The steep pebble beach of Start Bay begins at Pilchard Cove, and shortly after at Strete Gate, the road descends steeply to join the beach near a car park (835 455). Land here or continue along the (monotonous) beach to Torcross.

VARIATIONS

Shortening the trip by finishing at Kingswear (883 513) makes the shuttle easier. Land at the Darthaven Marina; the car park is across the railway. Finishing at Strete Gate (835455) is another possibility.

Tide and weather

Tide races are encountered around Berry Head, and also near the Mew Stone. Strong currents can be encountered flowing out of the River Dart. With swell from the east, the steeply shelving pebbles of Start Bay can be a dangerous landing.

Additional information

Upton Manor Farm camping (926 549) is 500m from St Mary's Bay in Brixham, tel. 01803 882384, www.uptonmanorfarm.co.uk. Slapton Sands camping (825 450) is 500m from the beach tel. 01548 580538.

Exercise Tiger

Beside the car park at Torcross is a WWII Sherman tank. It was placed here in 1984, but had previously spent forty years underwater.

On the night of 27-28th April 1944, Slapton Sands were the location of a full scale rehearsal for the D-Day landings. Due to communication errors, poor planning and (alleged) Royal Navy negligence, German E-boats slipped into the exercise area and torpedoed three of the landing ships, two of which sank. Many more soldiers died after clambering ashore, when they were accidentally shelled by live ammunition.

At least 946 US servicemen died in the exercise, the bodies buried in mass graves on local farms. This disaster was hurriedly hushed up with all participants sworn to secrecy. The full story of Exercise Tiger only emerged decades later. The 34 ton tank was raised from the seabed due to the prolonged efforts of local businessman Ken Small. He bought it from the US Government for $50 in 1974 and raised it from the seabed a decade later. The tank now serves as a memorial to the forgotten US soldiers and sailors of Exercise Tiger.

Small's book *The Forgotten Dead* is recommended to those wishing to learn more.

Prawle Point

14

No. 14 | Grade B | 28km | OS Sheet 202

Tidal Ports	Plymouth and Dover
Start	△ Torcross (824 423)
Finish	◯ Hope Cove (674 398)
HW/LW	HW Salcombe is around 5 hours and 35 minutes before HW Dover.
Tidal times	Inshore at Start Point, the WSW going (ebb) stream begins around 2 hours and 20 minutes before HW Dover. The ENE going (flood) stream begins around 3 hours and 55 minutes after HW Dover.
	At the mouth of the Kingsbridge Estuary, the ingoing stream begins 5 hours and 45 minutes before HW Plymouth and the outgoing stream begins 15 minutes after HW Plymouth.
Max Rate Sp	Inshore at Start Point, streams reach 4 knots, at Prawle Point, 3 knots, at Bolt Head, 2 knots. The out-going flow at the mouth of the Kingsbridge Estuary reaches 3 knots.
Coastguard	Brixham, tel. 01803 882704, VHF weather 0110 UT

Introduction

Although South Hams derives its name from Hamme (Old English: *Sheltered Place*), its south coast is anything but! These unforgiving cliffs and reefs have seen hundreds of shipwrecks. With

its famous lighthouse, wave-cut reefs and high cliffs, this excellent trip showcases the very best of South Devon's coastal scenery.

Description

Torcross with its Sherman Tank memorial is a more convenient spot to shuttle from, but launching at Hallsands (818 388) avoids 3km of pebble beach. The steep shingles of Start Bay recede after Hallsands. If you were wondering where Hallsands actually is, note the shattered ruins on the rocks; a calamitous storm destroyed the village in 1917.

The ebb tide propels you along the curving coast to the jutting mica schist headland of Start Point. Start Point's tide race flows offshore to the south-east, so unless you require a head start to Brittany, some form of break-out is necessary (ask a white-water paddler). Reaching 62m above the water, 28m Start Point lighthouse is unusual, James Walker's 1836 design incorporating gothic battlements. The fog signal house collapsed into the sea in December 1989, necessitating substantial rebuilding. Directly below, the rocks of Black Stone harbour a seal colony.

The 11km of coast stretching to the Kingsbridge Estuary are extremely interesting to kayakers, not to mention extremely beautiful. The cliffs are generally low, with farmland stretching downhill behind. The unique aspects are the raised former beaches visible above the high water mark, and the wave-cut ledges extending out into the waves. These wave-battered platforms were formed when the sea was higher in an inter-glacial period, approximately 120,000 years ago. The bedrock is riven with criss-crossing faults and prolonged wind and wave erosion has widened these. The result is a natural rock-hopping playground, with innumerable channels to probe.

The reef is broken up revealing occasional small sandy beaches. The first is Mattiscombe Beach (817 369) where two peculiar earth pillars on the reef have resisted erosion, due to being capped by harder rocks. Lannacombe Beach (802 372) has road access, although there is only parking for one or two cars. The house here is a former corn mill, and the grinding stones can be found lying nearby.

About 2km after Prawle Point, the keen-eyed will spot a series of WWII fortifications hidden along the shore. These were to protect a radar station near the village of East Prawle.

The southernmost point of Devon and the most distinctive coastal feature is Prawle Point, an angular arch of green-tinted hornblende schist. It can be 'threaded' at high water but don't mess up as the Coastwatch station above will be watching! The rusting scrap metal nearby was formerly MV *Demetrios*. She was blown here by Force 10 winds on 18 December 1992 after a tow cable snapped. She broke her back within an hour of running aground. The subsequent salvage operation bankrupted the salvage company, perhaps explaining the amount of debris remaining. Incidentally, birders will want to know that this is one of the few places where the extremely rare cirl bunting has been spotted in recent times.

Maceley Cove is sheltered by Gammon Head, said to resemble Queen Victoria! Further sandy coves lead to Gara Rock (750 369), where few traces remain of the tramway and pier used in the nineteenth century to ship out iron ore.

Approaching the Kingsbridge Estuary, the coast often receives shelter from Bolt Head against wind and swell. Paddling up the estuary to visit Salcombe (route 15) is a possibility.

The second half of this trip could be described purely by shipwrecks, just a handful of which are mentioned here. The Bar guarding the Kingsbridge Estuary from swell was responsible for the loss of the Salcombe lifeboat *William and Emma* in 1916. The crew had rowed to the aid of the schooner *Western Lass*, grounded near Start Point. They arrived to find the crew already rescued, and returned towards home. The lifeboat capsized in steep breakers whilst crossing The Bar, drowning 13 of the 15 lifeboatmen.

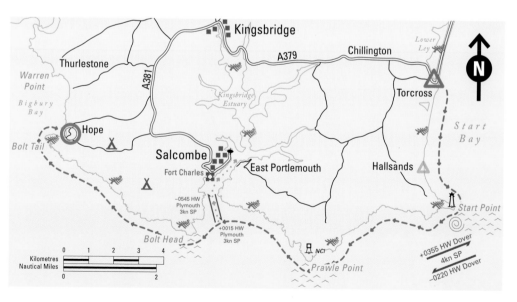

The approach to Bolt Head is beneath 130m cliffs, Starehouse Bay being surrounded by the spiky slopes of Sharp Tor. The rocks in Starehouse Bay are the Rags and the series of rocks extending out from Bolt Head are the Mew Stones, where a tide race might be encountered. The coast's character has transformed completely and 7km of cliffscape stretches away to the west, coloured by patches of thrift and thyme.

Two kilometres from Bolt Head, Steeple Cove is a sheer-sided inlet dominated by a tall stack which presumably supplied the name. In December 1932, the Spanish freighter *Cantabria* ran aground here in fog and all 24 crew made a misguided attempt to scale the cliffs. They were luckily discovered and rescued off the rocks by the lifeboat, narrowly averting a disaster. At LW, remnants of the *Cantabria* can be seen through the clear water.

Soar Mill Cove is the only good spot to land and stretch, before returning to face the cliffs. West Cliff (689 382) also claimed a fog victim. In 1925, the 10 crew of the tug *Joffre* were saved after the Mate swam ashore with rope, allowing a rescue team to rig a 'breeches buoy'. Sadly, the Captain died of exhaustion after rescue. Just to the west, look for 'Ralph's Hole', named after a smuggler who used a pitchfork to prevent Customs officials from investigating what he had stored inside!

Redrot Cove is the location of a monumental cave, and then Bolt Tail is reached. In 1907 this headland witnessed yet another of South Hams' shipwrecks, again in fog. The 76 crew and 79 passengers of the stranded SS *Jebba* were all rescued to the cliffs above. The Hope Cove lifeboat *Alexandra* failed to reach the stricken vessel, but two local fishermen scrambled 60m down the cliffs and managed to rig up two bosun's chairs. Edward VII awarded the Albert Medal to both men.

Tucked behind Bolt Tail is sheltered Hope Cove, journey's end.

VARIATIONS

Salcombe is perfectly placed to divide up this trip; land at North Beach car park (732 381). Mill Bay (740 382) on the east side of the Kingsbridge estuary is a convenient landing to shuttle the first half. Looping into the Kingsbridge Estuary (route 15) to land at Frogmore reduces the shuttle to around 5km.

Tide and weather

A launch around HW will give tidal assistance for much of this trip, although it is concentrated around the headlands and can be weak in-between. Start Point tide race extends 1.5km SE, and forms large eddy currents. Smaller races occur at Prawle Point and Bolt Head. This coast picks up Atlantic groundswell more than other parts of South Devon.

Additional information

Higher Rew campsite (714 382) is 2km from Salcombe, tel. 01548 842681, www.higherrew.co.uk. Bolberry House Farm campsite (695 392) is 2km from Hope Cove, tel. 01548 561251, www.bolberryparks.co.uk.

Alternatives

Salcombe is perfectly placed to divide this trip; land at North Beach car park (732 381). Mill Bay (740 382) on the east side of the Kingsbridge estuary is a convenient landing to shuttle the

first half. Looping into Kingsbridge Estuary (route 15) to land at Frogmore reduces the shuttle to 5km.

The death of Hallsands

Paddling past the shattered ruins clinging to rocks at Hallsands (818 384), it's hard to believe that this was once a large village.

In 1897, work began in Start Bay dredging sand and gravel for the construction of Plymouth docks. Within a few years, locals living and fishing along the beach complained that the beach was receding and that the fishing industry was suffering. Eventually, the authorities took heed and the dredging ended.

On 26th January 1917, an Easterly gale blew along the Channel, combining with spring tides to create a storm surge. The beach was overtopped and water flooded into houses in Hallsands. The village's 128 residents were evacuated. By dawn, four of Hallsands' 30 houses had been destroyed. Locals returned the next day at LW, to retrieve what they could of their belongings.

The following night saw a second storm surge. The village was completely demolished, with only one house left standing.

Kingsbridge Estuary

South Devon Rias ⊙ ⬛ ⬛ ⬛

No. 15 | Grade A | 7.5 / 6 / 10 / 10km | OS Sheets 201 and 202

Tidal Port	Plymouth
Start	△ See below.
Finish	◯ See below.
HW/LW	HW at the mouth of the Yealm is at HW Plymouth. HW at the mouths of the other estuaries is 17 minutes after HW Plymouth.
Tidal times	In the Yealm, the ingoing stream begins 5 hours and 45 minutes before HW Plymouth and the outgoing stream begins 15 minutes after HW Plymouth. This is representative of all four estuaries, although the duration of the outgoing stream in the Erme, Avon and Yealm increases progressively upriver after heavy rain.
Max Rate Sp	At the mouths of all of these estuaries, ebb flows can attain 3 knots.
Coastguard	Brixham, tel. 01803 882704, VHF Weather 0110 UT

Introduction

The Kingsbridge, Avon, Erme and Yealm Estuaries all offer scenic paddles along rias, drowned river valleys fringed by steep shores and wooded banks; English 'lochs'! These sheltered havens

are part of sailing lore and in summer numerous yachts will be anchored here. Observing 'yachtie' culture is part of the enjoyment of these trips. Even so, solitude can be found further upriver.

Description

KINGSBRIDGE ESTUARY

The Kingsbridge Estuary doesn't have a river flowing into it. It is formed by nine separate streams, now muddy creeks. Kingsbridge (736 437) is the best launch point for the paddle to Salcombe (732 381). A car park is located right beside the water with a public slipway at the end. The slipway is usable for at least two hours after HW.

Clear of Kingsbridge's quays, the water opens out and your main companions are wading birds. The only obstacle you'll encounter is the Saltstone, topped by a striped pole. As this unprepossessing drying rock was outside the jurisdiction of local parishes, seventeenth-century non-conformists rowed out and held outlawed services here.

If you seek diversion, Southpool and Frogmore creeks both extend for several kilometres off the main channel to the East, with convenient pubs at the ends.

Approaching Salcombe, you weave among some of the 10,000 yachts that visit annually. On the east shore yellow sand beaches beckon, whilst the west shore is Salcombe itself.

The affluent Sloane culture of Salcombe contrasts sharply with the observations of a 1607 magistrate, *"full of dissolute seafaring men who murder each other and bury the corpses in the sands at night"*. Ashore at the slipway in Salcombe, the Lifeboat House Museum and Salcombe Maritime Museum are worth visiting and it would be rude not to sample 'Salcombe Dairy Ice Cream'.

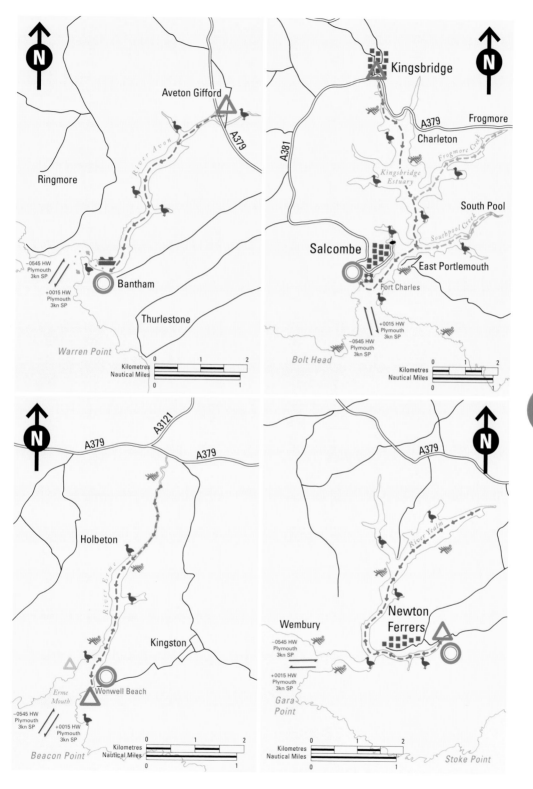

South Devon Rias

Parking and loading is difficult so it's best to paddle another 1.5km to finish at North Beach car park (732 381). This is just past Fort Charles, among the last Royalist strongholds to surrender in the Civil War. It was then slighted (blown up), explaining its current decrepitude.

RIVER AVON

Launch from the car park at Aveton Gifford (692 472) to paddle downriver to Bantham (668 438), or perhaps a make return trip upstream from Bantham. Shallow salt marshes along the upper river belie the fact that 50 years ago, large coal barges made passage here.

You will know you've reached Bantham when you start seeing moored yachts. The first landing spot is the thatched boathouse on the east bank, built in 1937 to commemorate George VI's coronation. This is also the landing place for the ferry, and a steep track leads up to the car park. The alternative is to continue a kilometre further around the corner to the beach at the far end of the car park. Surf is common on the beach and in the river mouth.

RIVER ERME

The Erme is the quietest estuary, and is the only totally undeveloped ria in the South West. It is located on the Flete Estate and awkward to access by road. Wonwell Beach (618 471) is the best access point, with limited parking. At Mothecombe (614 476) a lane leads to the river mouth, but the parking is a steep climb uphill. Whether you launch near the river mouth or paddle in from Bigbury Bay, the Erme rewards the effort. It can only be explored at HW and even then it is too shallow for yachts to penetrate so you will find yourself exploring alone. There isn't even a footpath alongside, real Swallows and Amazons stuff! Be unobtrusive, this is a wildlife sanctuary. The upper limit is a weir at Flete.

RIVER YEALM

The name Yealm is Celtic for 'kind'. The Yealm is the most impressive of the estuaries, being steepest-sided and narrow. The public quay in Bridgend (555 481) is a convenient access point to the 'Newton Arm' of the Yealm, which completely dries out for two hours either side of HW. A short paddle between the villages of Newton Ferrers and Noss Mayo brings you to the so-called Pool at Warren Point, where this side creek joins the Yealm proper. The upper reaches are part of the Kitley Estate and no yachts are allowed past Madge Point, due to oyster beds. Kayaks can potter north up the Yealm for 4km, but landing isn't permitted in this nature reserve.

Tide and weather

All these estuaries offer sheltered paddling, but flows are strong and return trips need to be well timed to avoid slogging against the tide. All the estuaries are protected from the open sea by shallow sand bars. If you follow the ebb out into the sea, be prepared for surf breaking over the bars.

Additional information

A summer ferry service runs between Kingsbridge and Salcombe, tel. 01548 853525.

The AONB website www.southdevonaonb.org.uk offers useful information. Higher Rew campsite (714 382) is 2km from Salcombe, tel. 01548 842681, www.higherrew.co.uk. Mount Folly Farm (661 447) is close to the mouth of the Avon, tel. 01548 810267, www.bigburyholidays.co.uk.

Thurlestone Rock

Bigbury Bay ▪▪▪▪

Bigbury Bay

No. 16 | Grade B | 28km | OS Sheets 202, 201

Tidal Ports	Plymouth and Dover
Start	△ Hope Cove (674 402)
Finish	◯ Bovisand (491 505)
HW/LW	HW in Bigbury Bay is 5 hours and 23 minutes before HW Dover.
	HW Wembury is 5 hours and 40 minutes before HW Dover.
Tidal times	In Bigbury Bay, the WNW going (ebb) stream begins 2 hours before HW Dover. The east going (flood) stream begins 4 hours and 15 minutes after HW Dover.
	At the mouth of the Yealm, the ingoing stream begins 5 hours and 45 minutes before HW Plymouth and the outgoing stream begins 15 minutes after HW Plymouth.
	Between Plymouth breakwater and Bovisand, the outgoing stream begins at HW Plymouth and the ingoing stream begins around 5 hours before HW Plymouth.
Max Rate Sp	Streams in Bigbury Bay reach a maximum of 1 knot on the flood. The ebb is weaker. Streams in Wembury Bay are normally weak, but note that the outgoing-stream from the Yealm flows west across the Bay. Ingoing and outgoing flows at the entrances to Plymouth Sound reach 1 knot.
Coastguard	Brixham, tel. 01803 882704, VHF weather 0110 UT

© *Erme Mouth*

Introduction

This coast is absolutely gorgeous. Pink thrift and yellow kidney vetch adorn cliffs of slate whilst at water level, gnarled reefs reveal phenomenal rock formations. Limited road access means that private beaches can easily be procured. Allow yourself much more time than might normally be needed to cover this distance.

Description

There are two beaches at Hope Cove, divided by the Shippen promontory. The easiest place to launch is the beach in Outer Hope (674 402) which has a car park close by.

From Hope Cove, a reef stretches west. The reef is characterised by tall pinnacles and sharp outlying rocks, great for paddlers but not so good for the *San Pedro*, a hospital ship from the Spanish Armada, wrecked on the Shippen in 1588. Thurlestone Sands is backed by a golf course and farmland, but the focus is Thurlestone Rock (Old English: 'holed rock'), an impressive arch standing solitary in the bay.

The reef recommences as far as Bantham, where the River Avon flows swiftly into the sea and surfers will be encountered. Across the river is Bigbury-on-Sea, connected at low tide by sand to Burgh Island. Detouring around the island allows a close look at the smooth slate cliffs on the east side, followed by exploration of the marvellous deep fissures and gulleys on the west side.

There is no easy road access for the next 16km. More slate cliffs around Toby's Point reflect the sunlight, and then two tiny landing spots appear amongst the rocks, Ayrmer Cove and

Westcombe Beach. Beacon Point is so named as (with every other Beacon Point on the south coast) it was lit to warn of the Armada's approach. Thousands of locals gathered to witness the entire fleet of 140 galleons sail close by.

Erme Mouth is a wide expanse of sand at the mouth of the River Erme, covered at HW. The east shore is Wonwell Beach and the west shore is Meadowsfoot Beach, a private residence. This is a beautiful and undeveloped spot, making a paddle up the river tempting.

Tearing yourself away from Erme Mouth, you pass Gull Cove, where a stream trickles down the cliffs. The bay is guarded by the imposing Bugle Rocks, named because of the noise made by waves compressing against these slate slabs. This is followed by enclosed Butcher's Cove and then you may spot St Anchorite's Rock, a small tor above the cliffs named after a hermit of prior residence.

Stoke Beach is a good spot to take a break, perhaps with a walk uphill to the still consecrated ruins of St Peter the Poor Fisherman Church. There is also a (less appealing) caravan park on the cliffs south of the beach.

The 6km to the River Yealm follows the base of steep cliffs below a disused CG station (the only building) and then The Warren, which as the name suggests was the site of a medieval rabbit farm. These cliffs are home to yellowhammers, kestrels, buzzards and sparrowhawks. Trips tend to slow down here. An astonishing rock-cut platform protrudes from the cliffs, forming a unique maze of small gulleys, arches, caves, and beaches. Those who explore will be rewarded!

Paddling up the Yealm to finish at Newton Ferrers or Noss Mayo is a possibility (see route 15), as is finishing at Wembury (517 484), landmarked by the tower of St Werburgh's Church. The outstanding Victoria sponge served in the beach café at Wembury is indeed tempting, but you really should carry on.

The 6.4km from Yealm Head to Bovisand are the Wembury Voluntary Marine Conservation Area (VMCA), extending out to sea to a depth of 10 metres. As the designation implies this is

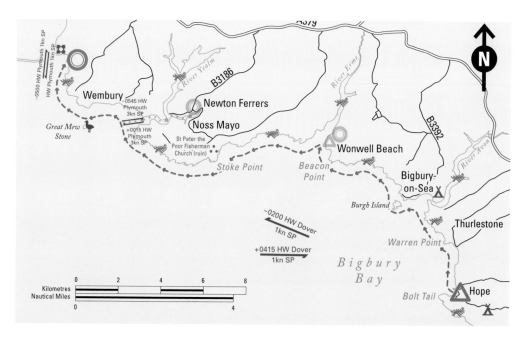

© Dunny Cove

a natural treat; consider jaunts ashore for rock-pooling or even carrying a snorkel. This author hasn't seen either, but apparently the things to look out for are the bloody-eyed velvet swimming crab below the waves, and the rare cirl bunting gliding above!

Offshore, Great Mew Stone Island is home to large numbers of shags, cormorants and herring gulls. The name comes from the mewing of the gulls. Landing isn't allowed, but spare a thought for the convicted man who in 1744 was 'transported' to this guano-smeared slanting rock for 7 years.

Past Wembury Point was formerly HMS *Cambridge*, the Royal Naval Gunnery School. However, the School closed in 2001, so you won't be used for target practice! The last 2km turn north into Plymouth Sound, to finish beneath the walls of Fort Bovisand at Bovisand's yellow sand beach. It's a bit of a carry to the car park.

VARIATIONS

Dividing this trip into shorter sections is difficult. One possibility is Wonwell Beach (617 472) in the River Erme, where there is very limited parking and water access is difficult at LW. Another possibility is to include sections of the tidal rivers (see route 15).

An overnight trip gives more time to explore the many diversions along these shores.

Tide and weather

Tide flows are not strong along the coast, but can be powerful at the river entrances. Bigbury Bay picks up plenty of groundswell, with Bantham and Bigbury being popular surf spots. In such conditions, landing and launching can be difficult. Consider carefully utilising the rips at the river mouths, which tend to flatten the surf.

Additional information

The Wembury Voluntary Marine Conservation Area (VMCA) has a visitor centre just behind Wembury Beach, www.wemburymarinecentre.org.

Bolberry House Farm campsite (695 392) is 2km from Hope Cove tel. 01548 561251, www.bolberryparks.co.uk). Mount Folly Farm (661 447) is a short stroll from the mouth of the Avon, tel. 01548 810267, www.bigburyholidays.co.uk.

Bigbury Bay

Burgh Island

The island is connected by a sand spit to the mainland at LW. At HW, the only way to reach it (unless you happen to possess a kayak) is by 'sea tractor', effectively a trailer on stilts.

There are two major buildings, the Pilchard Inn and the Burgh Island Hotel, which dates from 1336; in Elizabethan times, smuggler Tom Crocker was shot by excisemen outside.

Built 1929–32, Burgh Island Hotel showcases classic Art Deco design, intended to resemble a white ocean liner. The top floors were destroyed by WWII bombing, but this listed building has been fully restored. Luminaries such as Noel Coward, Wallis Simpson and Churchill have stayed here, but the most famous association is with Agatha Christie. She located her detective novels *And Then There Were None* and *Evil Under the Sun* at the hotel, the latter actually being written there.

How much does it cost to stay? Well, if you have to ask, then you can't afford it.

Near Blackstone Point | Heather Rainsley

The mean streets of Hope Cove

Despite its quaint appearance, Hope Cove has enjoyed a long and violent association with smuggling. In 1788, one revenue man had his head split open whilst his companion was crippled. In 1823, 18 local women were sent to Exeter gaol for assaulting a Coastguard when caught smuggling spirits. As recently as 1980 a group of guests at the Hope and Anchor Inn were caught removing 1.5 tons of cannabis from the cave, where it had been landed and hidden, to a waiting lorry.

Drake's Island

The Tamar
& Plymouth Sound

No. 17 | **Grade A** | **31km** | **OS Sheet 201**

Tidal Port	Plymouth
Start	△ Morwellham Quay (446 696).
Finish	◎ Phoenix Wharf, Plymouth (483 538).
HW/LW	LW in the Lynher River is about 20 minutes after LW Plymouth.
Tidal times	From the Tamar Bridge to The Narrows, the outgoing (ebb) stream begins at HW Plymouth and the ingoing (flood) stream begins around 5 hours before HW Plymouth. These times are strongly influenced by runoff from the River Tamar, adding or detracting up to 30 minutes in times of flood or drought. Strong north or south winds can prolong the streams by 15 minutes.
Max Rate Sp	Tide streams reach 5 knots on the Tamar, 1.7 knots in Hamoaze and can exceed 3 knots in The Narrows and The Bridge.
Coastguard	Brixham, tel. 01803 882704, VHF weather 0110 UT

The Tamar & Plymouth Sound

© The Garlandstone, Morwellham Quay

The Tamar & Plymouth Sound

Introduction

This engaging trip follows the River Tamar (and the Devon/Cornwall border) from the Historic quays in its quiet upper reaches, past Royal Navy dockyards to finish in Plymouth Sound, a bustling natural harbour fringed by a city of 250,000 people. Whilst those who came for scenery aren't too well served, those fascinated by maritime history and culture will be utterly riveted.

Description

RIVER TAMAR

Launching onto the tidal River Tamar after HW Plymouth utilises its strong ebb flow to help make this lengthy trip manageable.

The remarkable abandoned copper mining port at Morwellham Quay is being preserved and restored as part of the Cornwall and West Devon Mining Landscape World Heritage Site. Original wharfs, railways, buildings and a huge waterwheel are all intact, but the most impressive relic is the *Garlandstone*. This two-masted Tamar Valley ketch was built at Calstock in 1907. This is a wonderful spot from which to launch. At time of writing, accessing the river here is no problem. However, check www.morwellham-quay.co.uk for current news.

Calstock (435 686) is 5km downstream, unmistakeable by its towering viaduct. Launching from the public pontoon near the Tamar Inn is simpler but less entertaining than at Morwellham Quay. If you have missed out Morwellham, Cotehele Quay is 2km below Calstock and offers some recompense. The stone and slate wharfs and lime kilns are preserved, with a small offshoot of the National Maritime Museum in the quay buildings. Moored alongside is the *Shamrock*, a sailing barge which worked the river and local coast between 1899 and 1963, including transporting 'nightsoil' out of Plymouth. Just uphill, the medieval mansion of Cotehele House can be visited, courtesy of the National Trust.

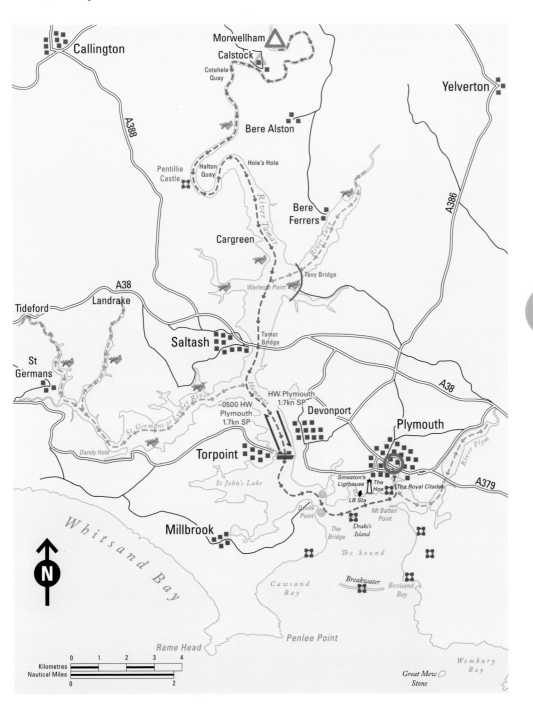

The river enters its quietest stretch, lined by reed beds hiding otters and curlews. Avoid stranding on the widening tidal flats. Pentillie Castle is hidden in trees on the Cornwall bank, but visible from further downstream as you negotiate 'Hole's Hole', a big loop where the river widens. Lines of moored yachts extend right past Cargreen, where the Spaniards Inn has a useful slipway, accessible at all tide states.

On the left bank at Weir Point, the River Tavy joins under a long railway bridge. The ancient woods across the bridge are Warleigh Point Nature Reserve (447 610), but an unprepossessing Naval ordnance depot follows. As with all the military sites that follow, don't approach within 50m or you'll earn a visit from the armed police launches that patrol vigilantly. Likewise, do *not* investigate the contents of the munitions barges moored hereabouts. Keep 200m clear of any submarines underway and pass them 800m astern.

The two towering bridges linking Saltash and Plymouth are oddly reminiscent of Anglesey's Menai Strait. The first is the Tamar Bridge, a suspension design opened in 1961. Close after is the Royal Albert Bridge, a mishmash of suspension cables and iron tubes. Brunel's 1859 design used 4,000 tonnes of iron in two 139m spans to link Cornwall to the Great Western Railway.

HAMOAZE

The Tamar is now known as Hamoaze, after the mud that used to ooze out of Ham Creek. Past the slipways of Saltash, the Lynher River joins from the right. Do not linger in the following 3km as the right bank is an MOD oil depot, whilst the left bank is Devonport Naval Base.

At Torpoint, keep clear of the three chain ferries clanking to and fro. The right bank opens out into the shallow basin of St John's Lake. Avoid this, unless you wish to run aground outside the firing ranges of HMS *Raleigh*, the Royal Navy's main training centre.

The tidal flow now squeezes and accelerates into The Narrows. This tortuous double bend generates strong eddy currents and confused waters. Keeping to the right shore ensures a clear passage through, but it's not a good idea to share this strait with large unmanoeuvrable ships (e.g. 21,578 tonne HMS *Ocean*, the Navy's largest vessel). A beach landing is possible on the right in front of the Edgecombe Arms, otherwise the Tamar opens out into …

PLYMOUTH SOUND

Any lingering claustrophobia now vanishes, but there is less freedom to manoeuvre than might first be imagined. Either side of Drake's Island shallows extend to the mainland, buttressed by submerged anti-submarine defences. Large vessels use Asia Pass, a wide opening north east of the island, whilst small vessels can go west of the island, either sneaking along the western shore or passing through the four tall beacons marking The Bridge. Kayaks can cross anywhere, but risk an encounter with rusty sharp metal. The most interesting option is to negotiate The Bridge, before turning back to view the fortifications on Drake's Island and head into Plymouth.

Crossing Asia Pass to Plymouth, ugly Millbay Silo and the Brittany Ferries dock welcome you to Plymouth. Things improve heading east, as you pass The Hoe where Smeaton's lighthouse stands proud of the walls of The Citadel.

The Mayflower Steps (483 540) are found just beside Sutton Harbour's gates, marked by a giant aquatic creature on a mast! Up the steps, plaques commemorate the departure of the Pilgrim

Fathers onboard *Mayflower* in 1620. Finish nearby at Phoenix Wharf Slipway (483 538), close to Elphinstone Car Park.

VARIATIONS

The Tavy and Plym estuaries offer alternative starts at HW. Before joining Plymouth Sound, the Plym becomes known as Cattewater and forms the Port of Plymouth (www.plymouthport.org.uk) as far as Mountbatten Breakwater.

The Lynher River (also known as the St Germans River) is a maze of drying creeks spreading into Cornwall. The Lynher always has enough water to paddle at least as far upstream as the yacht anchorage at Dandy Hole (383 553). The rising tide is needed to gain access to the shores and the creeks. The River Tiddy can be explored past the St Germans viaduct as far as Morvah Quay at Tideford (348 595). Tideford's limekilns bear witness to the 35 ton barges that somehow navigated the creek. The upper River Lynher leads to Notter Bridge (384 608). The Lynher creeks justify a separate trip, but the Tamar paddle could be extended into a longer adventure; rest after the Tamar until several hours past LW, then enter the Lynher.

Tide and weather

The Narrows generate powerful swirlies and currents on both the ebb and flood, especially behind Devil's Point.

Tide flows extend direct from The Bridge and Asia Pass to either side of the breakwater. In 'The Bridge', tide flows strongly NNW and SSE.

Additional information

In Hamoaze and Plymouth Sound, shipping movements are controlled by the 'Longroom', contactable on Ch14 and 16, call sign *'Longroom Port Control'*.

Single-car groups could utilise the Tamar Valley railway line for the shuttle, which links Calstock and Plymouth. Plymouth Boat Cruises, tel. 01752 408590, operate up and down the Tamar from Mayflower Steps, perhaps another shuttle possibility.

Information on Morwellham Quay can be found at www.morwellham-quay.co.uk, tel. 01822 832766. Information on the Tamar Valley's World Heritage status can be found at www.cornish-mining.org.uk.

The Tamar Estuaries Consultative Forum offer information on the management and ecology of the area; www.plymouth.gov.uk/tecf/.

Devonport Naval Base

Devonport is officially titled HMS *Drake*. 5,000 personnel work here on Western Europe's largest naval base, seeing 5,000 ship movements a year. The docks have 7km of waterfront providing a base for 14 frigates, seven submarines, two assault ships, four survey ships and HMS *Ocean*, a helicopter carrier.

Drake's Island

Drake's Island was previously called St Nicholas Island. The current name stems of course from the Elizabethan privateer Sir Francis Drake, who was governor of the island.

By Drake's time, the island was already fortified and the granite gun emplacements dominating the east shore date from the 1860s. Further concrete fortifications were added during the World Wars.

In 1963 the military departed and the island became an outdoor centre. After the lease expired in 1989, a former Plymouth Argyle chairman bought the island but was refused planning permission for a hotel. In 2005 Drake's Island was briefly designated a nuclear-free state, when protestors squatted in empty buildings to campaign against nuclear submarines.

This intriguing island is currently decaying in limbo, with no clear future plans. Landing is forbidden and due to a radioactive transmission mast, potentially dangerous.

The Tamar & Plymouth Sound

The Eddystone

No. 18 | Grade C | 36km | OS Sheet 201

Tidal Ports	Plymouth and Dover
Start	△ Cawsand (434 502)/Mountbatten Point (481 533)
Finish	◯ Cawsand (434 502)/Mountbatten Point (481 533)
HW/LW	HW Cawsand is as for HW Plymouth; 5 hours and 40 minutes before HW Dover.
Tidal times	At the entrances to Plymouth Sound, the outgoing stream begins at HW Plymouth and the ingoing stream begins around 5 hours before HW Plymouth.
	Between Rame Head and the Eddystone, the W going (ebb) stream begins around 2 hours before HW Dover and the E going (flood) stream begins around 4 hours after HW Dover.
Max Rate Sp	Ingoing and outgoing flows at the entrances to Plymouth Sound reach 1 knot. Offshore between Rame Head and the Eddystone, flows reach a maximum of 1 knot.
Coastguard	Brixham, tel. 01803 882704, VHF weather 0110 UT

Introduction

The first ever rock lighthouse is located 15km offshore from Plymouth Sound. The tale behind the Eddystone light is colourful enough in itself to warrant the paddle out to it. Those seeking a

bit of commitment will relish this experience. The Eddystone is also the focus of a great annual 'Challenge' organised by the Mayflower Offshore Rowing Club.

Description

The Eddystone is located firmly inside Devon, being within the city limits of Plymouth. It is a dangerous submerged reef hindering approaches to Plymouth Sound. In 1620, *Mayflower* captain Christopher Jones gave an apt description; *"Twenty-three rust red ragged stones around which the sea constantly eddies, a great danger … if any vessel makes too far to the south, she will be caught in the prevailing strong current and swept to her doom on these evil rocks."* After successive Herculean efforts to establish lighthouses on these 'evil rocks', there are now two structures adorning the reef, James Douglass' 49m lighthouse of 1882, and the truncated stub of a previous lighthouse.

The paddle out is fairly straightforward in settled and clear conditions. There are a number of launching points within Cawsand and Kingsand. These harbours are sheltered from weather and swell by the Rame Head peninsula, so check the 'real' sea state before launching. The main concern whilst heading out on your chosen bearing from Penlee Point is traffic, which will be lively for the first half, mostly cruising yachts but with some powerboats and the occasional cross-channel ferry! As you get further offshore, Rame Head blurs into the surrounding coast and the traffic thins, with only fishing boats and stray gannets to keep you company. Landing on the lighthouse (383 340) is not permitted, but paddling around the reef is a must, having come this far.

The other way to paddle to the lighthouse is through the excellent Eddystone Challenge, organised each year by the Mayflower Offshore Rowing Club. The Challenge was originally for rowing craft, but is now open to kayaks paddling in pairs. The Challenge departs from the breakwater off Mountbatten Point (481 533) making for a longer trip (44km), but many will appreciate the excellent safety cover.

This author is happy to confess that he hasn't actually been as far as the lighthouse, having been turned back 2km short when his husband-and-wife team missed the cut-off time during the 2007 Eddystone Challenge. Let us know what it is like!

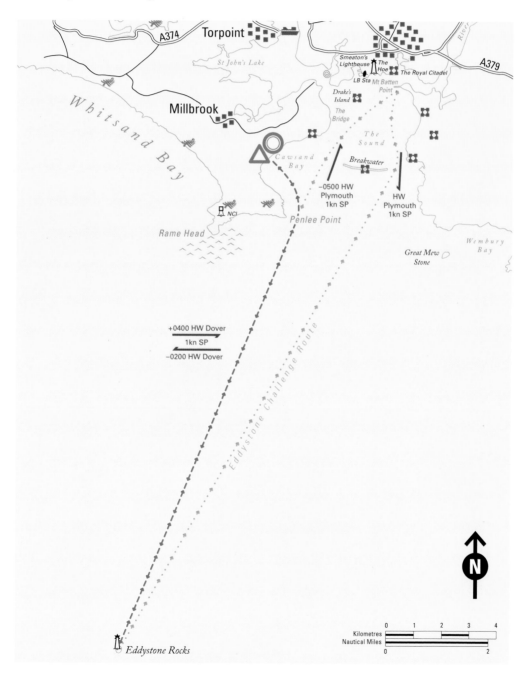

Tide and weather

North–south flowing tidal currents pass either side of Plymouth Breakwater. North of the breakwater is a triangular zone of slack water.

Off Penlee Head, the tide flows in a clockwise rotary direction. Rame Head forms overfalls for 1km offshore in wind over tide. The tidal streams around the Eddystone reef are complex and confused due to the shallow water.

Additional information

Details of the Eddystone Challenge can be found at www.mayfloweroffshorerowingclub.co.uk.

The Eddystone lighthouses

The Eddystone saw the first offshore 'rock' lighthouse and has been marked by five successive lighthouses. Trinity House was petitioned to light the Eddystone in 1655, but concluded that it was impossible. Enter Henry Winstanley, an eccentric innovator and shipping investor who had lost two vessels to the Eddystone. Regarding the Eddystone as a personal affront, he began construction work in 1696. HMS *Terrible* was deployed to protect his workers, but was unfortunately absent when the French arrived and destroyed the foundations. Winstanley was spirited across the Channel but Louis XIV ordered his release, declaring, *"France is at war with England, not with humanity"*.

Winstanley finally lit his lighthouse on 14th Nov 1698, a fantastical octagonal wooden pagoda. He was trapped there by storms until Christmas and winter damage necessitated a complete rebuild in 1699. Winstanley reaped acclaim, but also jibes and criticism. In 1703 he vowed to inhabit his creation during, *"The greatest storm there ever was"*. Winstanley's wish came true. A hurricane on 26th November wrecked 150 ships and drowned 8,000 sailors. It also left no trace of Winstanley or his lighthouse.

The second Eddystone light was completed from timber by John Rudyerd in 1709, but burned down in 1755. Two keepers were drunk but the third (aged 84!) battled the blaze alone. After rescue, his claim that molten lead had poured down his throat was discounted as madness. He died twelve days later and a seven ounce lump of metal was removed from his stomach.

John Smeaton completed the Eddystone's first stone lighthouse in 1759. His design principles were used by Robert Stephenson as the basis of the Scottish lighthouses. Smeaton's lighthouse survived the elements, but the rock underneath eventually fractured. Thus, James Douglass (fresh from Wolf Rock) constructed the present lighthouse. Despite being built on the underwater section of the reef, this 49 metre pinnacle was by now an almost straightforward undertaking, completed 18 months early and under-budget in 1882.

Smeaton's tower had protected Plymouth's shipping for over a century. Townsfolk raised funds for it to be dismantled and re-erected on Plymouth Hoe.

# South Cornwall

An Introduction

Maritime South Cornwall is redolent with mystery and history. The rugged headlands, traditional fishing communities and secluded anchorages have given rise to tales of nefarious smuggling exploits, legends of giants and 'piskies' and of course the novels of Daphne du Maurier.

The nineteenth century saw a regional boom in both fishing and mining, leading to dramatic expansion of ports and shipping. In time the pilchard shoals vanished, the mines failed and the miners emigrated. Those halcyon days left behind an attractive legacy of relics and ruins dotting the coast, as well as a plethora of stone wharfs and quays. Somehow, the industries have endured; china clay is still exported and sizeable fishing fleets continue to eke a living from the depleted Channel. Paddlers will relish these ever-changing environments; a typical day trip might encompass daunting cliffs, tide races, conversations with lobster fishermen, silent creeks and picture postcard harbours.

A significant characteristic of this coast is the manner in which it gradually accumulates wild exposure and beauty along its length, whilst intermittently relenting to offer sheltered harbours and creeks. A multi-day journey from Plymouth Sound to Land's End maintains interest at all times, with the best scenery held back for the final days.

Environment

The majority of South Cornwall's shores are designated as Heritage Coast; namely Rame Head, Gribbin Head – Polperro, Roseland, the Lizard and Penwith. The Cornish Area of Outstanding Natural Beauty (AONB) also incorporates pretty well all of those areas and as always, the National Trust own and manage large tracts of the finest coast. The Helford River is a Voluntary Marine Conservation Area (VMCA). The Navy maintain firing ranges near Rame Head and Dodman Point.

Tide and weather

As might be expected from South Cornwall's indented coast, the tidal situation varies considerably, from little discernable flow in sheltered spots like St Austell Bay to the complex and powerful currents and races around Land's End and The Lizard. The flood stream flows north and east, and the ebb stream flows south and west, into and out of the English Channel. There are plenty of areas that offer shelter from the prevailing south-westerly winds, but any coast facing south or west is likely to pick up groundswell with a fetch extending to Brazil!

Background reading

West Country Cruising Companion, Mark Fishwick, Nautical Data Ltd 2004,
ISBN 1-904358-25-X

Shell Channel Pilot, Tom Cunliffe, Imray 2006, ISBN 0-85288-894-5

Atlantic Edge – West Cornwall, Des Hannigan, Penwith District Council 2007, ISBN 978-0-905375-09-0

Cornwall's Maritime Heritage, Alan Kittridge, Twelveheads Press,2003, ISBN 0-906294-50-9

Cornwall's Lighthouse Heritage, Michael Tarrant, Twelveheads Press 2000, ISBN 0-906294-20-7

Cornwall's Archaeological Heritage, Nicholas Johnson, Twelveheads Press 2003, ISBN 0-906294-52-5

Cornwall's Geological Heritage, Peter Stanier, Twelveheads Press 1990, ISBN 0-906294-61-4

Cornwalls Industrial Heritage, Peter Stanier, Twelveheads Press 2005, ISBN 0-906294-57-6

Cornwall's Literary Heritage, Peter Stanier, Twelveheads Press 1992, ISBN 0-906294-26-6

Wreck and Rescue around the Cornish Coast, Richard Larn, Tor Mark 2006, ISBN 0-85025-406-X

Wild about Cornwall, David Chapman, Alison Hodge 2007, ISBN 978-0-906720-51-6

Cornwall's Marine Guide & Directory – free annual publication from the Cornwall Marine Network, available from Tourist Information Centres

Further information

www.cornwallwildlifetrust.org.uk – Cornwall Wildlife Trust.

www.cornwall-aonb.gov.uk – The Area of Outstanding Natural Beauty.

Basking Sharks

Basking sharks visit the South West in annually increasing numbers through spring and summer. The chances of encountering them are high in Cornwall, and there are now regular sightings off Devon's coasts.

Cetorhinus maximus is the world's second largest fish, growing to ten metres in length (your kayak is around five metres …) and seven tonnes in weight. They are harmless plankton feeders, ambling slowly on the surface to filter water through their enormous white mouths, which concertina outwards to twice the diameter of the shark's body. However, they are capable of jumping clean out of the water, at which time you wouldn't want to be close!

When you spot the telltale fin and following tail, allow your kayak to drift gradually closer with paddle blades out of the water, maintaining a parallel distance of at least four metres. Note that 'recklessly disturbing' a shark is a criminal offence. They will sometimes choose to swim closer to you, even rubbing their backs along your hull. The sensation of proximity to this primal-looking behemoth is beyond description in words.

More info from www.baskingsharks.org.

© Rame Head at dawn

Rame Head 🐾🏕️🏊🚗

No. 19 | Grade B | 25km | OS Sheet 201

Tidal Ports	Plymouth and Dover
Start	△ Kingsand (434 505)
Finish	◎ Looe (257 531)
HW/LW	HW Kingsand is as for HW Plymouth.
	HW Looe is 5 hours and 38 minutes before HW Dover.
Tidal times	At the entrances to Plymouth Sound, the outgoing stream begins at HW Plymouth and the ingoing stream begins around 5 hours before HW Plymouth.
	Between Rame Head and Looe the W going (ebb) stream begins around 2 hours before HW Dover and the E going (flood) stream begins around 4 hours after HW Dover.
Max Rate Sp	Between Rame Head and Looe, flows are weak inshore and reach a maximum of 1 knot. Ingoing and outgoing flows in Looe Harbour reach 5 knots.
Coastguard	Brixham, tel. 01803 882704, VHF weather 0110 UT

Introduction

This 'introductory' stretch of Cornwall's coast, stretching from Plymouth Sound to the resort of Looe, offers consistently pleasant scenery. The best bit comes early with the 7.5km of the Rame

© Near Portwrinkle

Head Heritage Coast, but once this is passed, paddlers are still spoiled with a cornucopia of unfrequented beaches.

Description

The villages of Kingsand and Cawsand are merged inextricably, and your launch spot will be simply determined by whichever parking space you manage to secure amongst the narrow streets. These communities were historically infamous as Plymouth's smuggling base, with the entire population complicit; an eighteenth-century visitor described meeting '... *several females, whose appearance was grotesque and extraordinary ... we found that they were smuggling spiritous liquors by means of bladders fastened under their petticoats.*'

The promontory around Rame consists of steep grassy slopes reaching down to low angled slabs. There are two headlands: Penlee Point and Rame Head, both forming tide races. Woodland extends out to Penlee Point where the 'grotto' marked on the map is a cave, used as a lookout point in the eighteenth century. Approaching Rame Head, inviting coves are encountered, but don't make the same mistake as a friend of the author. His tent now has a tide mark, 60cm above floor level!

Rame Head is unmistakeable, a bare conical hill topped by fourteenth-century St Michael's Chapel with a Coastwatch station nearby. Look out for the peregrine falcons that nest here, although the tide race may preoccupy your attention.

After Rame Head, Whitesand Bay sweeps 8km north-west without direct road access until Portwrinkle. Much of the beach disappears at HW, the sea flooding to the base of the jumbled grassy cliffs. In February 2001, this beach made the headlines after the *Kodima* was blown ashore. The ship disgorged mountains of timber, much of which vanished into the sheds on the cliffs. Another Whitesand wreck is HMS *Scylla*, bought by the National Marine Aquarium after decommissioning and scuttled as an artificial reef in 2004.

The west end of Whitesand Bay passes under Tregantle rifle range. Red flags (red lights at night) denote firing.

At Portwrinkle, reefs surround a tiny drying harbour. This lovely spot is officially the World's Nicest Place for peering into rockpools. The reefs extend along the shore past Downderry, passing the 18m Longstone stack and the dense 'fan' formations of bushes adorning Battern Cliffs. Naturists frolic hereabouts, be warned.

Downderry is a stultifyingly bland place, and awkward to access anyway due to the Sherberterry Rocks. Seaton's sand beach is more appealing, allegedly formed after a mermaid was spurned by a local sailor. She took rejection badly and cursed the town – then larger than Plymouth – to be submerged beneath dunes.

The final 5km pass the pink granite outcrop of Bodigga Cliffs and then popular Millendreath beach (268 540), marked by successive terraces of holiday chalets. Finishing here is a possibility if Looe's car parks are overwhelmed, not uncommon in the summer months.

Looe's beach is often crammed full of sunbathers, best paddle past the beach and around the Banjo Pier, named on account of its shape. This takes you into the Looe River where there are slipways and the Quayside car park on the east shore beside the road bridge.

VARIATIONS

For a shorter trip avoiding Rame Head's tide races, launch from Portwrinkle's twee harbour (354 538). Arrive early as the small car park fills quickly.

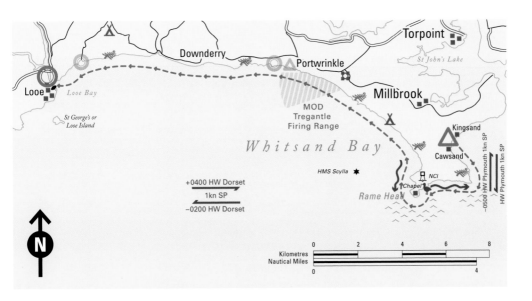

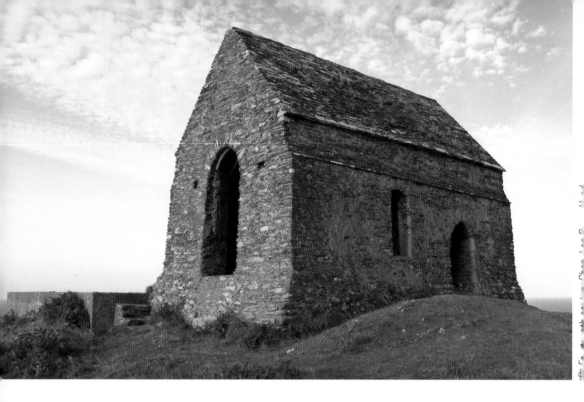

Tide and weather

Off Penlee Head, the tide flows in a clockwise rotary direction. Hence, it's possible to encounter a back eddy current flowing against you, after rounding the Head. Rame Head's tide race can form breaking waves for at least 1km offshore when wind from the west meets the ebb tide.

Additional information

Tregantle Range firing times can be checked with the Coastguard, or by calling 01752 822516.

Tregonhawke Farm campsite (413 514) is a tough climb up from the sea, telephone 01752 823210. Polborder House campsite (283 555) is 3km from Looe, telephone 01503 240265, www.peaceful-polborder.co.uk.

Polperro

Polperro

No. 20 | **Grade B** | **18km** | **OS Sheets 201 and 200**

Tidal Ports	Plymouth and Dover
Start	△ Looe (257 531)
Finish	◯ Fowey (118 510)
HW/LW	HW Looe is 5 hours and 38 minutes before HW Dover.
	HW Fowey is 5 hours and 40 minutes before HW Dover.
Tidal times	A weak W going (ebb) stream begins approximately 4 hours after HW Plymouth. It turns E around 2 hours before HW Plymouth.
	In Fowey Harbour, the ingoing stream begins 6 hours and 10 minutes after HW Plymouth and the outgoing stream begins 15 minutes before HW Plymouth.
Max Rate Sp	Flows in Looe Harbour reach 5 knots. Along the coast weak inshore streams do not exceed 1 knot. In Fowey Harbour, the ingoing stream reaches 1 knot and the outgoing 1.5 knots.
Coastguard	Brixham, tel. 01803 882704, VHF weather 0110 UT

Introduction

This trip includes a quiet island and some wonderful cliff scenery, with the highlight being the sheltered fishing village of Polperro. Deservedly amongst Cornwall's most popular attractions, its

113

20

Polperro

charm is inevitably diminished by hordes of tourists crowding the streets in summer. Arriving by water is the perfect antidote, permitting you to appreciate Polperro without elbowing someone's ice cream.

Description

In summer, securing parking space in Looe can be brutal. You have the option of launching from Looe beach, or (preferably) from the Quayside car park into the Looe River, past the baskets and lobster pots of Looe Port. Looe has a fishing fleet of around 60 boats, sustaining a thriving fish market in East Looe. Passing the Banjo Pier, St George's Island hoves into view. Paddle around to view the shore and meet the island's small seal population. The south-east tip stretches out to the Ranneys, a chain of sharp-looking rocks generating tidal rapids.

Back on the mainland, two pairs of white beacons with black stripes denote a measured nautical mile (1800m), leading past the Hore Stone to Talland Bay. Landing and launching is possible here, although inhibited at HW by a wave-cut platform.

The tall mast on Hard Head indicates Polperro's imminence. You pass a light mounted on the rocks, but the small opening in the cliffs leading to the harbour is hidden until the last moment. Polperro genuinely is a remarkable place. The winding inlet is filled with sheltering fishing boats, with tightly packed cottages lining the steep shores. Follow the inlet to the slipway at the end. You are assured of an appreciative audience, but consider arriving late in the day to ensure it's modestly sized. The street ahead is The Coombes, with decent places to eat and drink amongst the naff gift shops.

Paddling in, you will have passed the Heritage Museum of Smuggling and Fishing, located in a former pilchard factory and worth patronising. Polperro was one of the major smuggling bases on the Cornish coast (along with Cawsand and Mevagissey) and the museum relays the notorious tale of the *Lottery*, a Polperro boat. When the *Lottery* was caught in the act of smuggling by a customs vessel, a customs man was shot dead. A local was convicted and executed for this crime, but there are various versions of the truth and some locals maintain (to this day) that the victim was accidentally shot by his own men.

Leaving Polperro, you'll pass a tidal swimming pool and then the coast is completely undeveloped. The final 10km showcase some stunning cliffs merging into wave-cut platforms, with razor-sharp serrated strata angled upwards from the water. Perhaps not a place for rockhopping! Almost the only sign of civilisation is a lonely hut high above Lantivet Bay. Lantivet and Lantic Bays both have 'secret' beaches to discover.

Entering the River Fowey beneath Polruan's Coastwatch lookout, you have the choice of landing either at Readymoney Cove (118 510) or, for an easier shuttle, on the Polruan side (125 510). Getting a car down Polruan's steep streets to the quay is a bit of a feat.

Tide and weather

Overfalls form on the Ranneys, south-east of Looe Island. Although you're unlikely to take this trip on in heavy seas or strong onshore winds, note that Polperro Harbour closes its storm gate in such conditions, whilst the sea breaks in the entrance to the River Fowey.

Additional information

The Polperro Community website has useful information; www.polperro.org.

Boat trips run between Fowey and Looe, offering an unconventional shuttle possibility.

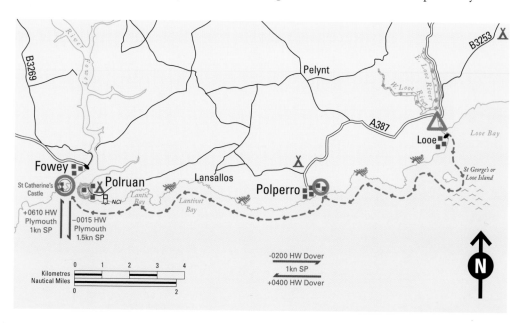

Polborder House campsite (283 555) is 3km from Looe, tel. 01503 240265, www.peaceful-polborder.co.uk. Great Kellow (200 521) is 1.5km from Polperro, tel. 01503 272387. Polruan Camping (132 507) is 1km from the water in Polruan, tel. 01726 870263.

Variations

One option is to explore the East and West Looe Rivers at HW. Both wind 2km inland from their confluence in Looe. The quieter West Looe River is noted for its ancient sessile oaks, with a heronry in Kilminorth Woods.

St George's Island

Also known as Looe Island, this was the site of a Benedictine Monastery in the Middle Ages (bombed during WWII, mistaken for a battleship). The island was infamous for rat infestation, the nineteenth-century novelist Wilkie Collins reporting how they were, *"eaten with vindictive relish by the people of Looe"*. In 1965 the island was bought by the Atkins sisters who lived there for four decades, described in *We Bought an Island*. There are still private residents, but it is now owned by Cornwall Wildlife Trust which maintains it as a sanctuary for the large population of black-backed gulls. A footpath leads around the island, taking in the highest point at 45m.

Access to the island for kayakers is contentious. Above the north spit beach is an enormous 'No Landing' sign. Although the CWT currently 'tolerate' paddlers landing on the beach, they request that visits to the island proper be made in summer only, be pre-arranged with the Trust and be met by the warden, for 'Health and Safety' reasons. A landing fee of £2.50 is payable. More information from http://www.cornwallwildlifetrust.org.uk/reserves/stgeorge.htm

Mevagissey inner harbour

St Austell
& Mevagissey Bays

No. 21 | **Grade A** | **31km** | **OS Sheet 204**

Tidal Ports	Plymouth and Dover
Start	△ Lostwithiel (106 598) or Fowey (118 510)
Finish	○ Gorran Haven (013 416)
HW/LW	HW Fowey is 5 hours and 40 minutes before HW Dover.
	HW Mevagissey and Gorran Haven are 6 hours before HW Dover.
Tidal times	In Fowey Harbour, the ingoing stream begins 6 hours and 10 minutes after HW Plymouth and the outgoing stream begins 15 minutes before HW Plymouth.
Max Rate Sp	Tidal flows are irregular, weak and unpredictable within the Bays. In Fowey Harbour, the ingoing stream reaches 1 knot and the outgoing stream reaches 1.5 knots.
Coastguard	Brixham, tel. 01803 882704, VHF weather 0110 UT

Introduction

There is something for everybody here, from the wooded River Fowey, to the picture postcard fishing village of Mevagissey. Daphne du Maurier fans will be in raptures.

Description

Including the River Fowey is recommended. Launch from Lostwithiel at HW to ride the ebb downstream. The picnic spot below the fifteenth-century bridge (106 598) is a pleasant launch spot. The limekilns and quayside buildings through town remind you that barges came this far upstream less than a century ago. The river opens out after several meanders, with wooded hills either side and egrets wading in the shallows. The fifteenth-century church of St Winnow is passed at the water's edge, and then the River Lerryn Creek joins. The river flows tightly through two bends, where moored 8,000 tonne freighters are a surprise. The tiny River Fowey is the UK's eleventh largest port, exporting 1.5 million tons of china clay a year from the IMERYS Minerals dock.

Entering Fowey town, houses rise direct from the water. At Bodinnick Ferry, the house on the left with a figurehead is Ferryside, home of Daphne du Maurier from 1926 to 1943. Here she wrote *Frenchman's Creek*, *Rebecca* and *Jamaica Inn*.

Fowey's quaint appearance masks an anarchic past. During the Middle Ages, the 'Fowey Gallants' waged a private war against French vessels. A Royal messenger sent to remind the local pirates that England wasn't at war with France had his nose and ears cut off. Later 'free trading' was rife, with 81 Fowey vessels confiscated for smuggling between 1786 and 1815. Two block-houses guard the exit to the sea, built in 1547 to defend against (aggrieved) Frenchmen. In WWII an anti-submarine boom was slung between. The Polruan (east) blockhouse can be visited.

If the Fowey River was enough, land at Readymoney Cove (118 511). If venturing onwards, you enter the sea below St Catherine's Castle.

The 2.5km to Gribben Head follows a series of tiny coves. The largest is Polridmouth. Hidden on the hill behind is Menabilly, *Rebecca*'s 'Manderley' and du Maurier's home from 1943. Gribben Head is unmistakeable, topped by a 104m striped square tower, an 1834 Trinity House daymark. A beach below allows you to survey St Austell Bay. The horizon is dominated by the 'Cornish

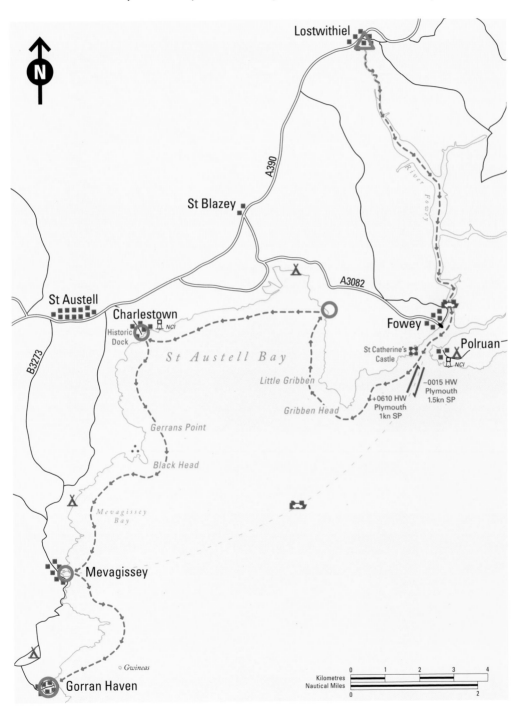

Alps', conical china clay hills that gleamed white until they were boringly 'greened up'. Polkerris is a pleasant harbour 2.5km north, but smoke-belching china clay works follow. Par Sands and Carlyon Bay are beaches largely consisting of silted mineral waste, with dubious water quality. Consider taking a shortcut across the bay.

Next stop is Charlestown; land 500m west of the Coastwatch lookout, at the outer harbour's ridiculously steep slipway. Named after entrepreneur Charles Rashleigh, Charlestown's harbour and dock were designed between 1791 and 1801 by John Smeaton (of Eddystone fame). China clay was still being shipped out in the 1990s, but the dock is now home to three historic ships belonging to the Square Sail Shipyard. The photogenic dock has been a filming location for productions as diverse as *Onedin Line*, *Hornblower* and *The Eagle has Landed*. The Shipwreck Rescue and Heritage Centre (tel. 01726 69897, www.shipwreckcharlestown.co.uk) looks tacky but has a huge collection of shipwreck artefacts.

St Austell Bay's south rim is a succession of sheltered cliffs, caves and hidden beaches. This leads to Black Head with its ancient cliff fort, entrance to Mevagissey Bay. The latter starts unpromisingly, with Pentewan beach backed by a gigantic holiday park. Pentewan was actually a quarry port from 1829 when the railway arrived, to 1918 when the harbour choked with waste.

The bay's highlight is Mevagissey itself. Entering past the cast iron lighthouse, you'll appreciate how active the local fishing industry is, with boats constantly coming and going. This is Cornwall's shark fishing capital, but Mevagissey previously thrived on pilchard fishing, landing 30,000 fish a boat until the shoals dried up. During the Napoleonic Wars, Mevagissey's fast boats smuggled tobacco and brandy. Exploring the small alleys ('squeeze bellies') allows sampling of the quayside chippies and a visit to the town museum.

All that remains is to round low Chapel Point, perhaps with a detour to see the Gwineas Rocks seals, and land at Gorran Haven.

VARIATIONS

The Fowey River is a lovely sheltered paddle in its own right.

Tide and weather

The sea breaks when wind blows strongly against the ebb in the River Fowey entrance. The Bays are sheltered from swell by Dodman Point.

Additional information

Information on Fowey, Charlestown and Mevagissey Harbours from www.foweyharbour.co.uk, www.square-sail.com and www.mevagisseyharbour.co.uk. In summer a ferry service runs between Fowey and Mevagissey, tel. 07977 203394, www.mevagissey-ferries.co.uk.

Broad Meadow House (039 517) is a B&B by the quay in Charlestown offering 'tent and breakfast', tel. 01726 76636, www.broadmeadowhouse.com. Two Holiday Parks offer beachside camping; Par Sands (082 533) near Par Docks, tel. 01726 812868, www.parsands.co.uk and Pentewan Sands (018 468) on Pentewan Beach, tel. 01726 843485, www.pentewansands.com. Trelispen Camping (005 422) is just outside Gorran Haven, tel. 01726 843501, www.trelispen.co.uk.

St Austell & Mevagissey Bays

St Anthony Head Lighthouse

The Roseland Peninsula

No. 22 | **Grade A** | **29/31km** | **OS Sheet 204**

Tidal Port	Dover
Start	△ Gorran Haven (013 416)
Finish	○ St Mawes (848 331) or Falmouth (803 312)
HW/LW	HW Gorran Haven is 6 hours before HW Dover.
	HW Falmouth is 6 hours after HW Dover.
Tidal times	Off Dodman Point, the W going (ebb) stream begins 3 hours before HW Dover. The E going (flood) stream begins 3 hours after HW Dover. The tide begins to ebb S out of Carrick Roads 6 hours and 5 minutes before HW Dover.
Max Rate Sp	Flows reach a maximum of 1 knot along the coast, but 2 knots off Dodman Point. Tidal flows ebbing out of Carrick Roads reach 1.5 knots, 2 knots after heavy rain.
Coastguard	Brixham, tel. 01803 882704, VHF weather 0110 UT, (from Dodman Point) Falmouth, tel. 01326 317575, VHF weather 0110 UT

Introduction

The Roseland Peninsula extends south, to the east of Carrick Roads. The Roseland Heritage Coast is comprised of quiet sandy beaches, pretty fishing villages and craggy headlands. This

makes for a wonderful paddle in a secret corner of Cornwall that is the diametric opposite of bustling Newquay!

Description

Launching from Gorran Haven's harbour is possible at any state of the tide, although it does dry out. Right away, Pen-a-maen Point gives the flavour of this coast, 50-100m cliffs covered in yellow lichen and topped by gorse and ferns, fronted by granite reefs. Shortly after, lovely Vault Beach is a reminder that there are no long exposed sections, with beaches never far away. Additionally there is hardly any tourist development to be seen.

Dodman Point is a distinctive 114m promontory, topped by the largest cliff castle in the South West with two enormous earthwork banks (The Bulwarks). Due to its alleged coffin-like profile, Dodman is often referred to as the 'Deadman'. The east-facing cliffs are fairly sheer, and a tide race awaits you at the end, which can be almost bypassed close inshore. The west side is more interesting, with inlets and caves. You'll now be able to see the tall granite cross on the summit, built as a day mark in 1896 by a local parson.

Two kilometres into Veryan Bay is Porthluney Cove, and behind you'll glimpse the entrance to Caerhays Castle (open to the public, oddly, from February to May), tel. 01872 501310, www. caerhays.co.uk. Built in the seventeenth century, Caerhays is best known as the location for Manderley House in Hitchcock's 1940 film of Daphne du Maurier's novel *Rebecca*. Try to visualise it burning, with evil Mrs Danvers screaming within.

The smattering of buildings named East and West Portholland are a failed fishing port, but 2.5km on is more successful Portloe. There is no harbour, so crab and lobster fishing boats are simply dragged up the landing beach, almost obscured in a tiny inlet. Close by is a steep slipway leading up to the former lifeboat house.

80m Nare Head bars the entrance to Gerrans Bay. The 38m pointed islet 500m offshore is Gull Rock, hosting a breeding population of cormorants, shags, razorbills, and kittiwakes. Just around the head, look out for the remains of a fisherman's hut in Mallet's Cove. Gerrans Bay has lower cliffs and wider beaches. This sleepy backwater had 15 minutes of fame in 1985 when Simon Le Bon's* yacht *Drum* lost its keel and capsized during the Fastnet Race.

Carne Beach is the largest beach in the bay. It has an ancient raised beach behind and at its east end are odd Tor-like outcrops of quartzite. Legend has it that a giant called Tregeagle lobbed them here from Cornwall's north coast.

Just past a Coastwatch lookout is the sandy harbour of Portscatho. This delightfully time-warped village is the last place in England where small boys wear shorts.

The 7km to Zone Point are punctuated only by two unfrequented beaches, Towan and Porthbeor. Zone Point's jagged rocks and caves are a rallying point for cormorants and seals. Just past is St Anthony Head, with the remains of successive gun batteries discernable. The lighthouse was built by Trinity House in 1835 to guide vessels clear of The Manacles Rocks to the south into Carrick Roads. It was built just a few metres above the water's edge and may seem familiar to those of a certain age … it featured in the children's TV show *Fraggle Rock*!

You now have the choice of rounding the Roseland Peninsula into Carrick Roads, in which case St Mawes Harbour is 2km north (see route 21). Those continuing down the coast will

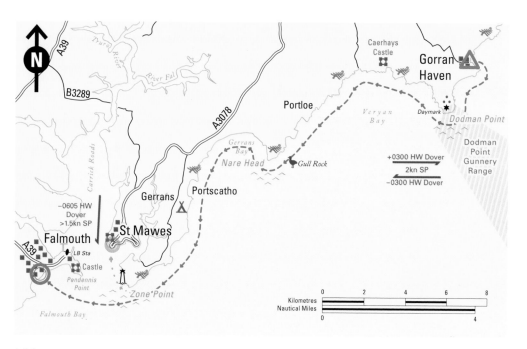

Ask your parents.

© Nare Head

need to carefully cross the busy entrance to Carrick Roads to Pendennis Point and then land at Swanpool Beach, 4.5km from the lighthouse.

VARIATIONS

This could be combined with Route 21 to make a fine overnight trip right around the peninsula.

Tide and weather

The degree of commitment is mild as although there are exposed headlands and cliffs, you are never far from a beach. Tide flows are very mild within Veryan Bay and Gerrans Bay, but heavy tide races can be found off Dodman Point, extending up to 1.5km offshore. Nare Head and Zone Point also generate tide races. Rough water can be encountered in the entrance to Carrick Roads when ebbing tide meets wind from the south.

Additional information

Dodman Point Gunnery Range fires seaward once or twice weekly, except during August and the two weeks over Christmas. Details of firings are given within the Coastguard's Maritime Safety Information broadcasts, or can be obtained direct from the Training Operations Room via VHF Channel 74 or by phone on 01752 557550.

Trelispen Camping (005 422) is just outside Gorran Haven, tel. 01726 843501, www.trelispen. co.uk. Treloan Coastal Farm (874 348) is close to Portscatho beach, tel. 01872 580989, www. coastalfarmholidays.co.uk, and has a camping barn for groups.

Carrick Roads 🔘🏄🚗🚢

No. 23 | Grade A | 20km | OS Sheet 204

Tidal Port	Plymouth
Start	△ Truro (833 437)
Finish	◯ Falmouth (812 325)
HW/LW	HW Falmouth and Truro is 5 hours and 58 minutes before HW Dover.
Tidal times	The tide begins to flow S (ebb) out of Carrick Roads 6 hours and 5 minutes before HW Dover.
Max Rate Sp	Tides can reach 3 knots in the upper reaches. Tides flows ebbing out of Carrick Roads reach 1.5 knots, 2 knots after heavy rain.
Coastguard	Falmouth, tel. 01326 317575, VHF weather 0110 UT

Introduction

Carrick Roads is the natural anchorage (roadstead) formed by the drowned valley of the River Fal and its tributaries, a 'ria' dating to the last Ice Age. Ports such as Falmouth, Penryn and Truro flourished around the harbour during the nineteenth-century tin trade. Although only Falmouth is still functioning as a major port, Carrick Roads is still important as the first and last port of

call for large ships approaching or leaving England. It is also a major breeding ground for wading birds. The paddle from Truro to the sea is a gem, exploring wooded creeks followed by a major harbour, with all manner of diversions en route.

Description

The Port of Truro had many quays within the city centre, but most have silted up. Easiest access for paddlers is the slipway at Boscawen Park (833 437) 1km down the Truro River and usable for an hour either side of HW. Here there is free parking with a fine view of Truro Cathedral. At HW neaps you may have to launch 1.5km further from a slipway in Malpas (841 426), near the Heron Inn.

Downstream of Boscawen Park, a daunting pair of gates are part of a flood prevention scheme and are only closed on exceptional high tides. The river squeezes past a busy working wharf and then opens out into a glorious wooded valley, continuing for the first half of this trip.

At Malpas, there is an exclusive looking waterfront residential complex. The following 3km are the quietest part; look out for herons. King Harry Reach begins where the River Fal joins from the east, where the land is Lord Falmouth's estate. There are occasional glimpses of Tregothnan, his stately home. Surprisingly large ships are moored in the strong current, the narrow river being used for laying up redundant commercial vessels.

500m below is Tolverne Point, location of the Smuggler's Cottage, a famous tea room and restaurant. Whilst quaffing cream teas, take a look at the nautical memorabilia on display. Even if you don't land, you will see the Union Jack and Stars and Stripes flying side by side. This is the spot where General Eisenhower viewed a huge fleet of landing craft, assembled for the D-Day Landings.

Another 500m brings you to the rather large and rather blue King Harry Ferry, shuffling cars across to the Roseland Peninsula on the left. Directly below on the right is a pontoon for the Truro-Falmouth passenger ferry, serving the National Trust property of Trelissick Gardens (tel. 01872 862090). A landing on the pier's shoreward side allows you to pay the entrance fee and explore the gardens, where hydrangeas, rhododendrons, camellias and other exuberantly colourful plants bloom. The gardens surround Trelissick House, a Georgian mansion that is not open to the public but that can be viewed from the water around the next corner.

Turnaware Point forms a sandy spit where the river opens out into Carrick Roads proper, with a small tide race. The roadstead is up to 2km wide, offering numerous route choices. Traffic is always busy, so stay alert. The rocky east shore is quieter (but is a waterski area) and less developed with occasional sandy beaches, whilst the west shore is characterised by villages and private residences for much of the 5km to Falmouth. On the west shore, Mylor Harbour was used by the Free French during WWII as a base for cross-Channel raids. Close by, Penarrow Point (headland of drowned bodies) is so named as hundreds of corpses washed ashore here after the troopship *Queen* was wrecked in 1814.

The approach of the sea is indicated by St Mawes Castle and Pendennis Castle, constructed for Henry VIII between 1540 and 1550 in the 'concentric clover leaves' style. English Heritage manages both, with St Mawes the easiest to visit from the water. Incidentally, the large building below Pendennis is Falmouth Coastguard, covering the coast as far as north Devon.

Falmouth docks are an interesting place to complete the trip, but perhaps first dip your toe in the English Channel with an excursion south past Carricknath beach to St Anthony Head lighthouse.

Falmouth Port functions as a ship repair dock and can reward (careful) exploration. Land past the National Maritime Museum Cornwall (813 324), unmistakeable with its 'lighthouse' design. There are car parks nearby.

VARIATIONS

There is endless exploring to be had in the River Fal's side creeks. All dry out at LW. The Tresillian and upper Fal (Ruan) Rivers offer quieter starts to this trip, with exceptional birdlife. Restronguet Creek has the remains of a nineteenth-century shipyard and wharfs to view. Upstream past Falmouth, Penryn Creek was once a granite exporting port. Up past St Mawes, the delightful Percuil River bisects the Roseland Peninsula.

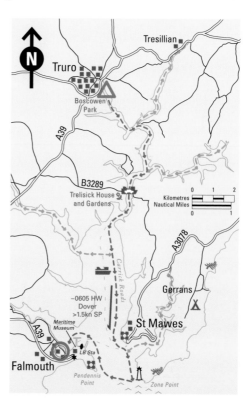

Carrick Roads

St Mawes Castle

Tide and weather

This trip is well sheltered from the sea state, but Carrick Roads is big enough to generate large waves, especially with wind from the N or S. The seaward entrance to Carrick Roads can be very choppy with a south wind and ebb tide.

Additional information

The National Maritime Museum makes an excellent finale. Kayaks belonging to Sean Morley and Derek Hutchinson have been displayed, tel. 01326 313388, www.nmmc.co.uk.

Ferries run a service between Truro, St Mawes and Falmouth, the hour-long journey offering a shuttle option - www.falriverlinks.co.uk.

There is useful port information at www.portoftruro.co.uk and www.falmouthport.co.uk.

Trewince Farm campsite (867 336) is hidden up the Percuil River, tel. 01872 580430, www. trewincefarm.co.uk, with access to the water.

Shark's Fin rock, Manacle Point

Helford River
& The Manacles

No. 24 | Grade B | 16/20km | OS Sheet 204

Tidal Ports	Plymouth and Dover
Start	△ Falmouth (803 312) or Gweek (706 267)
Finish	○ Coverack (784 182)
HW/LW	HW Falmouth is 6 hours after HW Dover.
	HW Helford River is 6 hours and 13 minutes before HW Dover.
	HW Coverack is 6 hours and 7 minutes after HW Dover.
Tidal times	Off Manacle Point, the SW going (ebb) stream starts 3 hours after HW Plymouth. The NE going (flood) stream begins 3 hours before HW Plymouth.
Max Rate Sp	Off Manacle Point, flows reach 2 knots.
	In the Helford River, flows reach 2 knots.
Coastguard	Falmouth, tel. 01326 317575, VHF weather 0110 UT

© Coverack

Introduction

South of Falmouth, the indented coast offers extremes of contrast, from the sheltered creeks of the idyllic Helford River, to the treacherous ships' graveyard of The Manacles.

Description

This paddle can commence near Falmouth, or alternatively from Gweek, the head of the Helford River. The latter option is more scenic.

Swanpool Beach (803 312) on the outskirts of Falmouth and (2km south past Pennance Head) Maenporth Beach (790 296) are both convenient for parking and launching. Outside Maenporth is the wreck of the *Ben Asdale*, which went ashore in a 1979 blizzard, costing three lives. Gorse-covered Rosemullion Head is recognised by its curved cliffs and level top. Grassy cliffs lead to Toll Point, mouth of the Helford River.

A short crossing brings you to Dennis Head, which hides successive defences from down the centuries beneath its overgrown flanks. A diversion into Gillan Harbour is possible, but the creek dries out quickly.

The cove of Porthallow is a lovely undeveloped spot, with free beachside parking and a pleasant café in the former 'pilchard palace' (fish cellars). Quarrying traces are discernable out to Porthkerris Point. An ugly dive centre at the Point was formerly an MOD torpedo test site.

Porthhoustock was a fishing cove, but also has old jetties for the quarries, from where river barges would carry stone to Falmouth. Several quarries are still active, the local gabbro used in road-building. The southern fringe of the cove is heavily quarried Manacle Point, but your attention will be drawn ahead to the Shark's Fin. This is part of the infamous Manacles, numerous sharp rocks punctuating the water for over 1km offshore. The name comes from the Cornish *maen eglos* meaning Church Stones; the spire of St Keverne can be seen from the rocks. Buried in the churchyard are 48 of 106 who drowned when the liner *Mohegan* struck the rocks in 1898. Paddling offshore to explore allows you to avoid the waste tips and working quarry on Dean Point.

Lowland Point is a wide area of raised beach with traces of prehistoric huts and medieval field strips. Landing is easiest on the east side.

At Coverack you have the option of landing on the beach or at the atmospheric harbour.

HELFORD RIVER

Part of the reason for this drowned valley's timeless beauty is that yacht anchorage is restricted, largely to protect the Duchy of Cornwall's oyster beds. The Helford River retains an almost religious status among yachtsmen. The south shores are The Meneage (Cornish; *Land of the Saints*), consisting mainly of agricultural land, whilst the granite trading quays of the north shores bear marks of an industrial past. Both shores feature gloriously secretive side creeks, with tree branches trailing in the water.

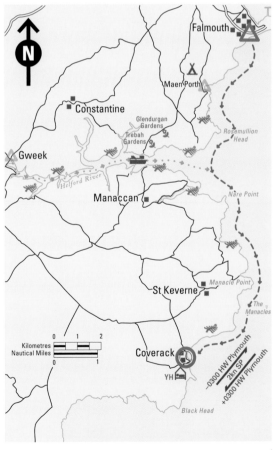

The river's seclusion means that parking is limited and usually located some distance from the water. Thankfully, parking and launching from Gweek, the head of the river, presents no problems for two hours either side of HW springs. Gweek's abandoned wharves and old rotting hulls and warehouses suggest that it was once much busier.

There is nothing in the upper river except you … so enjoy. After 3km is Tremayne Quay, built for a visit by Queen Victoria. The river widens at Groyne Point and just south is the narrow entrance to Frenchman's Creek, of literary fame. Calamansack is the upper limit of yacht anchorages.

A detour north leads to Porth Navas, where two quays shipped granite in the nineteenth century.

A passenger ferry connects Helford on the south shore to Helford Passage on the north shore. Helford saw plenty of 'free trading' during the Napoleonic Wars. Today, 'private quay' signs predominate

Helford River & The Manacles

but The Shipwright's Arms serves an impressive variety of Ploughman's. Five hundred metres north, you can land right in front of Helford Passage's Ferry Boat Inn ('FBI'). For a horticultural interlude, it's a 1km walk to Trebah Gardens, tel. 01326 250448, www.trebah-garden.co.uk, and a little further on is Glendurgan Garden, www.nationaltrust.org.uk/devoncornwall.

Polgwidden Cove played a role in WWII. The US 29th Infantry Division embarked here in June 1944 for Omaha Beach, and a secret trawler service ferried spies of the Strategic Operations Executive (SOE) to France, and downed airmen back.

If you don't intend to continue into the open sea, landing is awkward. Parking is impractical in Gillan Harbour, so a return to Helford Passage is easiest. The car park is a steep climb uphill.

VARIATIONS

The Helford River is worth exploring in isolation, but parking near the river is tricky.

Tide and weather

In the Helford River, avoid stranding on mud as the tide recedes.

Strong tidal flows can be found between the rocks of The Manacles, and the whole area becomes rough with wind against tide.

Additional information

The Helford River is a Voluntary Marine Conservation Area, see www.helfordmarineconservation. co.uk for more information. Gweek is home to the National Seal Sanctuary, tel. 01326 221874, www.sealsanctuary.co.uk, with domestic and foreign flavours featured.

Tregedna Farm campsite (785 304) is 1.5km from Maenporth beach, tel. 01326 250529, www. tregednafarmholidays.co.uk. Coverack Youth Hostel (782 181) has camping, a steep climb uphill from the harbour, tel. 0870 770 5780, www.yha.org.uk.

Sign in Lizard village

The Lizard

No. 25 | Grade C | 27km | OS Sheets 204 and 203

Tidal Ports	Plymouth and Dover
Start	△ Coverack (784 182)
Finish	○ Gunwalloe Church Cove (661 205)
HW/LW	HW Coverack and Cadgwith are 6 hours and 7 minutes after HW Dover.
	HW Mullion Cove is 5 hours and 55 minutes after HW Dover.
Tidal times	Inshore at Lizard Point, the W going (ebb) stream begins 1 hour and 55 minutes after HW Plymouth and the E going (flood) stream begins 5 hours before HW Plymouth.
Max Rate Sp	Off Black Head, rates reach 3 knots. At Lizard Point, flows reach 3 knots on the ebb and 2 knots on the flood.
Coastguard	Falmouth, tel. 01326 317575, VHF weather 0110 UT

Introduction

The Lizard peninsula has been responsible for over 500 recorded shipwrecks. Today it remains an obstacle to trade, with an unending line of container ships punctuating the horizon around Lizard Point.

133

© Mullion Cove and Island

For paddlers, the southernmost point of Britain's mainland showcases superlative maritime scenery, wildlife and culture. The cliffs are particularly amazing; you won't need to be a geologist to enjoy the Technicolor slates, schist, gneiss, granite, gabbro, and serpentine in the remarkable cliffs.

Description

Coverack lies on the less exposed East side of the Lizard. The beach covers at HW, but the harbour has a slipway. The harbour wall is constructed from serpentine, a local reddish or greenish-brown stone so-named as it resembles a snake's skin when wet. Beside the harbour on Dolor Point are a disused lifeboat station and the Paris Hotel, named after local people rescued 700 passengers from the 10,449 ton liner *City of Paris* which grounded on Lowlands Point in 1899. Remains of the ship are displayed inside.

Cliffs of serpentine commence at Coverack, leading around Chynhallis Point and on to the tide race off Black Head, where you'll first feel Atlantic swell. The next 5km pass several rocky beaches and Carrick Luz, a promontory with spiky rocks offshore. The cliffs fall back briefly at Kennack Sands, a long beach fronted by a wide reef of pink granite.

The pebble beach of Carleon Cove (728 156) hides a treat. Between 1855 and 1893, the Lizard Serpentine Company processed serpentine here, and beachcombing reveals polished examples of their work. The fallen chimney, fish cellars, warehouses and the rounded capstan house are clearly discernable. Stone was supplied from the quarry which is seen paddling south, near Enys Head where a landslip bit a large swathe out of the cliffs.

The thatched cottages of picturesque Cadgwith are hidden inside a narrow inlet. The black shack on the cliff was a Victorian huer's hut. 'Huers' were lookouts who would shout out when pilchard shoals were spotted. Cadgwith's twin beaches are divided by a rock outcrop, The Todden. With no harbour, the fishermen drag their boats ashore on rollers. Keep your kayaks out of the way on this working beach. Cadgwith Cove Inn is adorned by photos of the fishermen, and hosts unique traditional music get-togethers; folk music Tuesday night, Cornish maritime singing Friday night.

It's tough to tear yourself away from Cadgwith, but the best is still to come. The Devil's Frying Pan is an arch leading to a massive collapsed cave, now a sizzling 'frying pan' pool. Shortly after comes another arch, between quarried Polgwidden and Parn Voose Coves. Church Cove is the last evacuation point, look for the converted capstan roundhouse. The Lizard lifeboat station is nearby at Kilcobben Cove.

There is a real sense of foreboding as the tide pulls you below the Coastwatch station on Bass Point, and the very base of Britain opens up ahead. The white building above Bass Point is the Lloyds Signal House, once among the World's busiest communications centres. One thousand ships a month had their arrival from the Atlantic relayed to their owners in London. In 1913 the *Queen Margaret* was wrecked on the rocks whilst waiting for an answer! In Housel Bay, look for the signal cable cut into the cliff, linking to Bilbao in 1872. Up the footpath are huts (712 119) used by Marconi in 1901 for the first over-horizon transmission, 186 miles to the Needles.

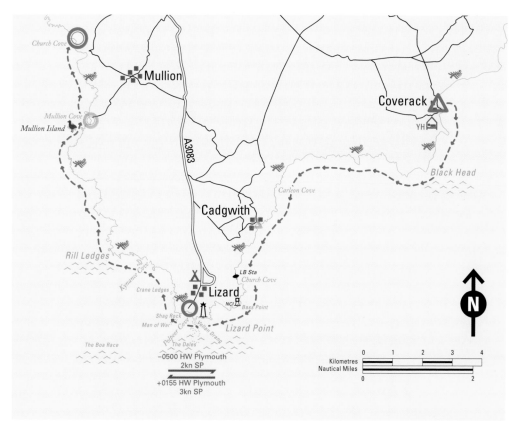

© *Conversing with seals, Polpeor Cove*

Past The Lion's Den (another collapsed cave) and Bumble Rock you can go no further south! Sawtooth reefs extend offshore; Vellan Drang, Shag Rock and Man o' War rocks are up to 500 million years old, the route through them dependent upon tide. This is a paddler's playground, with caves, arches and inlets to explore, but it's also an exposed position with swell and powerful tide races. Spare a thought for round-Britain paddler Mick Wibrew, who was backlooped here.

Landing is possible, on calm days at least, by the old lifeboat slip at Polpeor Cove. It's worth climbing up the track to visit the twin octagonal towers of the world's largest lighthouse complex. From 2008 the lighthouse will host much of the collection from the former National Lighthouse Museum at Penzance.

Around Lizard Point, the cliffs are draped with bright orange Hottentot fig, a South African interloper. More local is the Cornish chough, Cornwall's 'national' bird which after 50 years of absence returned to the county in 2002, breeding hereabouts.

On the west coast, swell breaks over reefs like Crane Ledges, but if you can stay inshore, do so! Kynance Cove is a famous beauty spot, with a strand of sand linking tall Gull Rock and Asparagus Island to the shore at low tide. The rocks are composed of multi-coloured serpentine and covered by wild flowers. There are numerous stacks look for blowholes and caves with names like Devil's Letterbox, Devil's Bellows, Ladies's Bathing Pool, Drawing Room …

Phenomenal cliffs continue. Past Rill Ledges, the jagged ridge of The Horse, the 70m sheer walls of Pigeon Ogo and the dark green serpentine of Vellan Head keep the gawp count high.

The cliffs of Mullion Island are inhabited by black-backed gulls, shags, cormorants, guillemots, razorbills and kittiwakes. Behind is the sheltered landing at Mullion Cove (666 178), where

one million pounds has been spent maintaining the battered harbour walls in the last decade. Finishing the trip is possible here.

Continuing north, Polurrian Cove is the boundary where the rock becomes slate. Poldhu Cove is a sandy bay popular with sunbathers. Atop the south cliffs is an obelisk (664 194) commemorating the first transatlantic radio transmission ('S' in morse code), made in 1901 to Marconi in Newfoundland. He really did get around.

Tiny Gunwalloe Church Cove is quite lovely, a great spot to finish. The small church in the dunes is gradually being surrounded by the sea as the beach erodes. The car park is some distance along a track, and whilst the beach of Jangye-ryn is slightly closer, it can be awkward for landing due to boulders dumped to stop the cliffs and beach eroding.

Those wanting to explore a little further will enjoy the contorted strata of Halzephron Cliff, and miniscule Dollar Cove 500m further at the end of the headland. The name refers to the silver dollar coins sometimes discovered here, reputedly from the wreck of a Spanish ship in the 1780s. However, the beach at Gunwalloe Fishing Cove shelves steeply and makes for a tough landing unless you have flat calm.

VARIATIONS

Consider making this an overnight trip, otherwise the journey from Cadgwith to Mullion Cove is a shorter 'asset strip'.

137

Tide and weather

The tide race off Black Head breaks in wind against tide conditions. A long and complex series of tide races extend from Bass Point around to Lizard Point, with conditions variable depending upon which reefs are uncovered. The races extend up to 5km offshore. The final coastal race is at Rill Ledges. The Boa Race forms 3km west of Lizard Point, should you find yourself out there.

Atlantic groundswell is first felt rounding Black Point. From Bass Point onwards, this trip is fully exposed to the prevailing swell. This may make the tide races 'exciting' and force an offshore course, with Mullion Cove becoming the only sheltered landing before Porthleven.

Additional information

Coverack Youth Hostel (782 181) has camping, a steep walk from the harbour, tel. 0870 770 5780, www.yha.org.uk. Henry's Campsite (701 125) is located in Lizard village, 1.5km from Polpeor Cove, tel. 01326 290596.

Lizard wild flowers

Even the most botanically ignorant paddler cannot fail to notice the exceptionally beautiful wild flowers that proliferate along the shores of the Lizard Peninsula. Sea campion and wild thyme are just two of the more common species to be found on the cliffs. The bloody cranesbill, recognisable by its purple flowers, grows on serpentine cliffs due to their high magnesium content. Cornish heath spreads across the plateau above, a heather species with multi-coloured blooms. This summary barely starts to do justice to the incredible botanical diversity, the booklet *Wild Flowers of the Lizard* (ISBN 1-903-798-01-9) is recommended for more information.

Mount's Bay

No. 26 | Grade B | 26km | OS Sheet 203

Tidal Port	Plymouth
Start	△ Gunwalloe Fishing Cove (653 223) or Porthleven (628 257)
Finish	○ Mousehole (470 263)
HW/LW	HW Porthleven is 5 hours and 51 minutes after HW Dover.
	HW Penzance is 6 hours and 35 minutes before HW Dover.
	HW Mousehole is 5 hours and 50 minutes after HW Dover.
Tidal times	Offshore between The Lizard and Gwennap Head, a SW going stream starts 2 hours before HW Dover and progressively swings WNW. An ESE stream begins 5 hours after HW Dover.
Max Rate Sp	Tidal flows are weak and irregular within Mount's Bay. Offshore, they reach 1 knot.
Coastguard	Falmouth, tel. 01326 317575, VHF weather 0110 UT

Introduction

Paddlers could easily overlook or discount the shores of Mount's Bay, nestling as it does between the magnificent peninsulas of The Lizard and Land's End. There is actually a great deal to see here, with enough variation and distraction to potentially fill several trips.

Description

Gunwalloe Fishing Cove (653 223) is a launch point for completists, accessing 4km of steeply shelving beach. This isn't completely monotonous, however. The Loe Bar is a barrier beach of flint shingles, formed by rising sea levels since the last Ice Age.

Most will probably launch in Porthleven, using the inner harbour's slipway. The harbour is recognisable from the clock tower beside the pier. After major storms, newspapers regularly carry pictures of waves overtopping this wall, which has been rebuilt more than once. The cannons around the harbour come from HMS *Anson* and above the North side of the harbour is a monument to those who've lost their lives in Mount's Bay.

Just outside, a wavecut platform of potholed dark slate commences the most scenic 5km of this trip. At low tide, the Giant's Rock is uncovered, a 50 tonne glacial 'erratic', of a form of gneiss unknown in the UK! The dark cliffs fall back to reveal two successive 'exclusive' beaches (exclusive to paddlers, anyway), and the keen-eyed will find a great tunnel located between them.

The underlying geology makes a dramatic transformation to columns and buttresses of lighter granite, streaked by damp mosses and riddled with caves. The two successive promontories of Trewavas and Rinsey Heads are a taster of the scenery around Land's End! Between the two is sandy Rinsey Cove, overlooked by the well-preserved engine houses and chimneys of Wheal Prosper Tin Mine. Rinsey Head's overhanging cliffs are home to a kittiwake colony.

Praa Sands is a popular holiday beach. Make an ice cream stop, or cross to Hoe Point where narrow channels between tall stacks keep the sit-on-tops from the beach amused. The next 4km are quite lovely, either side of the low headland of Cudden Point. Tiny coves and caves beg to be explored. Bessy's Cove and Piskies Cove come first; the names alone suggesting quaintness! Stackhouse Cove is surrounded by caves. One cave appears to lead right through the cliffs to Acton Castle.

St Michael's Mount

With its church and castle topping a 90m conical rock, the tidal island of St Michael's Mount is Cornwall's most recognisable landmark. There has been some form of religious site here since local fishermen experienced a vision of St Michael in the fifth century. In the past 500 years, various fortifications have sprung up, latterly a decorative Victorian castle. As the name implies, St Michael's Mount is a diminutive cousin of Brittany's Mont St Michel, the abbey that owned it for 300 years.

The island can become swamped by tourists, but the causeway is conveniently covered for two hours either side of low water. Arriving then should give you relative peace and quiet, although a ferry service still ships determined tourists across!

Through the nineteenth century, the harbour served the St Aubyn family in the castle (two rowing barges survive), Marazion's fishermen and local mines. Bollards on the piers are made from cannons and the East pier boasts Queen Victoria's footprint in cement. The gardens are worth strolling around (open several days a week) and the castle should certainly be checked out (surrender monies to the National Trust), an eclectic mix of stately rooms and eccentric artefacts … mummified cats and samurai armour, anyone?

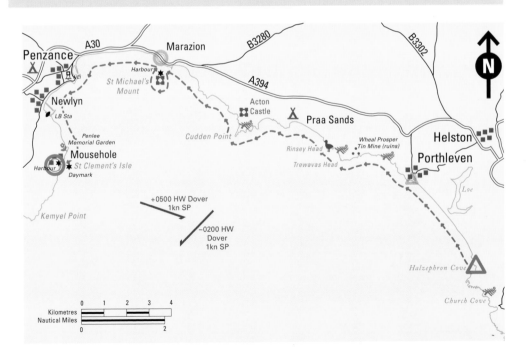

The character of Mount's Bay changes as St Michael's Mount is approached. The attraction now is the maritime heritage rather than the scenery. The unmistakeable silhouette of the Mount is a mainstay of postcards and tourist brochures, and landing in the harbour is a must. For around four hours either side of low water, the causeway is dry, forcing you to go long way around. At the shoreward end of the causeway is Marazion, once an important market town, now given over to galleries selling overpriced art of dubious quality. The car parks west of Marazion (514 309) may be a good place to finish if you don't want to visit the ports of Penzance, Newlyn and Mousehole.

A sandy beach reaches 4km across to Penzance, overlooked by Penzance's Coastwatch station and interrupted by a series of wide curlew-haunted reefs, including the Ryeman Rocks and Western Cressar Rocks. The south pier of Penzance Harbour is home to *Scillonian III* and the large white warehouse behind was the Trinity House Depot from 1866. The stones for Wolf Rock Lighthouse were prepared here.

Newlyn's harbour is more interesting to explore. Entering beneath the south pier's 1855 cast iron lighthouse (Penzance has a similar example), you'll be confronted by a now rare sight; row upon row of fishing boats. Sitting forlornly and disconnected in the centre of the bustling harbour is the original fifteenth-century granite pier, last departure point of the *Mayflower* before it conveyed the Pilgrim Fathers to the New World. Leaving Newlyn, look for the tidal observatory at the end of a pier, which monitors Ordnance Datum. In plain speak, this spot is the lowest baseline for Ordnance Survey maps.

The 2km from Newlyn to Mousehole are blighted by the massive scar of Gwavas quarry. There is a disused lifeboat station at Penlee Point. The last launch down this slipway was the *Solomon Browne*. Beside the station is a small memorial garden with a plaque naming the lost eight lifeboatmen. The current Penlee lifeboat is kept afloat in Newlyn Harbour.

St Clement's Island is a low windswept islet with a cross on top, marking the entrance to Mousehole Harbour. There is a slipway on the south side of the harbour leading to a car park. The last person to speak solely in Cornish died here in 1777. Dolly Pentreath's last words were *"Me ne vidn cewsel Sawznek!"* (I don't want to speak English!). Mousehole was an active fishing port (the earliest walled harbour in Cornwall), but has now almost totally given over to tourism. The tea shops and galleries are a world away from the warehouses and cranes of Newlyn.

Tide and weather

Rather boringly, it's hard to detect tidal flow for most of this trip. Swell is common at the east end of the bay, however. In such conditions, avoid landings on steeply shelving Gunwalloe Fishing Cove (653 223) and Porthleven Sands.

In northerly winds, a paddle from St Michael's Mount to Porthleven offers reasonable shelter.

Additional information

Penzance YHA (457 303) is 2km from the sea and permits camping, tel. 08707 705992, www.yha.org.uk.

The Old Farm (574 285) is a short walk from Praa Sands, tel. 01736 763221, www.theoldfarmpraasands.co.uk.

The Newlyn Fleet

With a fleet of over 100 working boats, Newlyn is the largest fishing port in England and Wales. Annually 9,500 tonnes of fish are landed, only 30% of which are eaten in Cornwall. If you are masochistic, the daily landings and auction can be watched at around 7am.

In 1896, the military were called to suppress rioting in Newlyn between east coast and local fishermen, the bone of contention being Sabbath Observance. The only riot today would be if you got in the way of fishing boats, remember that Newlyn is very much a working port. One bonus of this industry worth investigating is the extremely cheap and filling nosh served at the canteen of the Royal National Mission to Deep Sea Fishermen.

Henry Trengrouse

In 1807, Henry Trengrouse witnessed HMS *Anson* sink 100m offshore of the Loe Bar. To his horror, 120 men drowned before his eyes. This traumatic experience led him to spend ten years developing a rocket life-saving apparatus. His 'breeches-buoy' invention saved 10,000 lives between 1870 and 1911, and was still in service around the UK up to the 1980s. Poor Trengrouse invested £3,000 but was paid £50 by the Navy for his invention. The Tsar of Russia sent Trengrouse a diamond ring, but he was forced to sell it to support his wife and ten children, eventually dying in poverty.

Mousehole Harbour

Treryn Dinas

Land's End

No. 27 | Grade C | 20km | OS Sheet 203

Tidal Ports	Plymouth and Dover
Start	△ Mousehole (470 263)
Finish	○ Sennen Cove (351 264)
HW/LW	HW Mousehole is 5 hours and 50 minutes after HW Dover.
Tidal times	Inshore along the coast from Gwennap Head past Land's End, tide streams often flow contrary to the offshore streams. Inshore, the NW going stream begins 2 hours and 40 minutes after HW Plymouth and flows for about 9 hours 30 minutes, bending north at Land's End. A stream flowing east past Gwennap Head and south past Land's End begins 20 minutes before HW Plymouth and flows for 3 hours.
Max Rate Sp	Flows between the Runnel Stone and Land's End reach 3.2 knots on the ebb and 4.2 knots on the flood.
Coastguard	Falmouth, tel. 01326 317575, VHF weather 0110 UT

Introduction

Land's End completely lives up to its evocative name, offering a challenging paddle amongst astounding environs. Above heaving seas, fulmars and herring gulls wheel around castellated

towers of golden granite sparkling with quartz, feldspar and mica. This actually isn't Britain's westernmost point (that accolade goes to Scotland's Ardnamurchan Point) but out on the water, you may as well be at World's End.

Description

Dylan Thomas called Mousehole (pronounced 'mowzul') *the prettiest village in England* and it is indeed hard to beat its horseshoe-shaped granite harbour. Parking is available either side of the harbour, with the most convenient slipway on the south side. Arrive early to secure space.

Just outside the harbour is the cave that gives Mousehole its name. This first 3km skirt low shores adorned with daffodil fields, leading to the inlet of Lamorna Cove. The east side of Lamorna is scarred by quarries and waste tips. Until the quarries closed in the early twentieth century, stone was shipped from Lamorna's quay to the Trinity House depot at Penzance and used to construct lighthouses such as Wolf Rock and Longships. The cakes and fruit pies at the café come recommended!

Tater Du lighthouse stands on a black greenstone outcrop brightened by yellow xanthoria lichen, overlooking two rocks called The Bucks. This was the last Penwith lighthouse constructed by Trinity House, as recently as 1965. Mount's Bay is left behind now, and you have a good chance of meeting basking sharks, dolphins or porpoise.

Remnants of the *Union Star* can be seen between Tater Du and Boscawen Point. The crew of eight lost their lives here, alongside eight lifeboatmen.

The low bouldery beach of St Loy's Cove leads out to the Coffin Rock at Merthen Point, from where you'll spy Penberth Cove. Fishermen still land crab, lobster and mackerel at this tiny village's slipway, although they utilise an electric winch rather than the preserved old capstan.

The craggy promontory that follows is Treryn Dinas, site of an Iron Age cliff castle and (apparently) built by a giant. On the summit is 65 tonne Logan Rock, a Victorian beauty spot. The bay on the headland's west side is the bay of Porthcurno, floored by glorious white sand that shines through translucent water. Pedn Vounder is the bay's smaller beach, a naturist spot that 'covers up' at HW. Porthcurno beach is bigger and justifiably popular. The steep sandy hill behind will deter most from attempting to carry kayaks to the car park. The large building behind the car park is the Telegraph Museum. Extending under the sand from this building are 14 telegraph cables that stretched as far as Bombay from the 1870s, maintaining communication with the Empire.

Incidentally, if you happen to spot a black spectre ship whilst in the bay, this apparently denotes bad luck.

Spread up the cliffs to the west of Porthcurno is the famous Minack (Cornish: *rock*) Theatre, built by Rowena Cade and opened in 1932. Booking a seat here is a win-win deal; even if the performance stinks, there are worse ways to spend an evening than watching the light fade on Treryn Dinas.

The tiny beach in front of St Levan is Porth Chapel, named for a nearby early Christian site. Porthgwarra's narrow cove (371 217) is the last road access. A narrow tunnel leads steeply from the beach towards the car park, bored by miners to allow farmers to gather seaweed.

Henceforth, the coast is jaw-dropping. Between Gwennap Head and Sennen Cove, 60m cliffs face west into the open ocean, which is punctuated only by Wolf Rock and Longships lighthouses. The jointed buttresses and pinnacles resemble granite fortresses, pocked with innumerable zawns and caves, topped by pink lousewort and heather. Paddling here in late evening is incredible; the stone is set ablaze by the sun sinking into the Atlantic.

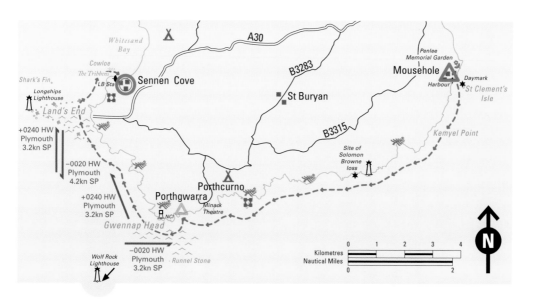

Gwennap Head is the most south-westerly point in the UK, the 'Fisherman's Land's End'. Beside the Coastwatch lookout on top are two conical daymarks, pointing offshore to the Runnel Stone. Chair Ladder Cliff is famous among climbers. It is also the seat of Madge Fiddy, a notorious witch who summons storms, allowing her coven to steal jewels from the drowned sailors washing ashore.

Porth Loe saw the wreck of the grain vessel *Khyber* in 1905, three crew members being rescued by ladders lowered to them.

Pendower Cove is a perfect granite amphitheatre, with Carn Les Boel forming the north rim. Squeeze between this headland and Bosistow Island into Nanjizal Bay, which is even grander. Zawn Pyg can be paddled right through the cliffs to the beach. Nanjizal's north edge is Diamond Horse Cove, surrounded by caves and so-named because the rich quartz veins here were mistaken for diamonds. Seals abound.

The best is still to come! Passing around Carn Boel and Pordenack Point, you spy two enormous stacks sheltering below the cliffs. The nearest is Enys Dodnan, pierced by an arch. Coming this far but not paddling underneath is actually a criminal offence. Further offshore is the turreted ridge of The Armed Knight.

You now reach Land's End proper, consisting of two successive outcrops, Dr Johnson's Head, and Dr Syntax's Head. A boulder-strewn cave passes right through the latter, and the rocks below this point channel a big tide race.

North of Land's End is Gamper Bay. Above the bay is Maen Castle, one of Cornwall's earliest cliff castles, dating from around 500 BC. In front of this is Castle Zawn, currently filled by the carcass of the RMS *Mulheim*, progressively disintegrating in successive Atlantic storms. Carrying toxic waste under a 'flag of convenience', she ran aground in March 2003 after the lone watch officer knocked himself unconscious.

The final headland is Pedn-men-du, marked by the pointed Irish Lady stack. Past this, Whitesand Bay opens before you. You may be unnerved to see surf breaking across the bay, but this can usually be avoided by following the Tribbens channel past the Cowlow rocks to the Sennen Cove breakwater.

That might just have been the best sea paddle in the South West.

VARIATIONS

To cherry-pick the best of this trip, launch from Porthgwarra (371 217). Even better, include a short trip across the tide to investigate the exposed Longships lighthouse (route 28).

Tide and weather

The Romans knew Land's End as Bellerium, seat of storms. Tides around Gwennap Head and Land's End are complex and erratic, with the flows of the English Channel and the Celtic Sea vying for dominance. Don't always trust calculated tidal flow times! The currents don't always follow the shore, meaning that respite can be had in the bays. However, numerous tide races form around exposed points, especially Gwennap Head and Dr Syntax's Head. There is almost always groundswell around Land's End and you are of course exposed to the weather from

most directions. www.landsendweather.info gives live reports from Gwennap Head Coastwatch station and surf websites like www.magicseaweed.com give swell readings from the Seven Stones Lightship, 25km offshore.

Service not self

Whilst paddling, consider the sacrifice made by the community of Mousehole on 19th December, 1981. The coaster MV *Union Star* suffered engine failure and was being blown ashore by a hurricane. The Penlee lifeboat *Solomon Browne* launched. Coxswain Trevelyan Richards refused to allow the son of one crew member to board, saying *"No more than one from any family"*.

Richards managed to bring the *Solomon Browne* alongside the *Union Star* through rocks and 16m breakers, the lifeboat actually being flung onto the deck at one point. Four survivors were somehow picked up but when the lifeboat returned for the remaining crew, radio contact abruptly ceased. What happened is unclear, but all eight volunteer lifeboatmen of the *Solomon Browne* were lost to the storm, as well as all eight crew of the *Union Star*.

The lifeboatmen were posthumously honoured with RNLI medals. The memorial at the lifeboat station is headed, *'Service Not Self'*.

SERVICE NOT SELF
IN MEMORY OF THE CREW OF THE PENLEE LIFEBOAT
SOLOMON BROWNE,
WILLIAM TREVELYAN RICHARDS, COXSWAIN
JAMES STEPHEN MADRON, 2nd COXSWAIN MECHANIC
NIGEL BROCKMAN, ASSISTANT MECHANIC
JOHN ROBERT BLEWETT, EMERGENCY MECHANIC
BARRIE ROBERTSON TORRIE, CREWMAN
CHARLES THOMAS GREENHAUGH, CREWMAN
KEVIN BRIAN SMITH, CREWMAN
GARY LEE WALLIS, CREWMAN
WHO GAVE THEIR LIVES IN SERVICE
19TH DECEMBER 1981

Penlee lifeboat memorial, Mousehole

Additional information

After paddling, you may be tempted to walk along the cliffs to Land's End. Don't do it. You'll encounter a theme park, offering, '*35,000 sq. ft. of undercover attractions and great shopping*'. How this blasphemy on the landscape ever gained planning permission is an enduring mystery.

Treen Farm (392 228) is 1km uphill from Penberth Cove, tel. 01736 810273. Sennen Cove Camping (370 273) is 3km from the harbour, tel. 01736 871818.

The Isles of Scilly

An introduction

The Isles of Scilly are a unique environment. Partly a piece of England, partly a piece of the Atlantic. Legend tells that the Isles are the sunken remnants of the Arthurian Kingdom of Lyonesse. Scientists have a less colourful theory, that the archipelago is an extension to Cornwall that has been drowned by rising sea levels since the last Ice Age. Picture Dartmoor, with only the craggy tors peeking above the water … with Caribbean beaches.

The name 'Scilly' derives from 'Sully' meaning Sun Isles. The islands are 40km WSW of Land's End and measure a tiddly 16km by 10km. There are about 100 islands and rocks, of which six are inhabited. The total land area is a mere 6.25 sq miles at HW and the population numbers just 2,000.

Although the area is small, the variety is great and kayakers will be captivated. Each of the main islands has its own character and interest. They cluster around a central lagoon which permits sheltered island hopping in most weathers. On the other hand, the open Atlantic is just a few miles away, characterised by impressive reefs and lighthouses offering real exposure. If this isn't challenging enough, there is of course the paddle out from the mainland.

Environment

Most of the Isles of Scilly belong to the Duchy of Cornwall, although the uninhabited islands are leased to the Isles of Scilly Wildlife Trust. The entire area is designated as Heritage Coast and encompassed by a Marine Park, as well as being a Special Area of Conservation and Britain's smallest Area of Outstanding Natural Beauty. This level of environmental protection and management has implications for paddlers. Wild camping is not permitted, and even landing is not permitted on certain islands to protect nesting birds. Ordnance Survey Explorer Map 101 shows the protected islands. Use discretion and common sense in interpreting these restrictions.

Tide and weather

Tide streams among the Isles of Scilly rarely reach more than 2 knots on exposed fringes and headlands. The Atlantic streams approach the Isles from a different direction at each hour of the tidal cycle, rotating right around clockwise in twelve hours. Inshore, tidal streams tend to hug the coast, flowing into bays at one end and out at the other. Offshore, streams flow in a more direct line up and down channels. Calculating when and where tides will rise, fall or flow involves a degree of luck and flaw. Complex and often unpredictable local currents are further confused by the effects of high or low pressure. Hence, the tidal data in this chapter should be treated as a guide only.

The inter-tidal zone is vast, huge areas of sand and rock drying out at low tide. Channels between islands disappear (don't trust that OS map!) and some trips become more sheltered at low tide when reefs shut out the Atlantic swells.

Scilly is famous for year-round mild temperatures, humid air and of course sunshine.

Background reading

Isles of Scilly Pilot, Robin Brandon, Imray 1994, ISBN 0-85288-411-7

Secret Nature of the Isles of Scilly, Andrew Cooper, Green Books 2006, ISBN 1-90399-851-4

Walking in the Isles of Scilly, Paddy Dillon, Cicerone 2000, ISBN 1-85284-310-1

Scilly's Wildlife Heritage, Adrian Spalding and Pat Sargent, Twelveheads 2000, ISBN 0906294-44-4

Scilly's Archaeological Heritage, Jeanette Radcliffe, Twelveheads 2003, ISBN 0-906294-53-3

Shell Channel Pilot, Tom Cunliffe, Imray 2006, ISBN 0-85288-894-5

West Country Cruising Companion, Mark Fishwick, Nautical Data Limited 2004, ISBN 1-90435-825-X

Further information

www.ios-wildlifetrust.org.uk – Isles of Scilly Wildlife Trust.

www.ios-aonb.org.uk – Isles of Scilly AONB.

Tel. (01720) 422536 / www.simplyscilly.co.uk – Tourist Information.

Tel. 0845 7105555 / www.ios-travel.co.uk – The Isle of Scilly Steamship Company.

Mid-crossing

The Scilly Crossing

No. 28 | Grade C | 42km | OS Sheet 203

Tidal Ports	Plymouth and Dover
Start	△ Sennen Cove (351 264)
Finish	○ Great Ganilly (948 144)
HW/LW	HW Great Ganilly is 55 minutes before HW Plymouth.
Tidal times	Around Land's End and Longships, streams often flow contrary to the offshore streams. Inshore at Land's End, the N going stream begins 2 hours and 40 minutes after HW Plymouth and flows for about 9 hours 30 minutes. A stream flowing south past Land's End begins 20 minutes before HW Plymouth and flows for 3 hours. Offshore, tide flows weaken and rotate in direction, but tend towards ENE beginning 3 hours after HW Dover, and tend towards WSW 3 hours before HW Dover.
Max Rate Sp	Rates around Land's End and Longships reach 4.2 knots. Further offshore, they weaken and do not exceed 1 knot.
Coastguard	Falmouth, tel. 01326 317575, VHF weather 0110 UT

Introduction

The 'Longships' are the rocks offshore of Land's End. Imagining its lighthouse as a tall mast, this extensive reef can certainly give the impression of a Viking flotilla when viewed from shore

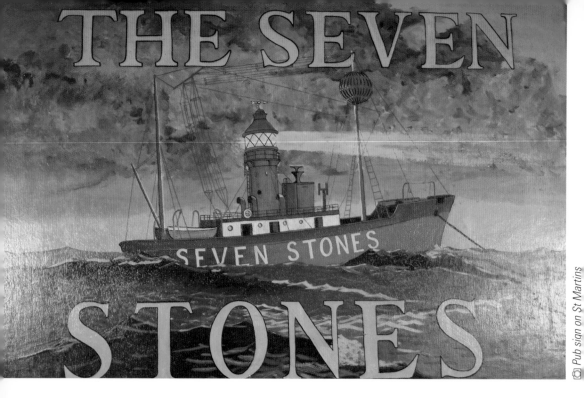

THE SEVEN STONES

SEVEN STONES

© Pub sign on St Martins

with the sun setting into the Atlantic. Much further out, the lights of the Isles of Scilly twinkle and beckon. Their appearance from Land's End is best described by novelist John Fowles: *'There they float, an eternal stone Armada of over a hundred ships'.*

With the right conditions, paddling out into the west is irresistible.

Description

Sennen Cove's harbour is described in Route 33. Passing the end of the breakwater, pick a path past the surf on Tribbens reef and paddle out into the tidal stream. You have just left the shores of England behind!

The Longships reef stretches for about 250m north and south of the lighthouse and rewards close exploration. A visit at low tide will obviously give you more to look at. Numerous tide races form around and between the sharp rocks and you share this aquatic playground with seals galore, sunbathing, sleeping, fishing, swimming, occasionally all at once. The lighthouse itself is the second on Longships, the 1795 original having been replaced in 1873 by the current 43m tower. A keeper of the first lighthouse had his hair turn white in a single stormy night, during which the lantern was smashed.

Pleasant as Longships is, your day has barely begun.

The shortest distance between Sennen Cove and the Isles of Scilly is 42km, bringing you to Great Ganilly in the Eastern Isles (see route 30). Given that the Isles of Scilly present a target just 10km wide, some pre-planning is a good idea. Consider a GPS for back-up. You may not see your destination for much of the distance and much of the pleasure of the crossing comes from seeing empty seas stretching to the horizon all around.

That said, there is a surprising amount to see between Longships and Great Ganilly. Encountering dolphins, porpoise, basking sharks or sunfish is pretty much a certainty. The Scilly helicopter flies low overhead at regular intervals (start worrying when you stop seeing it) and Traffic Separation Scheme (TSS) will certainly give you something to look at. The TSS crosses the middle third of your voyage, a massive maritime motorway. The two 'lanes' that you cross (north going, then south going) are each 4.5km wide with a 3km 'central reservation'. Despite the wide lanes, the big ships tend to form up in a single line cutting the corner from the Channel to the North Atlantic by the shortest route. The sight of container vessels stretching back to the horizon is pretty memorable.

If all has gone to plan, your first touch of the Isles will be Hanjague rock. For the final kilometre to Great Ganilly, you'll be guarded by an escort of seals.

VARIATIONS

A more challenging variation could be to take in the infamous Wolf Rock lighthouse (270 119). During 1862, the first year of the lighthouse's construction, workers were only able to land on 22 days. Don't plan on a picnic stop!

Tide and weather

The tide streams off Land's End are complex, flowing strongly across your route with tide races forming around the Longships reef. Further offshore, the main tidal stream is weaker and changes direction of flow at markedly different times. Further out again, the tide conveniently bends to flow weakly between Land's End and the Scilly Isles. If contemplating the crossing, look for settled high pressure and a smooth sea state.

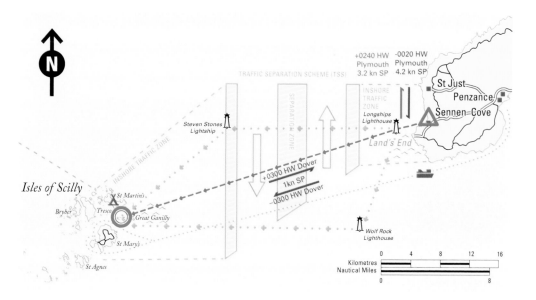

Additional information

Camping on Great Ganilly is not permitted. The nearest campsite is 4km further on at St Martin's (route 30).

The Seven Stones Lightship

A visit to the Seven Stones reef adds several kilometres to the crossing. There has been a lightship here since 1841, although in 1967 direct warnings from the lightship crew failed to prevent the *Torrey Canyon* running aground in broad daylight. 31 million gallons of oil spilled, causing a catastrophic slick along the Cornish coast and killing 15,000 sea birds. Classic British amateurism was displayed in botched attempts to ignite the spilling oil by dropping napalm bombs (they kept missing the 300 metre long tanker) and also in confused efforts to disperse the oil from beaches (it was often ploughed into the sand). The current lightship (087 257) is distinctively red-hulled and has been unmanned since 1987, subsequently being filled with buoyancy foam. Despite the thickness of the mooring chains, it has broken adrift on several occasions.

Don't be close when the foghorn goes off!

© *Peninnis Head*

St Mary's ⟳ 🛶 🔍 🍴 📐

No. 29 | Grade B | 14 km | OS Sheet 203

Tidal Port	**Plymouth (Devonport)**
Start	△ Hugh Town (903 107)
Finish	◯ Hugh Town (903 107)
HW/LW	Local HW is 55 minutes before HW Plymouth.
Tidal times	Within Crow Sound, the E going stream begins 15 minutes after HW Plymouth. The W going stream begins 5 hours and 40 minutes after HW Plymouth. These streams flow for about 3 hours and then weaken.
	In St Mary's Sound, the SE going stream begins 5 hours and 45 minutes before HW Plymouth. The NW going stream begins 45 minutes after HW Plymouth.
	In St Mary's Road, a tide stream varying in direction of flow between NW and SW begins 1 hour and 45 minutes before HW Plymouth. The east going (and stable) stream begins 5 hours and 40 minutes after HW Plymouth.
Max Rate Sp	In Crow Sound and in St Mary's Road, flows reach 1 knot. In St Mary's Sound, flows reach 1.7 knots at springs and 0.7 knots at neaps.
Coastguard	Falmouth, tel. 01326 317575, VHF weather 0110 UT

Introduction

St Mary's is the 'big' island of Scilly. The circuit of the island makes a good introduction to Scilly, especially if combined with forays ashore to explore further.

Description

Scillonian III offloads visitors at the quay in the 'capital' of St Mary's (and indeed Scilly), Hugh Town. There is a convenient launching beach beside the quay if you wish to paddle off right away. However, Hugh Town has a useful supermarket and cash machine, so a wander up the street may be your first priority

Be careful in Hugh Town harbour (known as 'St Mary's Pool'); the water is chock full of nippy little inter-island launches that don't take prisoners.

St Mary's west coast slopes gradually from the sea, with landing usually possible. Here in Scilly's central lagoon ('The Road'), it is possible to visualise Scilly's appearance a 1,000 years ago. The islands were all joined as one landmass 'Ennor', subsequently submerged by rising seas. When the settlement at Halangy Down (910 124) was occupied, it looked out over a wide wooded plain. Today, it is worth landing to view the oval houses of this excavated Iron Age village. Close by is Bant's Carn, an impressive Bronze Age entrance grave.

Rounding the northern tip of St Mary's at Bar Point, be aware that the deep water channel of Crow Sound only extends out for a few hundred metres. Offshore, a sand spit, the 'Crow Bar', forces ships like the *Scillonian III* close in.

St Mary's east coast is more imposing, with low granite cliffs often impeding landing. At Innisidgen more entrance graves (922 127) are close to shore, but the landing is rocky. Pelistry Bay is a secluded sandy cove linked to Toll's Island, a link severed at high tide. A stroll around the island reveals the Civil War defences of 'Pellows Redoubt' and a string of kelp pits.

Porth Hellick's narrow entrance is easy to miss. This beach is a shell hunter's paradise. Sir Clowdisley-Shovell washed up here after the 1707 disaster (see boxed text) and was briefly interred in the sand before reburial at Westminster Abbey. There are numerous entrance graves on Porth Hellick Down, including the so-called 'Giant's tomb'.

The next kilometre (passing under the end of the runway) has wrecked two ships in recent times, the *Cita* at Newfoundland Point in 1998 and the *Brodfield* in 1916. The *Brodfield's* steel plates are still visible.

Old Town Bay is a good place to stop if you don't fancy the exposure of Peninnis Head, Hugh Town being just a short walk away across a narrow isthmus.

The cliffs of Peninnis Head are topped by an ugly metal lighthouse, but are redeemed by engaging rock formations. The granite has eroded into shapes with names like The Pulpit, The Monk's Cowl and Big Jolly Rock. A tide race will need to be negotiated as you enter St Mary's Sound.

Porth Cressa offers another back route into Hugh Town, but it is worth completing the circumnavigation by paddling around The Garrison. This part of St Mary's was fortified in the wake of the Spanish Armada's threat, commencing with the building of the Star Castle in 1593. Battlements and cannons are visible beside the water, and make for a pleasant a walk around if staying at St Mary's campsite, located on The Garrison.

MV Scillonian III

Most paddlers reach Scilly by The Isles of Scilly Steamship Company's *Scillonian III*. From March to November, this sails six days a week (seven in August) between Penzance and Hugh Town. Kayaks are charged extra but it is possible to negotiate half price carriage for a second kayak.

Kayaks need to be ready on the quay, empty, at least two hours before sailing. Kayaks are placed on a pallet or in slings and craned onto the deck or into the hold, never a convincing process to watch!

The crossing takes 2 hours 40 minutes and may help you to understand why locals call the *Scillonian* the 'Vomit Comet'. Landing at Hugh Town on St Mary's, there is organised chaos as baggage is sorted into crates bound for different islands. If camping on St Mary's, your gear (but not your kayaks) will be driven uphill to the campsite, provided that you labelled it properly.

Paddle around tiny Rat Island which forms part of the quay and head into Hugh Town for fish and chips and medals.

VARIATIONS

Rounding Bar Point, a detour to the Eastern Isles is tempting! See route 30.

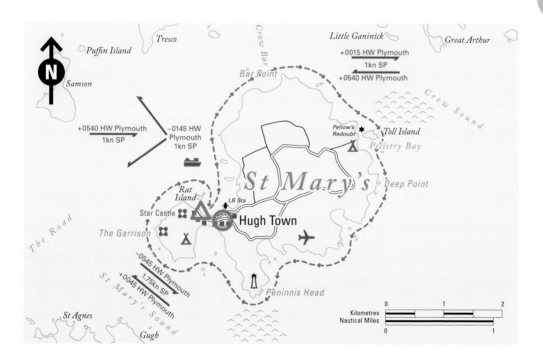

© Old Town beach

Tide and weather

Penninis Head forms a tide race which can be quite lively with wind or swell thrown into the mix. Rough water forms in Crow Sound with wind against tide.

Additional information

St Mary's campsite (898 104) is 1km inland from Hugh Town Quay. It is run by Mr and Mrs Moulson (01720 422670).

There is a basic campsite at Pelistry Bay (928 119), run by Cornwall Outdoors for groups, (01872 323356 www.cornwall.gov.uk/cornwalloutdoors).

St Martin's

St Martin's & the Isles ◌⬚◎⬚

30

St Martin's & the Isles

No. 30 | Grade B | 18km | OS Sheet 203

Tidal Port	Plymouth
Start	△ St Martin's campsite (919 159)
Finish	◯ St Martin's campsite (919 159)
HW/LW	HW is 55 minutes before HW Plymouth.
Tidal times	Tidal times for streams through Tean Sound are thought to be the same as for Old Grimsby Sound (route 31).
	North of Round Island, the E going stream begins 5 hours and 10 minutes after HW Plymouth. The W going stream begins 1 hour and 15 minutes before HW Plymouth. Streams through St Helen's Pool are similar.
	Within Crow Sound, the east going stream begins 15 minutes after HW Plymouth. The west going stream begins 5 hours and 40 minutes after HW Plymouth. These streams flow for about 3 hours and then weaken.
Max Rate Sp	In Tean Sound, flows can exceed 2 knots. North of Round Island, flows reach 2.5 knots, although 4 knot flows are reputed close inshore. In Crow Sound, flows reach a maximum of 1 knot.
Coastguard	Falmouth, tel. 01326 317575, VHF weather 0110 UT

© Round Island

30

Introduction

This trip takes in at least 18 islands in as many kilometres … enough said!

Description

This paddle is centred on crescent shaped St Martin's, which is accessed by a 5km paddle north from Hugh Town and conveniently has a good campsite (919 159) located right beside the south beach. Bring a trolley, as it might not feel so close at LW when the water has retreated several hundred metres across the sand. St Martin's is simply wonderful, adorned with high hedges sheltering brightly coloured flower gardens and vegetable patches. 1.5km away in Higher Town, there is a well stocked shop and a scrumptious bakery. That said, the 'Seven Stones' pub is nearer and warmer.

THE NORTHERN ISLES

Launching from the St Martin's campsite, a short paddle west will bring you to St Helen's Pool, surrounded by uninhabited isles. This was Scilly's main harbour in the Middle Ages. The two largest islands around the pool are hilly and overgrown. Tean and St Helen's are both named after early Christian saints; St Theona and St Elidius. Beside Tean's beach are traces of a settlement (908 164) which has been occupied for much of the past 2,000 years, including an eighth-century stone chapel. St Helen's also boasts early Christian remains, in the form of St Elidius' hermitage (901168). This small complex includes a circular living cell. Nearby is the less romantic Pest House (899 168), built in 1764 to quarantine sailors. A 1756 law stated, *'if plague shall appear on any ship, being northward of Cape Finisterre, the master shall immediately proceed to the harbour of St Helen's Pool'.*

Both Tean and St Helen's have small populations of puffins, an overspill from nearby Men-a-vaur (Old Cornish for 'great rock'). Men-a-vaur is three vertical granite slabs with narrow channels between, directly approachable from St Helen's when Golden Ball Brow reef is submerged. Men-a-vaur is home to Scilly's largest auk colony, with razorbills particularly numerous.

Rearing 40m from the water, Round Island is the most inaccessible Scilly isle. Due to the deep surrounding waters, the Atlantic swell hits the north cliffs full force. An 1886 storm left limpets stranded on the roofs of the lighthouse construction site! Appropriately, large numbers of storm petrels have colonised the island. Landing by kayak is virtually impossible; precarious steps rise direct from the water. The lighthouse is now only accessed by helicopter.

ST MARTIN'S AND WHITE ISLAND

The north coast of St Martin's is a maze of islets and rocks. Low tide forces a detour north of White Island, otherwise a shortcut is possible. Through the seventeenth and eighteenth centuries, the Nance family eked a subsistence living on White Island through processing seaweed (for soap and glass manufacture). A kelp pit (924 173) survives above Porth Morran, as do much older entrance graves and a chambered cairn (924 176). Take care not to step on fulmar or kittiwake nests.

The north coast of St Martin's begins with beaches but gradually rises to cliffs around St Martin's Head. The red striped pinnacle on the headland is Chapel Down daymark, often visible from Land's End. It looks modern but was actually built in 1683 by a Thomas Ekin.

St Martin's & the Isles

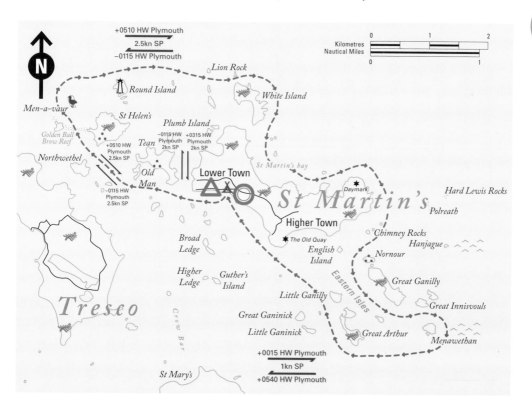

© St Martin's old quay

THE EASTERN ISLES

Rounding St Martin's Head, the jagged profile of the Eastern Isles is unmistakeable. This cluster of miniature islands is home to a significant grey seal colony, by day to be found basking on outlying rocks. The largest islands are Great Ganilly and Great Arthur, which both have prehistoric cairns and tombs, but the most interesting island is tiny Nornour. Coastal erosion has exposed eleven buildings of an Iron Age settlement and shrine (944 147). The circular walls are in remarkably good condition, but it is only a matter of time before the sea claims the site. Hundreds of votive offerings were excavated here, displayed in the Isles of Scilly Museum on St Mary's.

Close to the settlement, look out for a rusting ship's boiler. In 1872 a local pilot advised the *Earl of Aran* paddle steamer's captain to take a short cut through the Eastern Isles. The outcome was predictable. Incidentally, the pilot was banished from the Isles!

Returning along the south beaches of St Martin's, you will paddle past Higher Town Quay (close to a splendid wholefood café) and then the Old Quay, before reaching the campsite.

Tide and weather

Tide flows between the islands and pools are complex and changeable. The times given should be taken as a rough guide. Races form east of the Eastern Isles, off Menawethan and Hanjague.

Additional information

St Martin's campsite (919 160), tel. 01720 422888, www.stmartinscampsite.co.uk.

Tresco, Bryher & Samson

No. 31 | **Grade B** | **20 km** | **OS Sheet 203**

Tidal Port	Plymouth (Devonport)
Start	△ The Town, Bryher (881 149)
Finish	○ The Town, Bryher (881 149)
HW/LW	Local HW is 55 minutes before HW Plymouth.
Tidal times	At the N end of New Grimsby Sound the tide changes direction four times in twelve hours! The NW going stream begins 15 minutes after HW Plymouth. It switches to SE going 3 hours and 45 minutes after HW Plymouth. It switches back to NW going 5 hours and 10 minutes after HW Plymouth and to SE going 4 hours and 15 minutes before HW Plymouth.

In the North West Passage (also known as 'The North Channel') west of Bryher and Samson, the SE going stream begins 6 hours before HW Plymouth. The NW going stream begins 30 minutes before HW Plymouth.

In St Mary's Road, a tide stream varying between NW and SW going begins 1 hour and 45 minutes before HW Plymouth. The E going (and stable) stream begins 5 hours and 40 minutes after HW Plymouth.

Over Tresco Flats, the N going stream begins 15 minutes after HW Plymouth. The S going stream begins 5 hours and 45 minutes before HW Plymouth.

In Old Grimsby Sound the NW going stream begins 1 hour and 15 minutes before HW Plymouth and runs for 4 hours 30 minutes. The SE going stream begins 3 hours and 15 minutes after HW Plymouth and runs for 8 hours.

Max Rate Sp In New Grimsby and Old Grimsby Sounds, flows can exceed 2 knots. At the N tip of New Grimsby Sound and in St Mary's Road, flows reach 1 knot. In the North West Passage and St Helen's Pool, flows reach 2 knots.

Coastguard Falmouth, tel. 01326 317575, VHF weather 0110 UT

Introduction

An outstanding paddle, characterised by dramatic and unlikely contrasts. The three islands explored boast craggy shores and reefs, abandoned settlements, dazzling white beaches and even sub-tropical foliage. The Caribbean meets the Hebrides?

Description

This trip's start point is the beach closest to Bryher's campsite, near to the Fraggle Rock Inn (880 155). Launching here is awkward at LW due to rocks, but if needed there are slipways and jetties a short distance south.

TRESCO

It's a short paddle to Tresco across sheltered New Grimsby Sound. Tresco is a unique island. From the Sound you will see that its northern half is craggy and windswept, whilst the south is characterised by woodland, sand dunes and some of Britain's finest beaches. Landing at New Grimsby to explore is essential, although at least half a day is needed to enjoy the famous Abbey Gardens. These were created by Victorian reformer Augustus Smith around the twelfth-century remains of Tresco Abbey. Scilly's mild winter climate has helped the gardens to flourish, with over 3,000 species of exotic plants assaulting your eyeballs; 'Kew Gardens with the lid off'. Whilst in the gardens, seek out the Valhalla collection, 30 figureheads from ships wrecked on Scilly's reefs.

Augustus Smith's descendants (the Dorien-Smiths) still lease and manage Tresco. Recent development has added an exceptional supermarket (*not* called Tresco's) but also an incongruous holiday village. Tresco wasn't always packaged and marketed. Some idea of the island's wilder past can be gleaned from the Viking *Orkneyinga Saga's* description of a violent raid on Tresco, whilst in 1209, Tresco's monks clamped down on anti-social behaviour by beheading 120 pirates in one day.

Scilly was the last Civil War Royalist stronghold, and one of the final battles was enacted on Tresco in 1651. Paddling north up New Grimsby Sound, 'Cromwell's Castle' dates from this year and guards the Sound. Much of the stone came from the older 'King Charles' Castle' on the hill behind.

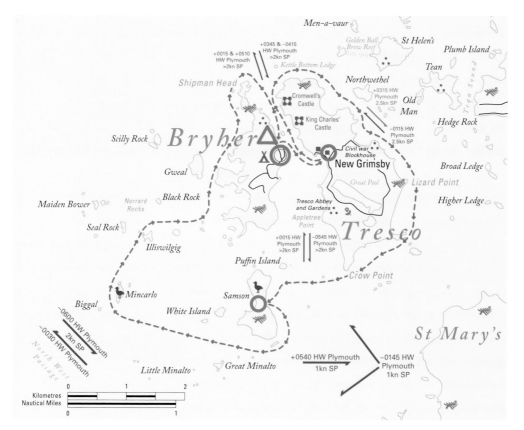

Tresco, Bryher & Samson

Common terns wheel overhead at the north end of Tresco, which is exposed to the Atlantic swell, with a tide race forming. The cave of Gun Hole is worth venturing into and another cave forms on a raised beach at Piper's Hole.

The east coast of Tresco sees you back in sheltered waters. Just past the cottages of Old Grimsby are the remains of a Civil War blockhouse (897 155), but it is the dazzling white beaches that will hold your attention. These extend uninterrupted to the southern point at Carn Near.

If you curtail your trip by heading north up New Grimsby Sound, note that the Tresco Flats between Tresco and Bryher become narrow and convoluted at LW springs.

SAMSON

Samson is instantly recognisable by its twin hills. Paddling across, look for traces of settlements and field boundaries, visible in the shallow water. Whilst also blessed with perfect beaches, Samson could not be more different from Tresco. The ruins of cottages bear witness to a harsh past and now the twin hills are populated solely by black backed gulls, over a 1,000 pairs in fact. In the early nineteenth century, around 40 residents eked a living from potatoes and limpets, always suffering from fresh water shortages. Augustus Smith persuaded most to leave to St Mary's, but evicted the defiant remainder in 1855.

Paths allow exploration of the ruined cottages and also the much older entrance graves to be found on both hills. Be careful to avoid disturbing nests, and check for seasonal access restrictions.

Rounding the south of Samson, the Southward Well rocks saw the wreck of Sir William Hamilton's HMS *Colossus*, returning victorious from the Battle of the Nile in 1798. Hamilton and his crew survived, but his irreplaceable collection of ancient Greek pottery was lost, only retrieved (in 30,000 pieces) in recent years. Also lost was his dignity as his wife Emma was elsewhere, busy sleeping with Lord Nelson.

BRYHER AND THE NORRARD ROCKS

Bryher is perhaps the bleakest of the inhabited Isles and you could be forgiven for thinking you'd arrived in the Hebrides. The Norrard Rocks are a scattering of islands and reefs extending 2km offshore along Bryher's west coast, looking not unlike a submerged mountain range. The paddle up this west coast is fully exposed to the Atlantic and favours calm conditions, but it is rewarding to pick a route which takes in as many of these rocks as possible. This is an entrancing area, comparable to the Western Rocks (route 32).

Large populations of grey seals inhabit the Norrard Rocks, and the bird life is also a draw. Mincarlo has Scilly's largest cormorant colony, along with many storm petrels. Puffins burrow here, and also on Castle Bryher and Scilly Rock. Landing isn't permitted on any of the Norrard Rocks apart from Gweal.

Uninvitingly named Hell Bay marks the top end of Bryher. The seas here occasionally justify the name, with storm waves breaking *over* Shipman Head. Shipman Head is separated from Bryher by a channel which forms a paddleable short cut. Paddling right around the Head is satisfying, however. The rampart of an Iron Age fort can be glimpsed atop the cliffs, now the home of kittiwake and herring gulls.

Back in New Grimsby Sound, Hangman's Island guides you back to where you set out from. A pint in the tiny Fraggle Rock Inn will allow you to relax and digest the day's amazing experiences.

© Samson

The Emperor of Scilly

Scilly's appearance and affluence is largely due to Augustus Smith, who acquired the lease of the islands in 1834. Shocked by poverty and destitution, he philanthropically vowed to 'improve the lot of the labouring classes'. He settled on Tresco (previous landlords were always absentees) and built schools, quays and churches. He expanded the ship-building industry and promoted island tourism. When the population of Samson hit starvation point, Smith built homes for them on St Mary's. Most imaginatively, he instigated flower cultivation; due to Scilly's mild climate, they could be sent year-round by steamer and railway to London. Smith's legacy is still visible; most obviously in the Abbey Gardens that he created around his home, but also in Scilly's numerous flower gardens and in the ruined cottages on Samson.

Tide and weather

A tide race forms off Kettle Bottom Ledge (N end of Tresco), starting 3-4 hours after HW Dover. Combined with Atlantic swell, this can become a bit too exciting.

Tresco Abbey Gardens

Additional information

Bryher Campsite (878 154) is several hundred metres from the water, accessed by a steep track behind the Fraggle Rock Bar. It is run by Kathy Stedeford, tel. 01720 422886, www. bryhercampsite.co.uk.

Information on Tresco Abbey gardens at www.tresco.co.uk.

St Agnes & the Western Rocks

No. 32 | Grade C | 23km | OS Sheet 203

Tidal Port	Plymouth (Devonport)
Start	△ Hugh Town (903 107)
Finish	○ St Agnes campsite (875 081)
HW/LW	Local HW is 55 minutes before HW Plymouth.
Tidal times	At the N end of Smith Sound, the N going stream begins 1 hour and 30 minutes after HW Plymouth. The S going stream begins 3 hours and 30 minutes before HW Plymouth.
	In St Mary's Sound, the SE going stream begins 5 hours and 45 minutes before HW Plymouth. The NW going stream begins 45 minutes after HW Plymouth.
	In Broad Sound, the streams rotate clockwise in direction. The stream flows NNE 5 hours and 40 minutes after HW Plymouth, and SSW 45 minutes before HW Plymouth.
Max Rate Sp	At the N end of Smith Sound, streams reach 2 knots and in St Mary's Sound, 1.7 knots at springs and 0.7 knots at neaps. In Broad Sound, the clockwise rotating stream is strongest when going NNE or SSW (1.2 knots) gradually weakening to 0.5 knots or less.
Coastguard	Falmouth, tel. 01326 317575, VHF weather 0110 UT

32

St Agnes & the Western Rocks

Introduction

The Atlantic starts here. The coast of lush St Agnes is a real gem, but the moment that you leave it behind, you enter a truly oceanic environment. Heaving seas, savage rocks, abundant sea birds. Bishop Rock is, literally, the edge of the world. Next stop Manhattan.

Description

ST AGNES AND GUGH

St Agnes faces the prevailing Atlantic weather and reaching it involves a ferry glide across the tide flow of St Mary's Sound. St Agnes separated from the combined Scilly landmass of 'Ennor' at least 500 years before the other populated islands, which perhaps helps to explain why – despite being so close to St Mary's – it feels remoter than the other inhabited islands. St Agnes is easily recognisable by the disused white lighthouse on the highest point. This was the first lighthouse built by Trinity House, in 1680. The coast of St Agnes is a mix of sandy bays and isolated granite tors, backed by brightly coloured bulb fields and wild flowers. St Agnes' campsite is right beside the water at Periglis Bay, a gorgeous location overlooking Annet and the Western Rocks. The ruined slipway here launched the St Agnes lifeboat up to 1920, the crew comprising a tenth of the island's population.

Paddling around the north coast, the inlet of Porth Conger reveals the Turk's Head Pub and The Bar, a perfect sandy spit joining St Agnes to the island of Gugh at low tide. Kittern Hill on the north of Gugh has a wealth of prehistoric remains, including a well preserved entrance grave,

Obadiah's Barrow (888 085). The south of Gugh is completely covered with the nests of black backed gulls, out in the open among the pink thrift.

Passing to the south of The Bar, you are back at St Agnes and reach Wingletang Bay. A Venetian ship carrying ceramic glass beads was wrecked here, and beachcombers still find beads among the sand grains. The coast around to the campsite features more peculiarly shaped wind sculpted tors. Look out for the peculiar Troy town maze (875 078), the origins of which are obscure.

Rounding the south tip of St Agnes past the Wingletang Rocks, tide races and confused water may be encountered.

THE WESTERN ROCKS

Looking south-west from St Agnes, a series of serrated reefs extend to the horizon. At low tide – when this trip is best enjoyed – the rocks almost bar passage. Known to sailors as the 'Dogs of Scilly', this is the graveyard of hundreds of ships. This is partly because, well into the nineteenth-century, charts misplaced the rocks ten miles to the north!

Paddling out is captivating. The nearest rocks are the wonderfully named Hellweathers, followed by the islets of Melledgan and Gorregan leading you to the Western Rocks proper. These form a 2km wide barrier to the Atlantic swell, and paddling along the inside rim can be calm and sheltered whilst the seas outside are raging. Grey seals bask in large colonies and thousands of cormorants and shags crowd every surface. Puffins and razorbills are also present. Tide flows can be strong between and along the rocks and races form.

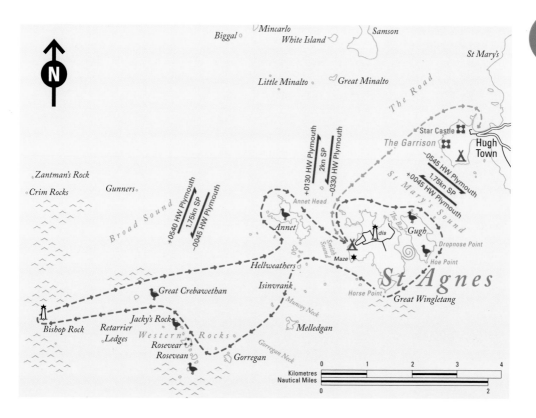

© The Western Rocks

The island of Rosevear can barely be described as such, but was home to navvies working on Bishop Rock lighthouse for ten summers between 1849 and 1858. The remains of cottages and the blacksmith's workshop can be viewed from the water. Despite having no flat surfaces and no turf, the men made the best of the unimaginably harsh conditions. They grew vegetables in rotting seaweed and guano, and in 1854, Scillonians were invited to a 'Grand Ball' on Rosevear.

Looming large behind the Western Rocks is the remarkable edifice that the men created. Britain's tallest lighthouse is only approachable on the calmest of days, and once you get there, there is nothing to do but come back! You actually aren't too far from dry land, but the sense of commitment is absolute.

ANNET

A circuit of uninhabited Annet's rugged coast forms an engaging finale to this magnificent paddle. Only rising 18 metres above sea level, Annet is a windswept maritime heath that is totally covered by pink thrift and bird nests. Landing is not permitted as nests full of eggs and squawking chicks extend to the water's edge. Annet is home to populations of storm petrels, black backed gulls, puffins and Manx shearwaters. An evening paddle will encounter large floating rafts of the latter socialising before returning to their burrows.

VARIATIONS

The circuit of Agnes and Gugh, or of Annet, or a paddle out to the Western Rocks are all worthwhile trips in themselves.

Bishop Rock

32

This is Britain's most exposed lighthouse, on account of the massive fetch of the waves which strike it, combined with the deep water directly in front. Construction began in 1847 on a design with cast iron posts supporting a lighthouse above the waves. In 1850 the finished lighthouse was washed away in a single night, thankfully whilst empty. Work re-started, using a design of Cornish granite. The resulting structure, lit in 1858, was 35m high and was rightly judged an engineering triumph. However, it still proved barely adequate. Cracks appeared, and in 1874 it was *submerged* by waves, with tonnes of water pouring down inside. The keepers recorded fish swimming past the kitchen window, 25m up. In 1882 a reinforcing outer skin of stone was added, extending the height to 53 metres.

Tide and weather

After St Agnes and Gugh are left behind, there is no permitted landing, adding to the commitment of this trip.

The Bar between St Agnes and Gugh submerges at HW springs. A strong south flowing tidal stream then flows across The Bar into The Cove. This creates an anti-clockwise eddy current flowing around The Cove.

St Agnes & the Western Rocks

175

During spring tides, heavy tide races form on either side of Broad Sound, especially around Bishop Rock and the Western Rocks.

Tidal currents are particularly unpredictable to the north of Annet and Smith Sound, as the North Channel, St Mary's Sound and Smith Sound intermingle here.

Additional information

Troy Town Farm campsite (875 081) on St Agnes is run by the Hicks family, tel. 01720 422360, www.troytown.co.uk.

Clowdisley-Shovell's fleet

1707 saw the Western Rocks' greatest tragedy. On 22nd October, 22 ships of the Royal Navy were battling storms in the Western Approaches. The Fleet Admiral was Sir Clowdisley-Shovell, as famous a naval hero in his day as Nelson. With no accurate way to determine longitude, it was impossible to judge their position. No one spotted the Saint Agnes lighthouse and at around 9 pm, the leading warships struck the Gilstone Ledge (832 053). Clowdisley-Shovell's flagship *Association* sank, as did the *Eagle* and *Romney*, with a single survivor between them. The *Firebrand* struggled on and sank in Smith Sound, a quarter of the crew surviving. The *Phoenix* ruptured its hull, but ran aground safely between Bryher and Samson.

Around 2,000 men drowned. Clowdisley-Shovell himself washed up at Porth Hellick on St Mary's. An islander reputedly confessed on her deathbed that she had discovered him alive, but strangled him for his emerald ring.

The catastrophe led Queen Anne to offer a £20,000 prize for an accurate means to calculate longitude at sea. Consequently, clockmaker John Harrison developed accurate chronometers which solved the problem and saved countless lives. A more recent consequence was the 1973 *Protection of Wrecks Act*. After the *Association* was discovered and surveyed by Navy divers in the 1960s, a free-for-all ensued, with private dive teams using explosives to search for sunken treasure. This led directly to protected status for sensitive wreck sites.

St Agnes & the Western Rocks

North Cornwall

An introduction

The north coast is among our grandest and finest coastal scenery. Cliffs stretch north and east for around 200km from Land's End to Marsland Mouth, fully exposed to the prevailing weather and the North Atlantic swells. This is the classic imagined coast, with innumerable coves, inlets, caves, reefs and stacks. This wave-battered wall holds back the Celtic Sea, with few breaches; beaches comprise only a small proportion of the coast.

North Cornwall's heritage is inextricably intertwined with the maritime environment. Even in the wildest places, the signs of past activity are plain to see. Cliff castles, smuggling, fishing, mining and tourism have all left their mark on the landscape and perhaps it is this complex convergence of scenic beauty and human activity that makes exploring the north coast such a memorable experience.

The reasons why relatively few sea kayakers frequent this fabulous coast remain a mystery. Perhaps some imagine the North Cornish coast as a giant tourist park? If so, this is simply not the case. The resorts of Bude and around Newquay comprise a very small proportion of the whole and the coast is often wild and committing within minutes of leaving popular beaches behind.

Environment

England's finest coastal scenery is protected by Heritage Coast status for most of its length, respectively the Penwith, Godrevy-Portreath, St Agnes, Trevose Head, Pentire Point-Widemouth and Hartland Heritage Coasts. Seven stretches are within the Cornish Area of Outstanding Natural Beauty (AONB) and the National Trust own and manage many of the most beautiful sections. In 2006 the remarkable post-industrial landscape of Cornwall was designated as being of international importance; the coasts around St Just, Hayle and St Agnes are now included within the newly created Cornwall and West Devon Mining Landscape World Heritage Site.

Tide and weather

The lack of sheltered ports means that this is not a classic cruising ground for yachts. Because of this, North Cornwall's tidal flows are not well documented. The tidal flow times included in this chapter are often based on tidal stream atlases and should be considered approximate. Local HW is often a better indication of when the flow will become favourable. Tides can retreat a long distance across sandy beaches, making a trolley very useful.

Although the climate is warm, strong winds from the south-west are common and the lack of sheltered water means that swell is a constant concern. North Cornwall's huge surf subculture is an indication of the regularity of groundswell. With calm seas, most of the trips outlined here are straightforward to access and complete. With even small amounts of surf, they become entirely different experiences. Choosing and safely utilising landing and launching sites becomes a very real concern. One metre of beach surf can mean offshore groundswell at least double that height.

Background Reading

Lundy and Irish Sea Pilot, David Taylor, Imray 2001, ISBN 0-85288-448-6

West Country Cruising Companion, Mark Fishwick, Nautical Data Ltd 2004, ISBN 1-904358-25-X

Atlantic Edge – West Cornwall, Des Hannigan, Penwith District Council 2007, ISBN 978-0-905375-09-0

Land's End, Oliver Hawker, Halgrove 2003, ISBN 1-84114-258-1

Cornwall's Maritime Heritage, Alan Kittridge, Twelveheads Press 2003, ISBN 0-906294-50-9

Cornwall's Lighthouse Heritage, Michael Tarrant, Twelveheads Press 2000, ISBN 0-906294-20-7

Cornwall's Archaeological Heritage, Nicholas Johnson, Twelveheads Press 2003, ISBN 0-906294-52-5

Cornwall's Geological Heritage, Peter Stanier, Twelveheads Press 1990, ISBN 0-906294-61-4

Cornwalls Industrial Heritage, Peter Stanier, Twelveheads Press 2005, ISBN 0-906294-57-6

Cornwall's Literary Heritage, Peter Stanier, Twelveheads Press 1992, ISBN 0-906294-26-6

Wreck and Rescue around the Cornish Coast, Richard Larn, Tor Mark 2006, ISBN 0-85025-406-X

The Maritime History of Cornwall, Helen Doe, Tor Mark, 2006, ISBN 978-085025-407-5

Wild about Cornwall, David Chapman, Alison Hodge 2007, ISBN 978-0-906720-51-6

Cornwall's Marine Guide & Directory - free annual publication from the Cornwall Marine Network, available from Tourist Information Centres

Further information

www.cornwallwildlifetrust.org.uk – Cornwall Wildlife Trust.

www.cornwall-aonb.gov.uk – The Area of Outstanding Natural Beauty.

www.cornish-mining.org.uk – The Cornwall and West Devon Mining Landscape World Heritage Site.

www.magicseaweed.com – Swell size readings from offshore buoys.

© Cape Cornwall

Cape Cornwall ▨▨▨▨

33

No. 33 | **Grade C** | **28km** | **OS Sheet 203**

Tidal Port	Dover
Start	△ Sennen Cove (351 264)
Finish	○ St Ives (519 407)
HW/LW	HW St Ives is 6 hours and 5 minutes before HW Dover.
Tidal times	From Sennen Cove, the N going (flood) stream begins 1 hour after HW Dover. This stream has turned to flow NE between Cape Cornwall and St Ives by 3 hours after HW Dover. The SW going (ebb) stream begins 5 hours before HW Dover. An inshore current begins flowing between Sennen and Cape Cornwall 3 hours before HW Dover, but has reversed direction by 2 hours after HW Dover.
Max Rate Sp	Rates reach over 4 knots at exposed points.
Coastguard	Falmouth, tel. 01326 317575, VHF weather 0110 UT

Introduction

Penwith's north shores are among the wildest in England, offering breathtaking environs and plentiful wildlife. Choose a fine day for this long committing paddle among strong tides, deep zawns and ghostly ruins.

Description

Mainland England's most westerly village has a car park beside the harbour. Launch in front of Sennen Cove's imposing Round House, which formerly housed the capstan for winding in fishing boats. The 4.5km between the 1908-built pier and Porth Nanven (355 309) can be missed out for a shorter trip, but Whitesand Bay could well be the best place in the UK for seeing basking sharks (often congregating here in large groups). It's also a classic surf spot, although any surf here will make the remaining trip 'lively', at best.

Porth Nanven faces the Brisons, a pair of 25m offshore rocks. It's illegal to remove the ancient rounded boulders from this beach, ever since a certain northern city was found to be using them for ornamentation! Carn Gloose cliffs lead to tiny Priest's Cove (352 317), where a slipway serves local fishermen. This is the last road access.

England's only cape is recognisable by the chimney on top and the Coastwatch hut below. Once believed to be Britain's westernmost point, Cape Cornwall still marks the divide between the English Channel and St George's Channel. On the north side, seals can be found sleeping in Porth Leddon.

Heading inshore to clear the Cape's tide races, you are now committed to the full distance! The good news is that from hereon, the cliffs are nothing short of awe inspiring. It would take a separate book (and a lifetime's exploring) to describe every zawn, cave, inlet and cove. The rock varies between pale 270 million year old granite, and dark slates and hornsfels, laid as sediment 400 million years ago and baked by the heat and pressure of the granite's intrusion. Colour is added by yellow xanthoria lichen above the waterline, and plants such as sea campion, sedge, thrift, samphire and sea beet growing higher up. In the water seals, sunfish and sharks are commonplace sightings.

The Iron Age fortifications on Kenidjack headland give way to 3km of more recent ruins, namely the mining landscape. Buildings and chimneys stand on rock-hewn levels in the stained cliffs, with rusting chains and bolts visible on the rocks below. It's no coincidence that many of the workings sit atop gaping zawns in the cliffs, as these indicate the presence of vertical ore lodes. Most dramatic is Botallack Crowns Mine (362 336), where two engine houses perch barely high enough to clear storm waves.

Pendeen Watch Lighthouse sits on a slate promontory, built in 1900 to counter the notable amount of wrecks caused by fog. A kilometre further is Portheras Cove, the safest landing of the day. Wear something on your feet, as shards of metal lurk in the sand, the legacy of a botched attempt to dynamite a wreck!

After a kittiwake colony is passed at Whirl Pool, the cliffs are increasingly indented, characterised by successive jutting headlands and deep inlets. Porthmoina Cove is quite a sight, with its knife-edge island. It is hemmed in by craggy Bosigran Ridge to the south (aka Commando Ridge, a WWII training ground) and Bosigran cliff castle to the north.

The 'Great Zawn' is boastfully named, as the deepest zawn of all Zawn Duel (429 383); comes shortly after Porthmeor Cove.

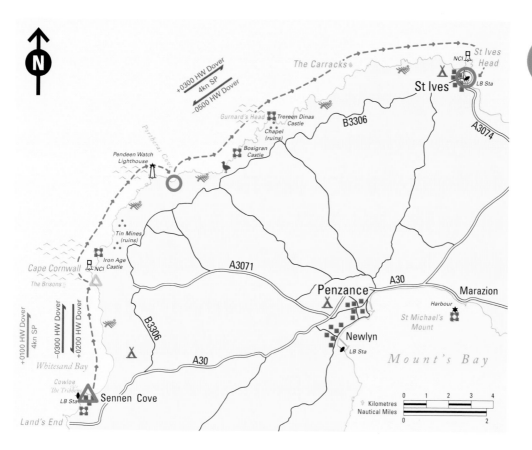

Gurnard's Head has a particularly exposed cliff castle, Trereen Dinas. Whilst the west side is a sheer cliff, traces of Iron Age houses are visible on the east side. Three rocky coves stretch between Gurnard's Head and Zennor Head: Treen, Porthglaze and Pendour. Landing is possible with care at LW. Mine remains and the site of an early Christian chapel can be seen behind Treen, whilst Pendour Cove is the place to listen for Matthew Trewella's singing, a local man seduced into the sea by the Mermaid of Zennor.

D.H. Lawrence lived at Zennor during WWI. Although much of *Women in Love* got written, it wasn't a successful stay. His German wife Frieda (the Red Baron's cousin!) was regarded as a spy by xenophobic locals. Their moonlit walks along Zennor Head's tors and Porthzennor Beach were suspected of being used to signal U-Boats. After three ships were torpedoed locally, the police forced the Lawrences to leave.

Along the final 8km, the cliffs become less sheer but remain imposing, with few signs of civilisation. Wicca Pool is surrounded by fine granite castellations and then The Carracks are reached, a group of islets with a sizeable colony of seals.

St Ives creeps up with little warning, and seeing the packed apartments (and the Tate Gallery) behind Porthmeor Beach is a bit of a shock after what has come before. If you still have the energy, paddle beneath the Coastwatch lookout on 'The Island' (St Ives Head) to finish at Downlong, the harbour area. The fishing boats, narrow streets and granite cottages make an atmospheric end to an outstanding expedition.

The St Just Mining District

The St Just Mining District extends from Porth Nanven to Porthmeor, part of the Cornwall and West Devon Mining Landscape World Heritage Site. Viewed from the water, the plethora of chimneys, engine houses, levels and tips do not jar. On the contrary, they are a hauntingly beautiful sight, blending as integral components of the landscape. Undoubtedly, the actual experiences of those who worked these mines and the contemporary environmental impact were considerably less romantic.

'Hard rock coastal mining' was profitable on account of Cornwall's unusually rich tin and copper lodes. Early in the nineteenth century, the introduction of steam pumps led to astounding expansion. For example, Levant Mine reached 600m below sea level, with tunnels extending 1.5km out under the sea and worked to within metres of the seabed.

A miner's life expectancy was under 40, due to dangerous working conditions. In 1893, at Wheal Owles, twenty men drowned when a flooded adjacent mine was accidentally breached. The owners refused to pay £4,000 for the pump needed to retrieve the bodies. At Levant in 1919, an aging lift failed, sending thirty-one miners to their deaths.

Geevor Mine (375 345) was the last to close, in 1990. The site can be visited (www. geevor.com, tel. 01736 788662), as can Levant (368 345) where the beam engine has been restored by the National Trust.

World Heritage Site – a tin miner's view

I am so proud of having been, if for only a short time, a tin miner. I am delighted at the prospect of the mines being re-opened for all kinds of reasons - economic, the tidying up of some of the sites, and the return of some true wealth generation.

From my experience and conversations with some of the last generation of tin miners there are still huge amounts of ore left in Cornwall. It will alter the landscape, change the demography, and give some local people the chance to own their own home in the place they grew up. It will give some of those miners caught up in the last Cornish diaspora the chance to return.

There will of course be those people who want to maintain the living museum that they have bought into. I agree that the development should be sensitive, but the derelict mine engine houses we now so love were the simplest, least expensive way of building at the time.

To have ridden the cage from deep within the earth, to arrive at the surface tired and filthy after a night shift, and see the sun rise over Carn Brea is to have lived. World heritage is in the experience as much as the legacy.

Dillon Hughes (a Cornish sea kayaker)

© Sennen Cove

ALTERNATIVES

Combined with route 27, a circumnavigation of Penwith forms one of the finest 2-3 day trips in British waters. Shuttling by car, bus or rail between Penzance and St Ives is simple.

Tide and weather

Atlantic groundswell is pretty well the norm hereabouts. Fog is also common, often the first harbinger of a change from fine weather.

Consider launching two or three hours before HW Dover to utilise the inshore current as far as Cape Cornwall. A powerful tidal race forms off the Cape and in the following 3km, with further races around exposed points. These races form a dangerous trap if approaching on the ebb from St Ives into SW groundswell.

Additional information

Sennen Cove Camping (370 273) overlooks Whitesand Bay but is 3km from the harbour, tel. 01736 871818. Ayr Holiday Park (511 405) in St Ives is very close to Porthmeor Beach, tel. 01736 795855, www.ayrholidaypark.co.uk).

godrevy Island from Godrevy Point

Godrevy Island

No. 34 | Grade B | 18km | OS Sheet 203

Tidal Port	Dover
Start	△ St Ives (519 407)
Finish	○ Portreath (656 453)
HW/LW	HW St Ives and Hayle are 6 hours and 5 minutes before HW Dover.
	HW Portreath is 6 hours before HW Dover.
Tidal times	The NE going (flood) stream begins 2 hours after HW Dover. The SW going (ebb) stream begins 4 hours before HW Dover.
Max Rate Sp	Rates reach 2 knots along the coast.
Coastguard	Falmouth, tel. 01326 317575, VHF weather 0110 UT

Introduction

St Ives Bay is not the most inspiring start, but this trip gradually accumulates interest until by the time Portreath is reached, you may not wish to finish! The appeal to paddlers of the Godrevy-Portreath Heritage Coast revolves around a strong tide race and numerous offshore stacks, with the highlight being Godrevy Island and its dramatic lighthouse.

© Godrevy Island

Description

Located on a headland surrounded by numerous beaches, the narrow whitewashed streets of St Ives are an attractive place to explore on foot. Artists flock to the town for the (apparently) unique light; thus every second building is an art gallery, with the Daddy being the Tate on Porthmeor Beach. Down in the harbour there is less pretension, with John Smeaton's 1770 pier protecting a working fishing fleet. Seals thrive around the harbour, as does a criminal element of herring gulls who steal chips and ice cream from your hand. Launching is possible here or at any of the beaches, your choice largely dictated by parking availability.

The first few kilometres of St Ives Bay are rather drab and the tide recedes 1.5km at Porth Kidney. A direct crossing to the eastern end of the bay gives an excuse to look for bottlenose dolphins, commonly seen here.

The sand dunes behind the bay have been infiltrated by holiday parks, but Upton Towans (579 397) is owned by the Cornwall Wildlife Trust. This site was a huge dynamite production complex up to the end of the First World War, and the ruins remain crumbling among the dunes. Look out for pyramidal orchids and cantankerous adders.

Godrevy Beach is found just before the cliffs close in at the east end of the bay. The water here is sometimes stained by (harmless) tin waste from the Red River. Surfers are often found here, implying surf. Until recently 25,000 tonnes of sand were extracted from the beach and dunes each year; thankfully it is now protected as the St Gothian Sands Nature Reserve.

Approaching Godrevy Point, the tide accelerates and the character of this trip changes completely. Tide races rage on both sides of Godrevy Island, necessitating a vigorous ferry-glide to cross the 300m gap to it.

Godrevy Island is deceptive; as you near you'll realise that it is actually two distinct islets with outlying rocks. Oyster-catchers and pipits screech noisily at paddlers negotiating the 'canyon' between the islets. The largest has a steeply sloped surface, with the lighthouse perched on top. This meagre environment is attractively colonised by heather, primroses and thrift. The 26m Godrevy Lighthouse was immortalised by Virginia Woolf in *To the Lighthouse*, although she relocated it to the Hebrides! James Walker completed it for Trinity House in 1859, after the horrific loss with all hands in 1854 of the steamer *Nile*.

Back inshore, the coast is equally dramatic. The folded strata of the cliffs between Godrevy Point and Navax Point have been exploited by wave action to form many caves and coves. Shags nest here, but the most impressive wildlife can be found on storm beaches like Mutton Cove (584 433) in the spring, when large numbers of grey seals congregate to give birth.

The 7km to Portreath encompasses an unbroken line of 70m cliffs. The beach in Fishing Cove is the last sheltered landing. Hell's Mouth is a vast portentous looking cave mouth in the black rock, followed by cheerily named Deadman's Cove. The final 3km to Portreath are stunning, lined by successive clusters of large stacks including the Crane Islands, Samphire Island and Gull Rock. Lodged between is Basset Cove, where the eccentric Basset family installed a winched cage to lower them down to the beach, and also Ralph's Cupboard, a deep zawn.

Portreath beach converts any swell into surf. Should you not fancy this, the harbour entrance is at the east end under the cliffs, looking decidedly unconvincing until the final moment. There is a slipway at the back end of this narrow harbour.

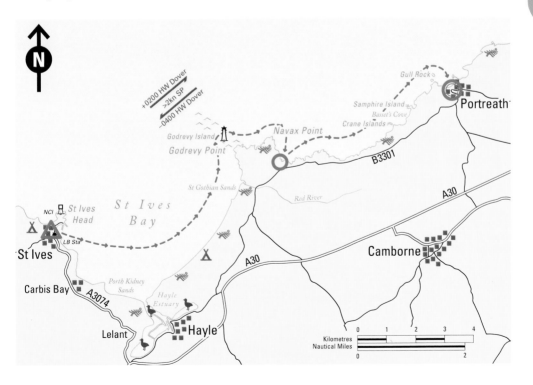

Birders may fancy a diversion into the Hayle Estuary, an RSPB Reserve. Wading birds thrive, rather strangely given that massive amounts of toxic heavy metals (mine waste) are trapped in the estuarine mud.

Tide and weather

In St Ives Bay, tide flows are very weak. The flood stream tends to flow north-east, whilst the ebb follows the shore of the Bay.

Significant races form offshore and inshore of Godrevy Island. On the flood, they push paddlers strongly north-east away from shore. Ferrygliding skills may be helpful.

Additional information

Tate St Ives (tel. 01736 796226, www.tate.org.uk/stives) saw its three millionth visitor in 2007! Seek out the 'naïve' sea paintings produced by local fisherman Alfred Wallis in the 1930s, inspiring artists to descend on the town and form the 'St Ives School'.

Ayr Holiday Park (511 405) in St Ives is close to Porthmeor Beach, tel. 01736 795855, www. ayrholidaypark.co.uk. Beachside camping is available at Beachside (563 390) near Hayle, tel. 0800 376 1599, www.beachside.co.uk, and similar sites along the same beach.

Wrath of Portreath

Wrath was a rather nasty giant who spent his days flinging immense boulders at passing ships to sink them, before snacking on the sailors. It was these boulders that created the outlying rocks around Godrevy Island. Wrath apparently resided in the deep zawn known as Ralph's Cupboard. Local fishermen claim of this chasm that, *'Nothing ever comes out, which was unfortunate enough to get in'*. Why not test this, by sending a (not very popular) paddler in?

34

Godrevy Island

St Agnes Head ⬛⬛⬛⬛

No. 35 | Grade B | 15km | OS Sheet 203

Tidal Port	Dover
Start	△ Portreath (655 454)
Finish	◯ Perranporth (755 546)
HW/LW	HW Portreath is 6 hours before HW Dover.
Tidal times	The NE going (flood) stream begins 2 hours after HW Dover. The SW going (ebb) stream begins 4 hours before HW Dover.
Max Rate Sp	Rates reach 2 knots along the coast.
Coastguard	Falmouth, tel. 01326 317575, VHF weather 0110 UT

Introduction

The St Agnes Heritage Coast includes some impressive sheer cliffs, punctuated by narrow coves and inlets. However, what makes this area memorable is the mining heritage. Industrial ruins and wasteland are interwoven into the fabric of the landscape, augmenting rather than detracting from its beauty. This is also *Poldark* country, the location of Winston Graham's novels and the associated BBC drama.

Trevaunance Cove entrance

Description

In the eighteenth century Portreath gained Cornwall's first railway when a pier and tramroad were constructed to handle the 100,000 tons of copper exported yearly. The harbour pier still exists to the east of the beach, popular with bodyboarders. Launch from either, the narrow harbour entrance offering shelter if there is surf. Eccentrically, the west end of the beach features 'Lady Basset's Baths', six pools cut from the rock in 1800 for Lady Frances Basset, whose father believed in the sea's healing powers.

The 4.5km to Porthtowan leads the paddler below cliffs of slate and sandstone, with impressive stacks and rocks. Diamond Rock and Gullyn Rock lead to two coves with Sheep Rock between. The second cove is known as Sally's Bottom, passing which you'll spot the chimney above Kites Shaft. This is the first of numerous similarly evocative remains, justifying the area's inclusion within the Cornwall and West Devon Mining Landscape World Heritage Site. The final landmark of these cliffs is Tobban Horse, a triangular mass.

At LW, the coves of Porthtowan and Chapel Porth are joined by a long strand, whilst at HW the sea reaches the cliffs and only Porthtowan has a sandy landing. Porthtowan is popular with holidaymakers as it receives sun all day. The Beach Hotel offers awesome cream teas! Between Porthtowan and Chapel Porth, look for multi-coloured mine waste spilling down the cliffs into the sea. Although they can be seen from the sea, a landing at Chapel Porth is recommended to investigate the remains of the Charlotte United Mine and the three tall engine houses of Towanroath and Wheal Coates tin mines uphill on the cliffs 500m to the north (700 502). The site operated between 1802 and 1913 and may seem familiar, being a perennial favourite of photographers.

No landing is possible for nearly 5km, with imposing 100m cliffs looming overhead. Tubby's Head is a buttress extending out from the cliffs before St Agnes Head itself. Two large rocks called the Crams sit at the base, around which a big tide race surges. This is an intimidating location, always noisy with the local breeding population of kittiwakes, fulmars and guillemots swirling on all sides.

The tide race begins to subside by Newdowns Head, allowing you to enjoy a fantastic series of huge caves and arches, extending to (and under) Trevaunance Head, which shelters Trevaunance Cove. The beach here vanishes at HW springs, but normally offers some shelter from wind and swell. Watch out for rocks lurking underwater, the remains of five successive stone piers built and swept away since 1632. The final pier lasted from 1794 until the early twentieth-century, and at LW the granite foundation blocks are a very real hazard. Ore was shipped from Trevaunance Cove, having first been lowered down the precipitous street. Coal landed in the cove was raised uphill by intricate horse-powered winding gear. A climb up to St Agnes takes in more impressive mine remains, as well as the wonderful 'Stippy-Stappy' ('uphill') terraced cottages.

The quieter cove just north of Trevaunance is Trevellas Porth, site of the Blue Hills Mine. The steep-sided valley is strewn with waste rock tips. The cliffs are now more indented, often with workings traceable on the cliffs themselves through coloured stains. The extent of a rock-cut reef is marked by Green Island.

Hanover Cove is a protected wreck site, where the so-named Falmouth Packet vessel was wrecked in 1763, with only three surviving from 67 onboard. The *Hanover* was travelling from Lisbon but overshot Land's End.

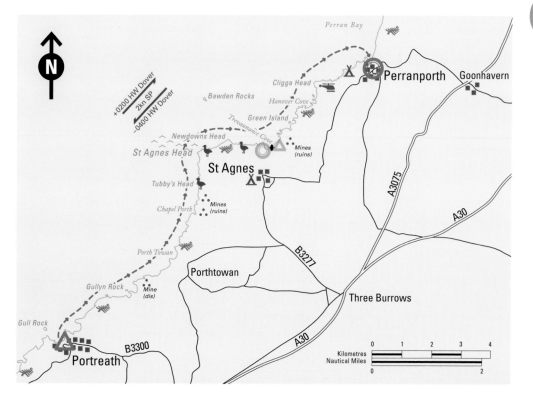

The cliffs of Cligga Head are distinctive smooth slabs, which presumably helped guide in fighter pilots using the airfield above during WWII. The original aircraft pens survive on this complex, which is riddled with mine remains as well as traces of the 'British and Colonial Explosives Factory' located here a century ago.

Approaching the long beach of Perranporth, the cliffs of Droskyn Point continue to bear witness to the past, with caves and arches enlarged by mining. A surf landing in this grim resort will help you return quickly to the present!

Tide and weather

A laconic fisherman informed the author that St Agnes Head would be 'a bit choppy' with the tide race running and 1m of surf at Trevaunance. He wasn't kidding.

Additional information

The free St Agnes Museum illuminates the local maritime heritage and mining landscape (www. stagnesmuseum.org.uk).

There are two campsites around St Agnes; Blue Hills (731 519) is 3km from Trevaunance Cove, tel. 01872 552999, www.bluehillscamping.co.uk, and Beacon Cottage (705 505) is 2km from Chapel Porth, tel. 01872 552347, www.beaconcottagefarmholidays.co.uk.

SAS

In May 1990, St Agnes saw the birth of the remarkably effective pressure group, 'Surfers Against Sewage'. Local boardies were sick of becoming sick from surfing at Porthtowan, Chapel Porth and Trevaunance. By year's end, they had 2,000 members and enjoyed wide media coverage.

Seventeen years later, SAS are still based in St Agnes and have enjoyed numerous successes in getting the issue of clean beaches and sea water taken seriously, playing a part in the passing of legislation such as the 2006 European Bathing Waters Directive. SAS represent the concerns of all water users concerned about water quality. They have widened their campaigns to address issues as diverse as safer shipping, toxic waste, climate change and marine litter.

Consider supporting their work by joining – www.sas.org.uk.

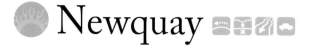

Newquay ▨▧◪◨

No. 36 | **Grade B** | **20km** | **OS Sheet 200**

Tidal Port	Dover
Start	△ Perranporth (755 546)
Finish	◯ Trenance (847 64)
HW/LW	HW Newquay is 6 hours and 4 minutes before HW Dover.
Tidal times	The NE going (flood) stream begins approximately 2 hours after HW Dover. The SW going (ebb) stream begins approximately 4 hours before HW Dover.
Max Rate Sp	Rates reach 2 knots along the coast.
Coastguard	Falmouth, tel. 01326 317575, VHF weather 0110 UT

Introduction

Newquay is Surf City UK, Mecca for crowds of attractive young people seeking excessive sun, sex, surf and lager. Where and how sea kayakers fit into this scene is anybody's guess, but don't despair, this is the North coast, and the power and beauty of the sea environment allures far more than anything that Newquay's nightclubs and extreme sports can offer … unless you are attractive and young.

Description

"Newquay looks almost smart by comparison", was poet John Betjeman's damning of Perranporth in the 1930s. It's still fair comment, but you didn't come for the amusement arcades. Launching across the sands can be hard work at low water.

Perran Beach is long enough at 3km to escape the holidaymakers. The expanse of dunes behind host pyramidal orchids and partially cover an important archaeological site, St Piran's Oratory. St Piran was a sixth-century monk who became patron saint of tin miners. The dunes extend into Penhale Army Camp at the north end of the bay.

Ligger Point is the start of a stretch of coast as attractive as any in Cornwall. Hoblyn's Cove has many caves to explore, and Penhale Point stretches out to an impressive pair of tall pyramidal islands. A law in Cornwall decrees that all offshore rocks must be named Gull Rock, and these are no exception. However, locals know them as 'Fishtail Rock', for obvious reasons. On rare swell-free occasions, it is possible to venture between. Behind the Fishtail, Holywell Bay might look familiar to Bond fans. The surfing sequence of *Die Another Day* was filmed here, with (un-convincing) enormous waves added by computer.

Kelsey Head is guarded by The Chick, and tucked between here and Pentire Point West is the secluded beach of Porth Joke.

Crantock Beach is backed by more dunes behind, and then around Pentire Point East is the most famous beach. Fistral can be identified by the large gothic-spired Headland Hotel at its north end. There is almost always surf here, and it is a contender for Britain's premier big wave spot. Sea kayakers will wish to give it a wide berth if it's working, and probably also Towan Head which follows. Shallow waters off Towan Head allow waves to break some distance offshore. This is the world-famous Cribbar Reef, forming a Hawaiian wave on big days. It probably still hasn't been surfed by kayak?

The gull colony on the north side of Towan Head is clearly unbothered by the large hotels nearby. Shortly after, look out for the Huer's Hut, a centuries old whitewashed lookout (805 623) used for spotting pilchard shoals.

Newquay – owned entirely by Prince Charles – was first called Towan Blystra ('boat cove in sandy hills'). Its present name dates from the sixteenth century when a 'new quay' established it as a port, and thus it remained until the railway arrived and with that, tourists. Newquay now sees 750,000 a year! In a town prowled by 'lairy' beer-boys and predatory hen parties, the harbour is still a quiet haven, frequented by urban seals who have learned how to surf (it's true) and beg for chips.

You should be safe passing Lusty Glaze beach, location of the National Lifeguard and Rescue Training Centre.

Trevelgue Head (825 630) is another of Newquay's surprises, connected by bridge to the mainland with Bronze Age barrows atop. The north side is indented with large caves. 'Banqueting Hall' cave has collapsed, but hosted festivities in the 1930s.

The next 2km follows Watergate Beach, passing the 'Extreme Academy' surf school and Jamie Oliver's restaurant 'Fifteen'. Purist sea kayakers will be glad to see normality now restored, with a final kilometre of quiet cliffs, coves and caves to Trenance.

Tide and weather

Tide races are found off all of the headlands. 1-2m of clean surf on Newquay's powerful surf breaks can equate to 3-5m of groundswell offshore. If caught out by the size of the swell having launched through the surf, your best bet for a sheltered landing is probably Newquay Harbour. Tucked behind Towan Head, this receives less swell. Entry is easiest around 3 hours either side of HW.

Additional information

There are numerous campsites, but most refuse all-male groups on account of Newquay's dubious status of UK stag night capital. Two campsites are accessible from the water: Porth Beach (834 629) near Newquay, tel. 01637 876531, www.porthbeach.co.uk, and Magic Cove (852 671) in Mawgan Porth, tel. 01637 860263, www.redcove.co.uk).

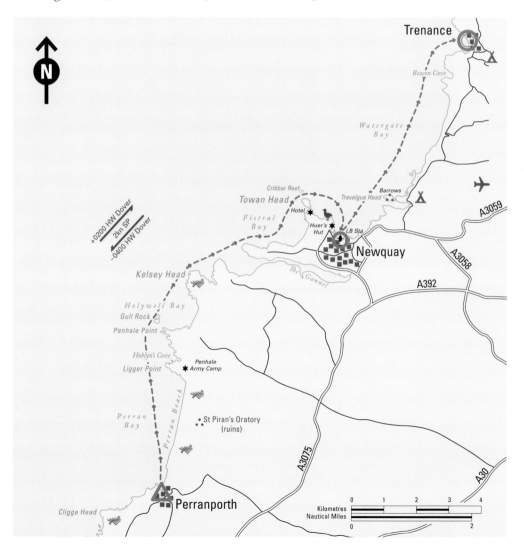

© Seal, Newquay Harbour

Speed Bumps

Two factors in combination add a unique challenge to sea kayaking on the North Cornish coast: tourists and surf. Whilst most beaches are relatively quiet and uncrowded, there will be times when you have to land or launch on a busy beach. This is no problem unless there is surf, in which case your 5.5m craft becomes a potential WMD.

In summer, popular beaches are monitored by lifeguards who flag out areas for swimmers, surfers and sometimes kayaks. Before launching, tell these itinerant Aussies your plans. Often they will be able to give good advice or even clear a path for you. Likewise, when arriving offshore at a packed beach, lifeguards may well paddle or jet ski out to advise you or guide you in.

At classic surf breaks like Newquay's Fistral, sea kayakers are advised – for their own health – not to mix it with the boardies. Choose a different landing spot (or beach).

Trevose Head lighthouse

Trevose Head

No. 37 | Grade B | 22km | OS Sheet 200

Tidal Port	Dover
Start	△ Trenance (847 64)
Finish	◯ Padstow (920 754)
HW/LW	HW Padstow is about 5 hours and 50 minutes before HW Dover.
Tidal times	The NE going (flood) stream begins 2 hours after HW Dover. The SW going (ebb) stream begins 4 hours before HW Dover.
	In the Camel estuary, the outgoing and ingoing flows correspond with HW Padstow.
Max Rate Sp	Rates reach 2 knots along the coast, exceeding 3 knots around Trevose Head. Rates reach 3.5 knots in the narrowest part of the Camel estuary's channels.
Coastguard	Falmouth, tel. 01326 317575, VHF weather 0110 UT

Introduction

Yet another swathe of North Cornish grandeur! Jutting into the Celtic Sea, Trevose Head forms a prominent hazard to shipping and claimed many wrecks before the lighthouse was constructed. Paddlers will relish paddling around the headland and amongst the numerous

offshore stacks. This trip offers more landing opportunities than most North Cornish ventures, and has a shorter shuttle.

Description

Busy Trenance beach is just one of many coves to launch from in the locality. The sea retreats some way out at low tide, consider bringing a trolley.

Directly outside the bay, High Cove is the first of many large caves to be seen along this trip. Bedruthan Steps (848 694) is something different however. A varied series of stacks litter the beach for 1km, with colourful names; Carnewas Island, Pendarves Island, Redcove Island, Samaritan Rock (named after a ship wrecked here in 1846), Queen Bess Rock and Diggory's Island. Steps descend the cliffs to the beach from the National Trust visitor centre above. Oddly, Bedruthan Steps can be a disappointing paddling experience as the stacks are often high and dry, surrounded by sand; their appeal to tourists comes from the fact that they can be explored on foot. However, if a paddle here is engineered at high tide, the stacks (and various arches through them) become the domain of sea kayakers once more.

Park Head is rounded (more big caves) and the following 2km is a wonderful medley of rock gardens, inlets and coves. The Trescore Islands and Minnow Islands are rather grandly named rocks. Wills Rock is just outside Porthcothan Bay, here a Customs officer was left by smugglers to drown, but somehow survived. Fox, Warren and Pepper are three tiny coves following in succession. Pepper Cove is named on account of the illegal shipments of spice landed there. Paddling in, you'll see why the cove is a perfect haven for smuggling, with its hidden profile and sandy landing.

Treyarnon Bay is overlooked by a Youth Hostel which obligingly serves cream teas. Constantine Bay follows, but you'll want to paddle straight out towards looming Trevose Head. Just before the end of the headland, look for Round Hole (890 763) which is exactly what the name suggests. The roof of a huge cave has collapsed, now being open to the sky.

The pace accelerates at Trevose Head. Tide races drag you around Dinas Head to Stinking Cove (it doesn't), overlooked by the lighthouse, 50m above atop grey granite cliffs. To sea, the jagged stacks you can see are The Bull and further out, the Quies. Races continue past Cat's Cove and the Merope Rocks chain. Follow one of the many gaps through these rocks, and you emerge beside Padstow Lifeboat station. The unlikely location of this enormous new £5.5 million building was achieved by placing it on stilts over Mother Ivey's Bay. The station is open to the public, a perfect point for a break?

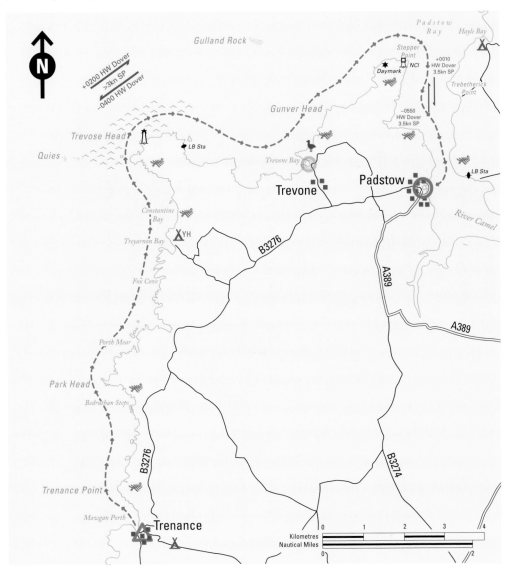

Behind heavily quarried Cataclews Point is Harlyn Bay, well-known among surfers as one of Cornwall's few north-facing beaches. Surfers come here when everywhere else is too big.

Trevone Bay features another collapsed 'Round Hole'. This 25m deep cave forms a spectacular blowhole when the sea emerges from the open roof. Trevone (891 760) may be a tempting spot to finish, but good things are still to come. Porthmissen Bridge (891 764) is a section of layered marble cliffs, home to a large gull colony who take advantage of the horizontal ledges. From here to Gunver Head is constantly entertaining, with reefs to negotiate and some tall stacks that can be sneaked behind. This is at least as pleasant as Bedruthan Steps, only without the crowds!

The approach of Stepper Point is indicated by the daymark tower on top, a Coastwatch station and also Pepper Hole, yet another collapsed cave, forming a gully in this instance. As you paddle around Stepper Point into the Camel estuary, spare a thought for the sailing ships which had to negotiate this difficult entrance. In 1829, capstans were fixed onto the quarry levels here, so that teams of men and mules could haul on ropes to 'warp' ships into the estuary against the prevailing south-west winds.

Padstow is 3km up the estuary past some glorious sandy beaches; see route 38 for details.

VARIATIONS

Many shorter variations are possible. The paddle across the tide race to explore the Quies rocks off Trevose Head could be an interesting challenge.

Tide and weather

As always with North Cornwall, exposed cliffs are the order of the day. However, this trip is broken up by plenty of sandy coves, offering more landing possibilities than is the norm.

A series of notable tide races extend around Trevose Head, from Merope Rocks to Dinas Head. They are less severe close inshore.

The tide stream off Stepper Point follows a rotary pattern, making it tricky to predict!

Additional information

Magic Cove (852 671) in Mawgan Porth, tel. 01637 860263, www.redcove.co.uk, and Tristram Camping (933 789) in Polzeath, tel. 01208 862215, www.rockinfo.co.uk, both offer camping close to the beach. The Youth Hostel (858 741) beside Treyarnon Bay has some space for camping outside, tel. 08707 706076, www.yha.org.uk.

© Harbour Cove

The River Camel

No. 38 | **Grade A** | **13km** | **OS Sheet 200**

Tidal Port	Dover
Start	△ Wadebridge (789 726)
Finish	○ Padstow (920 754), Polzeath (936 790) or Rock (928 758)
HW/LW	HW Padstow is about 5 hours and 50 minutes before HW Dover.
Tidal times	Outgoing and ingoing flows correspond with HW Padstow.
Max Rate Sp	Rates reach 3.5 knots in the narrowest part of the channels.
Coastguard	Falmouth, tel. 01326 317575, VHF weather 0110 UT

Introduction

The name Camel is thought to derive from two Cornish words, 'Cam' (crooked) and 'Hayle' (estuary). North Cornwall's only sheltered paddle is a pleasantly varied journey along Bodmin Moor's river, taking in tidal marshes and the bustling fishing port of Padstow.

© The Town Bar

Description

The bridge from which Wadebridge takes its name was built in 1468, and has somehow mislaid four of its arches over the centuries. The easiest place to launch is a slipway several hundred metres downstream on the south bank. Launching after high water allows the ebbing tide to quickly carry you past several dilapidated boatyards and under the bypass.

Trewornan Marshes give the flavour of the upper estuary. As the tide falls, salt pans are exposed, covered with salt-tolerant plants like scurvy grass. These marshes are bounded by metre-high 'salting cliffs' which mark the upper limit of neap tides and form the boundary where the mud begins. This is a perfect environment for wading birds such as oystercatchers, which flit about going 'peep peep'. Otters are also regularly spotted.

The estuary changes character when Cant Hill is reached on the right. The left bank is covered by overgrown stone tips, dumped in massive quantities until the Camel Slate Quarries closed in the 1890s. This is also a noisy waterski area. More positively, a railway bridge just after is the entrance to Pinkson Creek, home to breeding herons and little egrets. The railway is disused, now being the course of the cyclist-friendly Camel Trail.

Around the corner past a wreck at Oldtown Cove bridge, the estuary widens and Padstow hoves into view. You'll encounter the Town Bar, a 900m wide sand bank extending 2km up the estuary from Padstow Harbour.

Little Petherick Creek is marked on the left by a three arched iron bridge. Just past is a convenient campsite (see below) and then Padstow is reached, North Cornwall's largest port. The old inner harbour is worth investigating, but note that it is sealed off as the tide falls. Don't get trapped! Best landing place is a slipway to the left of the inner harbour entrance, leading up to the car park and toilets.

On the far side of the Town Bar, Porthilly and Rock are also worth a visit. There is always a deep channel across, follow the yellow ferry!

If there is surf at Polzeath, you might wish to finish your trip at either Padstow or Rock. Otherwise, the final 4km are a lovely gradual transition from estuary to sea. Both shores have sections of low cliffs and dunes. The largest dune is 50m high Cassock Hill behind Rock, part of a raised beach extending to distinctive Brea Hill. The churchyard behind Daymer Beach is the resting place of poet John Betjeman, who holidayed here through his life. A green banded rock – trebetherick slate – extends into the sea along the Greenaway past Trebetherick Point.

The ominously named Doom Bar is a shallow sandbank cutting off much of the estuary from the sea. This natural hazard to shipping – apparently a curse awarded for shooting The Mermaid of Padstow – has wrecked numerous ships and restricted Padstow's growth. On the bright side however, it means that this end of the estuary has some stunning beaches and it gave its name to a great local beer, brewed at Rock.

Polzeath is a simple beach landing, as long as there is no surf. You checked beforehand, right?

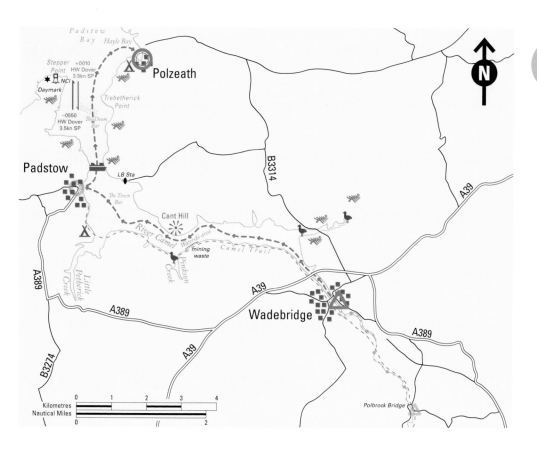

The tidal limit is actually 4km above Wadebridge at Polbrock Bridge (014 695). Although the Camel really *is* a river for most of this stretch, it makes for a beautiful extension.

Tide and weather

The outgoing stream flows fairly weakly along the channel between Padstow and Trebetherick until the Doom Bar is uncovered by the falling tide, then it strengthens considerably. The ingoing stream does the same in reverse.

Additional information

In theory, a fee is owed to Padstow Harbour Authority for launching anywhere along the Camel, as far as Pentire Point.

As noted, the Camel Trail closely follows the Padstow side of the estuary, utilising a disused railway line. One possibility is for a cycle shuttle 8km back up to Wadebridge. There are cycle hire businesses right beside the water at both Wadebridge and Padstow, and they are happy to collect the bikes from the other end afterwards.

Dennis Cove Camping (920 745) is adjacent to the Camel in Padstow, tel. 01841 532349, www.denniscove.co.uk. Tristram Camping (933 789) is right beside the beach in Polzeath, tel. 01208 862215, www.rockinfo.co.uk.

Padstein

Padstow prospered in the nineteenth century, with twenty-seven registered shipbuilders and a large fishing fleet supplying herring by rail to London's Billingsgate Market. These industries declined sharply during the twentieth century.

Padstow has undergone something of a renaissance, largely due to TV chef Rick Stein. Stein's popularising of the fruits of Cornwall's coasts has helped to resuscitate the ailing fishing industry and has put Padstow on the tourist map. Stein opened a seafood college at the harbour and owns several restaurants in town. Whilst dripping paddlers in stinky thermals might be admitted into Stein's Fish and Chips, they certainly won't be allowed into The Seafood Restaurant, even if they could afford the £70-a-head menu.

Not everyone is enamoured of Stein; old salty seadog types can be found moaning in the backstreet pubs about the 'good olde days' before 'Padstein' was full of expensive cafés and gawping tourists.

Tintagel

No. 39 | Grade B | 28km | OS Sheets 200, 190

Tidal Port	Dover
Start	△ Polzeath (936 790)
Finish	◎ Boscastle (096 214)
HW/LW	HW Polzeath is 5 hours and 50 minutes before HW Dover.
	HW Boscastle is 5 hours and 43 minutes before HW Dover.
Tidal times	The NE going (flood) stream begins 2 hours after HW Dover. The SW going (ebb) stream begins 4 hours before HW Dover.
	In Port Quin Bay, tides run ESE for 3 hours 30 minutes and WNW for about 9 hours.
Max Rate Sp	Rates reach 2 knots along the coast, exceeding 3 knots off Pentire Point. In Port Quin Bay they reach 1.5 to 2 knots.
Coastguard	Falmouth, tel. 01326 317575, VHF weather 0110 UT

Introduction

The coast between the River Camel estuary and Boscastle is exceptionally scenic with headlands, caves, historical sites and pretty villages maintaining constant interest.

Description

Polzeath is a very popular surf spot with a car park just uphill and another on the beach itself, best avoided unless you can be back before HW! If the surf is pumping, you'll probably want to make alternative plans. Otherwise, head out to the headland of Pentire Point. Tide races will be encountered here and at also at Rumps Point, the promontory 1km further on. This is a dramatic start, with the offshore stacks of Newland and The Mouls seeking to distract from the cliffs and caves of the peninsula. Rumps Point is the site of Cornwall's finest Iron Age cliff castle, and from the water you will see the thrift-covered ramparts and ditches constructed to keep out uninvited guests. Keep an eye out for puffins, which nest on The Mouls.

Port Quin Bay is ringed by cliffs, with a long tunnel to be discovered near Carnweather Point. The inlet of Port Quin (970 806) is the first sheltered landing. This 'port' was abandoned in the late nineteenth century after the local quarry failed. The *Poldark* TV series (ask your parents) was filmed here. Just a few cottages remain, as well as the nineteenth-century 'castle' on Doyden Point.

The inlet of Port Isaac, 3km east, couldn't offer a greater contrast. This whitewashed fishing village (recognisable from TV Drama *Doc Martin*) is always crammed with visitors, crowding the steep narrow streets around the harbour. Pleasant as it is, Port Isaac isn't recommended as a launch point; the village is often closed to traffic, and the only parking is on the beach. Port Isaac originates as a pilchard fishery from Tudor times, and the earliest pier is visible inside the stone breakwaters at low water. The inshore lifeboat is housed inside old fish cellars. Just east, the subsidiary inlet of Port Gaverne (002 809) is a quieter bet.

After the bustle of Port Isaac, 8km of cliffs make for a quiet contrast. Not too quiet though; Bounds Cliff has a large and screeching seagull colony, followed by Barrett's Zawn, a collapsed tunnel through which slate was once hauled for loading onto ships. The seabed is largely sandy along here and a sunny day will allow you to watch seals and cormorants swim beneath. Tregardock beach will suit those who want a private lunch spot, otherwise Trebarwith Strand, marked by monolithic Gull Rock looming just offshore, has pubs, toilets and of course, the public. Note that these beaches vanish at HW.

Trebarwith was a busy quarry port long before tourists ever came. Evidence of this can be seen in the tall rock spires behind Hole Beach, actually the unworked remains of Lanterdan Quarry. Cutting the stone and loading it onto boats was harsh work, and could be lethal; in 1889 three men vanished into sea when the face that they were boring sheared off the cliff.

Between Penhallic Point and Tintagel Head, the vertical Glebe Cliffs feature some monumental caves, not unlike scaled-up versions of Anglesey's 'Parliament House Cave'.

Tintagel Head is of course home to the famous castle, but to access this you must first paddle around to Tintagel Cove on the north side. At high tide, it is possible to take a shortcut directly underneath via a tunnel. Known as 'Merlin's Cave', this is where the poet Tennyson had the magician discover the boy Arthur in *Idylls of the King*. English Heritage has obligingly provided steps up from the cove, although this author remembers a desperate cliff scrabble a decade ago! Less romantically, Tintagel Cove was the site of another nineteenth-century quarry port, with slate loaded onto boats after being lowered beside the waterfall via a 'Heath Robinson' system of pulleys and derricks.

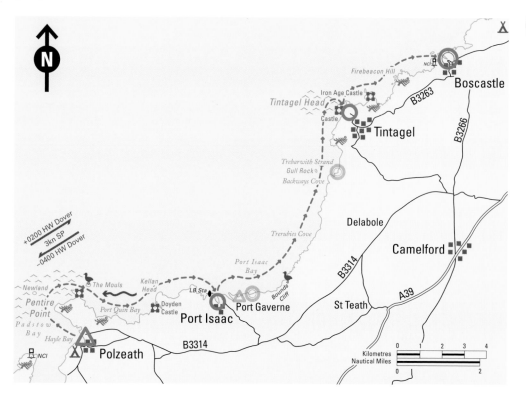

© Port Isaac harbour

Opposite Tintagel Head, Barras Nose became in 1897 the first piece of coast to be purchased by the National Trust. The land was purchased as a memorial to Tennyson, more specifically to rescue it from rapidly encroaching developments such as the vast and awful King Arthur's Castle Hotel. It wasn't of course their last coastal acquisition; they now own 38% of Cornwall's coast, 327km!

Perhaps the best scenery is still to come. Rounding the promontory of Willapark with its Iron Age cliff castle, The Sisters (look out for guillemots) are the first of many steep-faced islets ranged along the cliffs to Boscastle. This is followed (at low tide) by sandy Bossiney Haven, one of Cornwall's most beautiful secluded beaches. Next to Bossiney is Elephant Rock, named for the arch which resembles a 'trunk' dipping into the water. At the far end of the beach is Rocky Valley, the name leaving little to the imagination. In this inlet, water tumbles around boulders and potholes to meet the sea.

Long Island is the spectacular spire rising from the sea 2km before Boscastle, recognisable by its jagged horizontal strata. This and Short Island are breeding grounds for auks, especially razorbills. Caves and blowholes literally abound now, but you may be able to identify the 'Ladies Window' rock formation.

The entrance to Boscastle Harbour is marked by the white tower atop Willapark, not to be confused with the previous Willapark! The tower was built in 1823 as a summer house, but was later used by Customs men. It is now a Coastwatch lookout.

Boscastle harbour is described in route 40.

Tintagel

Like many of the South West's highlights, Tintagel Head is best visited from the sea. Landing at Tintagel Cove, you avoid Tintagel village, a temple to tackiness and kitsch. Here you can visit 'King Arthur's Hall', buy crystal balls from New Age shops and eat 'excaliburgers' (no, really). Sea paddlers bypass this drivel and land beside The Island itself. The entrance is just up the steps from the beach. Cheapskates who don't wish to cough up can follow the path left, up steps to some interesting ruins on the mainland and also the visitor centre. Otherwise, the entrance booth is to the right and English Heritage will negotiate a paddlers' discount.

The Island isn't quite an island as the sea hasn't quite broken through yet. This easily defended headland has seen millennia of occupation. The remains of thirteenth-century Earl Richard's castle are the most obvious remnant of the past, but more enigmatic are the traces of over 70 buildings perched on terraces above the north cliffs. Archaeologists have unearthed heaps of sixth-century pottery here, originating from Malaga in Spain.

Although Tintagel's historical importance has been somewhat obscured by all the daft Arthurian associations, it's not hard to see how it has become progressively entangled with mythology. Whether or not you go looking for Merlin, Tintagel Head is a truly magical location.

Those not already suffering from scenery overload may wish to extend this trip past Boscastle to Crackington Haven, see route 40. A shorter trip can be had by starting or finishing at Port Gaverne (002 809).

Tide and weather

With long cliff sections, exposed headlands and tide races, this is clearly a trip for good weather. Groundswell will make for an intimidating experience and may prevent landing at Tintagel, however the sheltered harbours at Padstow, Port Quin, Port Isaac and Boscastle make the trip feasible in such conditions.

Additional information

Tristram Camping (933 789) is right beside the beach in Polzeath, tel. 01208 862215, www. rockinfo.co.uk. Lower Pennycrocker Farm (124 925) is 4km from Boscastle, tel 01840 250257, www.pennycrocker.com).

Sunfish

Despite originating from tropical climes, the Ocean Sunfish *(Mola Mola)* is increasingly sighted around Cornwall. You'll first recognise it by its peculiar habit of lying on the surface lamely slapping its long dorsal fin from side to side. One theory is that this is intended to attract gulls, in order to remove parasites. The author has observed gulls pecking viciously into passive sunfish.

Sunfish don't seem to mind proximity. Up close, they appear to have been designed by committee; they have the appropriate piscine appendages, only attached in the wrong places, pointing in the wrong direction, with leftover bits to spare! The result is an asymmetric creature that doesn't have an obvious 'right' way up.

Brian Wilson's description can't be bettered: *'... a one-eyed inflatable deep pan pizza'.*

The Beeny Cliff

Boscastle

No. 40 | Grade B | 16km | OS Sheet 190

Tidal Port	Dover
Start	△ Boscastle (096 214)
Finish	△ Widemouth Bay (198 024)
HW/LW	HW Boscastle is 5 hours and 43 minutes before HW Dover.
	HW Widemouth Bay is 5 hours and 40 minutes before HW Dover.
Tidal times	The NE going (flood) stream begins approximately 2 hours after HW Dover. The SW going (ebb) stream begins approximately 4 hours before HW Dover.
Max Rate Sp	Rates reach 2 knots along the coast.
Coastguard	Falmouth, tel. 01326 317575, VHF weather 0110 UT

Introduction

This paddle takes in two lovely contrasting sections of coast. Although tourists throng around Boscastle, very few know about or see the amazing coast hidden just to the north.

Reefs near Dizzard Point

Description

The natural harbour of Boscastle is a drowned river gorge, augmented by two stone piers. In years past, Boscastle handled a busy ore shipping trade, with ships 'warped' into the tortuous inlet by fixed hawsers and pulleys.

You'll be amazed at the degree to which Boscastle has recovered from the flood of 2004. The buildings around the harbour have been repaired or rebuilt, whilst work continues to deepen the riverbed. Launching is possible at HW from the slipway beside the River Valency, past the quirky Witchcraft Museum (perhaps Someone punished Boscastle?). Otherwise, follow the track to the south pier and launch there. At low tide, rocky shallows will still be encountered around the corner. 84 cars were extracted from the harbour after the flood, but 32 cars remain unfound … rolling practice is a bad idea!

Boscastle is sheltered by Meachard Island and Penally Point. A cave passes right through the latter, being exposed at LW and forming the 'Devil's Bellows' blowhole. This is the first of dozens of caves riddling the black cliffs in the next few kilometres. Even if there is groundswell, there are still enough in sheltered inlets to satiate your explorer instinct. Note that the caves are often occupied by denizens of the local seal community; be especially careful when venturing towards the back (if you ever find it).

Pentargon Cove is a long inlet flanked by cave entrances, with a special treat at the end. A 40m waterfall (107 919) gushes to the cove, not all of Cornwall's treasures have car parks and visitor centres!

The Beeny Cliff is honeycombed by (of course) many more caves, tunnels and blowholes. Seals Hole cave is marked on the map, presumably as it has a particularly spacious front porch. The Beeny Sisters are rocks where seals snooze, out of the water, or 'cottling' (sleeping in the water with just their noses showing).

The following bay is full of interest, including a natural archway and Gull Rock stack, precipitous enough itself without factoring in the 170m cliffs behind.

The scenery now moves down a gear, but remains constantly interesting. High Cliff is so-named as it's the tallest point on the Cornish coast at 223m. The Northern Door is a big arch located at the north end of Strangles beach.

Misanthropists will lunch at sandy Little Strand, otherwise visiting Crackington Haven (142 968) is much recommended. The entrance to this cove is guarded by the severely folded headland of Cambeak. In the nineteenth century, plans were drawn up to transform sleepy Crackington into a major town, with associated harbour, dry dock railway, and lighthouse. Thank goodness that the plans were abandoned, this is a lovely quiet haven, served by a pleasant café.

The 8km to Widemouth Bay are attractive, if low-key in the light of what has come before. Striated cliffs form a backdrop to a long succession of pools and reefs begging to be snorkelled or fished. Millook Haven has seen its share of drama. In 1820, armed Customs men landed from the Boscastle Preventive Boat and seized 450 barrels of rum. A cutter then arrived and offloaded two boats of armed men. The Customs men fought back, but were outgunned by the smugglers who reclaimed the rum and also stole the Preventive Boat! This battle indicates the strength and

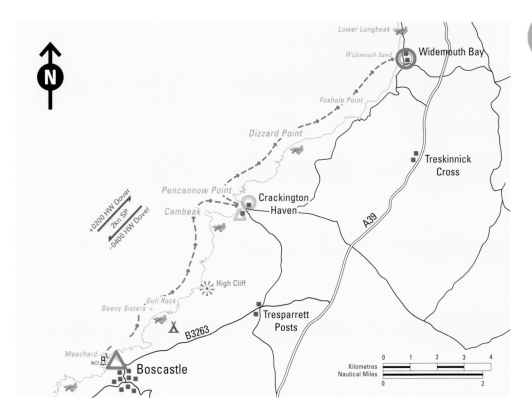

organisation of the 'free trading' industry, as does the fact that an offered £200 reward failed to retrieve the Customs vessel.

If landing in surf at Widemouth Bay, note that a few rocky patches lurk amongst the sand.

VARIATIONS

The first few kilometres are so good that this trip might be better done in reverse!

The stretch from Crackington Haven is less exposed and could be a reasonable fallback if the sea is lively.

Tide and weather

This is best saved for settled conditions, to appreciate the caves. Tide flows are barely discernable, other than around Cambeak. Surf landings may be required at Widemouth Bay and Crackington Haven.

Additional information

Lower Pennycrocker Farm (124 925) is 4km from Boscastle, tel. 01840 250257, www.pennycrocker.com).

The Boscastle Flood

On 17th August 2004, images of Boscastle adorned national newspapers. The astonishing flash flood of the 16th had seen River Valency transformed from bubbling brook to amorphous grey mass, demolishing buildings and carrying cars into the harbour. TV news carried dramatic footage of tourists being winched from the roof of the National Trust visitor centre whilst it collapsed around them. Incredibly everyone survived, although the desperation of the situation was made clear by helicopter pilot Pete McLelland's transmission:

"This is a major incident, repeat major incident ... we are in danger of losing Boscastle and all the people in it."

The rebuilt NT visitor centre has excellent displays on the flood. Historically, Boscastle and other steep-valleyed coastal settlements in the South West have been struck by flash floods many times. No one doubts that such floods will happen again, but the burning question is whether climate change will make them a commonplace occurrence.

The Hartland Heritage Coast

No. 41 | **Grade B** | **23 km** | **OS Sheet 190**

Tidal Port	Dover
Start	△ Widemouth Bay (198 024)
Finish	◯ Hartland Quay (222 248)
HW/LW	HW Bude is 5 hours and 40 minutes before HW Dover.
Tidal times	The N going (flood) stream begins approximately 2 hours after HW Dover. The S going (ebb) stream begins approximately 4 hours before HW Dover.
Max Rate Sp	Flows are inconsistent but rates can reach 3 knots around exposed points.
Coastguard	Falmouth, tel. 01326 317575, VHF weather 0110 UT, Swansea, tel. 01792 366534, VHF weather 0150 UT

Introduction

The long straight coast north to Hartland Quay is one of the South West's unique highlights. Although there are tall cliffs, the real interest is the reef that keeps you offshore. The rock strata

are folded upwards, with endless rows of sharp fangs pointing to the sky. Alongside the extraordinary solitude of this coast, this adds up to a wild and committing paddle.

Description

If the surf looks intimidating, then postpone to a more settled day. Although you can also launch from coves north of Bude, the scenery is interesting all the way from Widemouth Bay. The coast is characterised by cliffs protected by a wave-cut platform; in plain-speak, a bedrock reef up to 250m wide extends into the sea. At this southern end there are gaps in the reef revealing patches of ochre sand, especially at LW. The sand recedes as you head north and the landing at Hartland Quay is crunchy at the best of times.

Five kilometres north of Widemouth is Bude, among Cornwall's most popular resorts. Landing a sea kayak on Bude's crowded beaches could cause a massacre, approach carefully.

Sandy Mouth (201 099) is the final beach remaining sandy at all states of the tide, and 2km further is Duckpool, another road-accessed cove but rocky at some states of the tide.

What is all the fuss about? As you paddle north, the reef becomes increasingly serrated, with the appeal of landing decreasing proportionally for anyone not in a borrowed boat. Intimidating as this is, the resulting views are stunning, especially with a (mild!) swell foaming across the reef.

The reef's character is explained by the zigzagging patterns in the cliffs. Those who know about these things explain that around 290 million years ago the two continents of Eurasia and Gondwana collided in this general vicinity, the impact causing the zigzags. Waves eroded the mudstone away and the harder sandstone remains pointing to the sky, waiting to shred your fibreglass pride and joy. Lower Sharpnose Point is a case in point, with several vertical rock slivers explaining the name.

The waterfall of Stanbury Mouth follows. From near Higher Sharpnose Point, at least four large waterfalls can be seen at once, tumbling out of hanging valleys to the reef.

North of Higher Sharpnose Point, the white buildings of Hartland Quay can be seen, over 10km away with no houses in between. That said, nearby (197 152) is Hawker's Hut, a peculiar driftwood shack built by Victorian poet and eccentric, the Reverend Robert Hawker, and maintained by the National Trust.

Just after Gull Rock (with a tunnel blasted through by wave action) is the waterfall of Marsland Mouth. This indicates that you are entering Devon (Swansea Coastguard's remit). Fulmars nest between here and Welcombe Mouth (213 180), which has a car park and is comprised of grey shingles, but is sandy at some stages of the tide. A further 1.5km and you are below Embury Beacon, an Iron Age settlement and the highest point on this coast. The reefs become increasingly extravagant, look out for the section resembling ruined house gables! Just before Longpeak Point is Gunpath reef, which in 1962 wrecked the 3,000 ton tanker RFA *Green Ranger*. The 'Wrecker's Bar' at Hartland Quay is decorated by the *Green Ranger's* portholes.

The final 2km to Hartland Quay are the trip highlight. At Speke's Mill Mouth, Milford Water freefalls 16m and then a further 30m in four waterfalls. The reef relents slightly here, with a sandy gap offering a chance to land and appreciate the waterfall. St Catherine's Tor rises 84m above the beach, an isolated hill named after a mariners' chapel on the summit, long since lost to the sea. Behind the Tor, a final waterfall indicates that Hartland Quay is just 500m away.

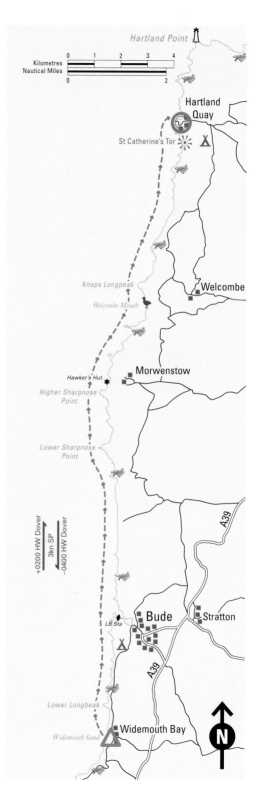

Landing at Hartland Quay isn't easy. For starters, there isn't a quay (see route 42) and the landing is at Warren Beach, located *past* the buildings. Note that it's a stony landing.

VARIATIONS

Combined with route 42, the entire Hartland Heritage Coast makes a magnificent overnight trip. A scrutiny of the map reveals small group camp spots on both routes, but none have easy or straightforward landings. Be flexible in your plans!

Tide and weather

Atlantic groundswell makes launching and landing a challenge. The only (moderately) sheltered landing is at Bude Harbour, accessible two hours either side of HW, provided you pick a route past the surf. If you arrive at Hartland Quay and can't land, then your best bet may be to continue around Hartland Point to Clovelly harbour (see route 42).

Additional information

Upper Lynstone Camping Park (204 052) is near Bude, tel. 01288 352017, www.upperlynstone. co.uk. Stoke Barton Farm (234 247) is 1.5km from Hartland Quay, tel. 01237 441238, www. westcountry-camping.co.uk.

This quiet coast is a national stronghold of the peregrine falcon. More information on the area at www.hartlandpeninsula.com, plus there is a Heritage Coast Exhibition at the Visitor Centre in Bude.

Westward Ho!

The remarkable Hartland coast was best described by local author Charles Kingsley in his 1855 novel *Westward Ho!*:

"Each cove has its black field of jagged shark's tooth rock which paves the cove from side to side … one rasp of which would grind abroad the timbers of the stoutest ship. To landward, all richness, softness and peace; to seaward, a waste and howling wilderness of rock and roller, barren to the fisherman, and hopeless to the shipwrecked mariner."

North Devon, Somerset, Avon & Gloucestershire

An introduction

The Bristol Channel has been a conduit for trade and transport at least since lintels for Stonehenge were rafted across from Wales to England, 5,000 years ago. Transatlantic trade commenced when John Cabot set sail from Bristol for Newfoundland in 1497. During the Industrial Revolution, coal and iron were shipped across from South Wales to small English ports like Porlock, whilst Bristol expanded and prospered from shipping manufactured goods to all corners of the Empire. The chain of lighthouses that stretch east from Hartland Point and Lundy Island indicate the continuing economic importance of the waterway, as does the large shipping always in view offshore.

This region offers plenty of excellent sea kayak adventures to be added to the wish list. The approaches to the Bristol Channel are marked by the folded cliffs of Hartland Point and 30km offshore, by the smooth granite cliffs and lush marine wildlife of magnificent Lundy Island. Barnstaple Bay's headlands punctuate some of the UK's most popular surf beaches, but the crowds are limited to road-accessed hotspots. Behind Barnstaple Bay, the estuaries of the Taw and Torridge Rivers quietly lead inland to the old ports of Bideford and Barnstaple, forming a birdlife haven. Past the headland of Morte Point, the high plateau of Exmoor falls away to the sea, forming Britain's highest mainland sea cliffs. Further east, the upper Channel is characterised by extensive mud flats and an often uninspiring coastal profile. Amidst this, the islands of Steep Holm and Flat Holm are something special, whilst the River Severn estuary makes for an extraordinary journey.

Environment

North Devon's shores are divided up into, respectively, the Hartland, North Devon, Lundy and Exmoor Heritage Coasts, almost all of which fall within the North Devon Area of Outstanding Natural Beauty. The coast between Croyde and Combe Martin (to an offshore depth of 20m) is a Voluntary Marine Conservation Area, and Lundy is England's only statutory Marine Nature Reserve. The National Trust manages large parts of the coast. Exmoor National Park extends east into Somerset. Whilst the upper Bristol Channel is dominated by industrial ports, power stations and mud banks, the region is a habitat for internationally important populations of wading birds and migratory fish, acknowledged by its protected status as a European Marine Site. Sand Point and Brean Down are nature reserves, and Steep Holm and Flat Holm are carefully maintained by charitable nature trusts.

Tide and weather

"I do not think the Bristol Channel at all suited for the amateur cruiser. The tides are too strong, the harbours but poor ones, and the traffic too busy." Frank Cowper, *Sailing Tours*, 1895.

Although the Bristol Channel is up to 45 kilometres wide, it has a phenomenal tidal range of up to 14.8m, Europe's largest, indeed the second largest worldwide. As a result, tide flows reach exceptionally high speeds, and vast expanses of sand, rocks and mud are uncovered at low tide. The tide's speed means that even light winds whip up choppy waves. Atlantic groundswell travels up at least as far as Weston-Super-Mare, often making surf landings necessary. Due to the constant stirring of bottom silt, the water is a rather unappealing murky brown in the upper reaches of the Channel.

Experienced sea kayakers should revel in the challenge presented by all of these factors.

Background Reading

Lundy and Irish Sea Pilot, David Taylor, Imray 2001, ISBN 0-85288-448-6

Secret Nature of Devon, Andrew Cooper, Green Books 2005, ISBN 1-903998-50-6

Devon Smugglers, Robert Hesketh, Bossiney Books 2007, ISBN 978-189938393-1

The Scenery of the North Devon Coast, Rick Abbott, Aycliffe 1991, ISBN 0-9517539-0-8

Somerset Coast, Rodney Legg, Halsgrove 2003, ISBN 1-84114-302-2

Shipwrecks of North Devon, Richard and Bridget Larn, Tor Mark 1999, ISBN 0-85025-381-0

Further Information

www.devonwildlifetrust.org, www.gloucestershirewildlifetrust.co.uk, www.avonwildlifetrust.org.uk, – Wildlife Trusts

www.exmoor-nationalpark.gov.uk - Exmoor National Park

www.northdevon-aonb.org.uk – the AONB

www.severnestuary.net – Severn Estuary Gateway

North Devon, Somerset, Avon & Glos.

© Lobster fisherman, Hartland Point

Hartland Point

42

No. 42 | **Grade B** | **28 km** | **OS Sheet 190**

Tidal Port	Dover
Start	△ Hartland Quay (222 248)
Finish	○ Westward Ho! (434 297)
HW/LW	HW Clovelly is 5 hours and 24 minutes before HW Dover.
Tidal times	Off Hartland Point, the NE going (flood) stream begins 1 hour and 20 minutes after HW Dover. The SW going (ebb) stream begins 4 hours and 40 minutes before HW Dover.
Max Rate Sp	Off Hartland Point, rates reach 3 knots.
Coastguard	Swansea, tel. 01792 366534, VHF weather 0150 UT

Introduction

Hartland Point was known to Roman navigators as the 'Promontory of Hercules'. As this grandiose title implies, the headland is something special. Those who have paddled the wild and committing first part of the Hartland Heritage Coast (route 41) will have some idea of what to expect.

Description

Hartland Quay's name is a bit of a con. There was a quay dating from the sixteenth century, but after the railway reached Bideford in 1855 it fell into disrepair and in 1896 a storm destroyed it. Today, paddlers can access the water by a steep track from The Street down to Warren Beach. Launching can be rocky and might not be viable at all if there is significant swell. At such times, console yourself with a visit to the 'Shipwreck Museum' or a pint in the 'Wrecker's Retreat'.

The view to the north is of a savagely jagged and serrated reef extending out from the cliffs. Bear Rock is the nearest isolated stack, where the mudstone has eroded away between two upright slabs of sandstone. The same process explains the forbidding 'spiky' look of the surrounding coast. Behind Bear Rock, Dyers Mouth waterfall plunges onto the reef.

Hartland Point lighthouse becomes visible above the endless rows of rock teeth extending from the cliffs, but before it is reached you paddle past enormous pieces of ship. On the last day of 1982, the Dutch-owned *Johanna* was driven ashore by gales, rudely interrupting its passage to Cardiff. The remains are a sobering sight.

The lighthouse is built on a promontory below the headland, 37m above the rocks which extend out forming a tide race. It was constructed by Trinity House supremo James Douglass, but was soon undermined by wave erosion. Successive sections of cliff were deliberately collapsed to form a shield, but each washed away. Eventually the present 6m sea wall was constructed in 1925.

Twice daily between April and September, Hartland Point is the site of a wildlife spectacle. At dawn and dusk, large numbers of Manx shearwaters fly past en route to their burrows in Pembrokeshire. The record is 15,000 counted in one morning!

Landing is possible in Barley Bay, overlooked by a garish radar tower. This more sheltered north-facing coast is less severe, and trees often extend towards the waterline. High above on Windbury Hill is the site of an Iron Age settlement, as well as a memorial to the crew of a crashed Wellington Bomber (284 266). Just after are another waterfall, and the rough beach of Mouth Mill. There are preserved lime kilns here, as at Clovelly and Buck's Mills. In past centuries, ships would deliver coal and limestone by doing 'beach work'; simply running aground and waiting for the next high tide. The impressive stack at Mouth Mill is Blackchurch Rock, its name explained by the spire-like shape and the sunlight blazing through two 'windows'.

The white-washed fishing village of Clovelly is justly famous, winding improbably steeply down to the fourteenth-century quay. Donkeys lug lazy visitors up 'up-along' as the pebbled street is known. Arriving by water gives a great view of Clovelly, and isn't the only advantage. Climb up and explore as far as the Queen Victoria fountain, but go no further. Beyond is a huge grotesque shopping complex, barring entrance to the village in order to extract a hefty admission fee. This carbuncle is the Devil's work, an example – like the Land's End theme park – of how the South West's heritage is often desecrated for profit.

Between Clovelly and Peppercombe, weakness in the rock strata has lead to several landslides. The largest formed The Gore (350 242), a 400m spit of boulders to be diverted around at LW.

Marked by another waterfall, Buck's Mills (354 236) is the only viable road access on this trip. Whenever the fishing industry declined, the men of this tiny community would sail to Lundy daily to work in the quarries! Buck's Mills is another rocky landing and the steep track isn't an inviting carry. In any case, it's worth persisting with the final 10km. From Peppercombe valley, the trees are replaced by green fields and rolling hills, whilst the cliffs become lower with more landing opportunities. An abandoned Coastguard lookout marks the turning towards Westward Ho! beach. At HW springs this beach vanishes, forcing landing on the shingle bank behind.

VARIATIONS

The only place with road access to shorten this trip up is Buck's Mills (354 236). Park and carry or trolley your boats downhill.

Hartland Quay is one possible base from which to cross to Lundy Island (route 45).

Tide and weather

The tide race at Hartland Point extends 3km NW of the shore. Picking a route through the chain of shallow rocks inshore avoids the worst of it.

As noted, groundswell makes launching from Hartland Quay and landing at Westward Ho! difficult. The reefs and rocky beaches also mean that there are few soft landings to be had for most of this trip. Clovelly harbour is the only landing sheltered from swell. The estuary at Appledore (routes 43 and 44) is another sheltered option, requiring a careful approach to find the deep channel.

Additional information

More information on the area at www.hartlandpeninsula.com, plus there is a Heritage Coast Exhibition at the Visitor Centre in Bude.

Stoke Barton Farm (234 247) is 1.5km from Hartland Quay, tel. 01237 441238, www.westcountry-camping.co.uk. Steart Farm Touring Park (356 229) is near Buck's Mills, tel. 01237 431836.

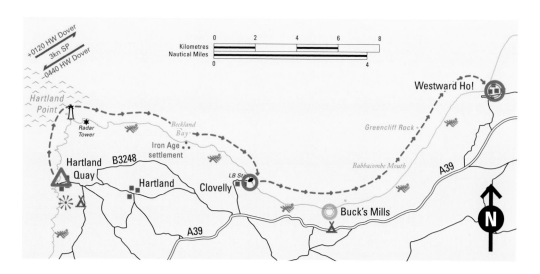

© *Hard landing at Mouth Mill*

The Taw & Torridge Rivers ⓐ🏕🌊🚗

43

No. 43 | Grade A | 12/5 km | OS Sheet 180

Tidal Port	Dover
Start	△ Barnstaple (553 333)/Bideford (455 268)
Finish	◎ Appledore (465 307)
HW/LW	HW Appledore is 5 hours and 20 minutes before HW Dover.
Tidal times	Times of ingoing and outgoing tides correspond with HW Appledore.
Max Rate Sp	In the mouth of the Taw and Torridge Rivers, flows of up to 5 knots have been recorded.
Coastguard	Swansea, tel. 01792 366534, VHF weather 0150 UT

Introduction

Between them, the Taw and Torridge Rivers drain around 2,000 sq km of Devon. Their estuaries join at Appledore, just prior to meeting the open sea. Submerging 4 to 13 sq km of land, the estuaries are small, but they are exceptionally important in ecological terms, encompassing several

225

© Instow

The Taw & Torridge Rivers

SSSIs, RSPB reserves and an UNESCO Biosphere Reserve. The main appeal for the paddler is the compelling landscape of tidal flats and the birdlife which inhabit them.

Description

TAW

Barnstaple's regional dominance as a port ended in the nineteenth century when the Taw silted up. Small boats (like kayaks!) will however have no problems, with Castle Quay just one of numerous launching possibilities, downstream of the Long Bridge on the right. There should be enough water for two hours either side of HW.

Downstream, Barnstaple's outskirts won't win any beauty contests, but these are soon left behind and the river is channelled into tortuous courses between wide banks of sand and mud. There is nothing much to see here, but that's pretty well the point. This bleak tideland has an appeal of its own, with only the cries of wading birds breaking the silence. In winter, these birds number in the thousands, crowding the salt marshes along the south shore.

Around Penhill Point, the high wooden walls of Fremington Quay (517 334) are reached, with a rusting ship or two usually moored. The Heritage Centre here can be accessed by muddy steps, ostensibly to examine the displays about the Quay's past (inconceivably, it was a major port) but really to sample the splendid café!

The Taw next ambles past RAF Chivenor airfield, before reaching inlets to the north and south. To the north is the River Caen, leading up past drained Horsey Island to Velator Quay in Braunton. To the south is Isley Marsh, an RSPB reserve.

Yelland Power Station is a rather unprepossessing sight on the south shore. Thankfully, the view north is better. The dunes of Braunton Burrows (a UNESCO Biosphere Reserve) are worth a venture ashore between the distinctive White House and Crow Point, but adhere to military signs. Hereabouts (463 326) there are several concrete landing craft used by the Americans to prepare for the Normandy landings.

Appledore is attractive from the water, with successive rows of houses stretching around the promontory beneath. There are numerous slipways to choose from, but one leads direct to a car park (465 307).

TORRIDGE

As with Barnstaple, launching at Bideford should be fine two hours either side of HW. Launching is simple at Bank End beside the park entrance, on the left several hundred metres downstream of Bideford's Long Bridge. Paddling up to the bridge is interesting; it was built c1280 with 24 irregularly spaced arches. For several years, the gorgeous *Kathleen & May* has been grounded just downstream of the bridge. The only wooden triple-masted sailing schooner remaining, it is on the National Register of Historic Vessels (with the *Cutty Sark* and HMS *Victory*). This relic from 1900 will be sold when restoration is complete, the current asking price being $7,000,000!

The 5km to Appledore are more developed than the Taw. Houses dot the banks past the A39 'New Bridge', which marks the start of a waterski area. A landing on the East bank, 1.5 km past the bridge, could be made to walk to the Italianate Gardens of Tapeley Park gardens (www. tapeleypark.com). The contrasting West bank is dominated by the cranes and workshops of Kingston Shipyard, possibly Britain's last remaining purely commercial shipbuilder. The yard has had some difficult years, but with new contracts, currently looks set to continue.

Before landing at Appledore, consider a visit across the river to its quieter neighbour Instow. The sandy beach here was used for D-Day rehearsals.

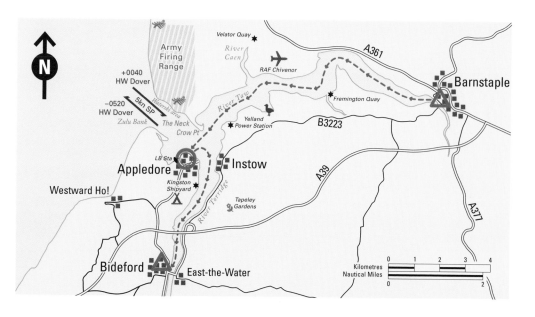

The Taw & Torridge Rivers

After the two rivers converge at Appledore, they flow north-west to meet the sea between Braunton Burrows and Northam Burrows Country Park. The shores are often shallow and deceptive. With swell running, follow the buoys and resist the temptation to cut the corner south across Zulu Bank unless you want a soaking! The north shore of the channel is a (boo hiss) jet ski area.

VARIATIONS

Joining both estuaries in one trip will inevitably involve tedious upstream paddling … but each to their own.

Tide and weather

Rough water can be encountered when the wind blows against the outgoing tide over Bideford Bar, the exit to the estuary.

Additional information

The Tarka Trail (www.devon.gov.uk/tarkatrail) follows both rivers, making a bicycle shuttle possible. Rental is possible in both Barnstaple and Bideford.

The Taw and Torridge Estuary Forum website has useful information on navigation and environment, www.ttef.org.uk.

North Devon Maritime Museum in Appledore has displays on the local maritime heritage, a short walk uphill from the quay (01237 422064 www.devonmuseums.net/appledore).

There is a campsite (456 295) beside the A386, 1.5km before Appledore's waterfront is reached.

Taw and Torridge birdlife

The estuaries are an extremely important sanctuary for wintering birds, with over 20,000 resident through the winter months. Sightings of birds of prey such as peregrine falcons and merlins are common, but this is really the kingdom of the wading bird. The variety of resident waders is impressive, even to non-twitchers: bar-tailed godwit, black-tailed godwit, common sandpiper, curlew, dunlin, golden plover, greenshank, grey plover, lapwing, oystercatcher, purple sandpiper, redshank, ringed plover, ruff, sanderling, snipe, spotted redshank and turnstone.

The Taw & Torridge Rivers

43

 Putsborough Beach and Baggy Point

Baggy & Morte Points

Baggy & Morte Points

No. 44 | Grade B | 30 km | OS Sheet 180

Tidal Port	Milford Haven, Dover and Avonmouth
Start	△ Westward Ho! (434 297)
Finish	◯ Ilfracombe (524 478)
HW/LW	HW at the mouth of the Taw and Torridge Rivers is 5 hours and 20 minutes before HW Dover.
	HW Ilfracombe is 5 hours and 25 minutes before HW Dover.
Tidal times	Off Morte Point, the NE going (flood) stream begins around 6 hours after HW Avonmouth. The SW going (ebb) stream begins around HW Avonmouth.
	Between Bull Point and Ilfracombe, the E going (flood) stream begins 5 hours and 40 minutes after HW Milford Haven. The W going (ebb) stream begins 25 minutes before HW Milford Haven.
Max Rate Sp	In the mouth of the Taw and Torridge Rivers, rates of up to 5 knots have been recorded. Rates in Barnstaple Bay are generally weak, but there is a noticeable N going (flood) stream between Westward Ho! and Baggy Point. There is little flow within Morte Bay, but rates reach 4 knots offshore of Baggy Point, 3.2 knots off Morte Point, and 3 knots at Bull Point.
Coastguard	Swansea, tel. 01792 366534, VHF weather 0150 UT

229

44

Introduction

This trip links two attractive headlands to cross Barnstaple Bay. The beaches in between are often packed, this being Britain's most popular surfing area outside Newquay. There is room for all however, as the surfers seem incapable of venturing further than 500m from the car parks and North Devon's fine sandy beaches are considerably longer than that!

Description

The beach fronting grimly characterless Westward Ho! can be a frustrating launch. At LW springs, the tide recedes several hundred metres and at HW springs the beach is submerged, the sea reaching up to the steep pebble bank, causing any surf to dump. Alternatively, consider a launch from Appledore (route 43).

The pebble ridge extends for 3km and protects the dunes of Northam Burrows Country Park. It is retreating at an annual rate of 1m. Local legend suggests, 'when Charles III reigns, the sea will reach Northam' (1700 years at current rate).

Passing the entrance to the Taw and Torridge estuaries can be tricky. Even the smallest waves break across Zulu Bank, an expanse of shallow water. There can also be a strong tidal pull into the estuary. In 1791 the *Abeona* was grounded here, proving to contain £5,000 worth of smuggled contraband, including silk and china!

The far bank is Saunton Sands, 5km of sand backed by Braunton Burrows, 1,000 acres of sand dunes. The dunes reach up to 30m high with names like Mt Vesuvius and Ayers Rock! English

Nature manages this site, its importance recognised by its status as an SSSI, an NNR and a Biosphere Reserve. This ecological significance doesn't seem to bar the Army from using the southern two thirds as a firing range.

During WWII, Saunton Sands was used by the Americans to prepare for the Normandy landings. Innumerable mines were buried in the seaward facing dunes. Post-war, massive damage was done when water hoses were used to clear the mines. Marram grass was planted to stabilise the dunes.

The north end of Saunton beach will be crammed full of surfers if there is even the merest ripple on the sea. 2km away around Saunton Down, this scene is repeated at Croyde Bay and then later at Putsborough and Woolacombe. Incidentally, these seem to be Britain's most popular breaks for kayakers, but banish any ideas you might have about wreaking havoc on the waves in your massive sea kayak!

In between the surf spots, Baggy Point is a highlight. The Devonian rock strata dips steeply, allowing wave action to bore out numerous caves. This is a superb place to explore on a calm day. Around the headland are incongruous quartz 'erratics', rocks carried by glaciers from Scotland. Watch for Manx shearwaters gliding past the Point en route to their burrows in Pembrokeshire.

From Woolacombe, tiny Barricane and Grunta Beaches are passed en route to Morte Point. Morte Point means … well, how is your French? The Point has a strong tide race and is low enough at the western tip for waves to break across it. In local lore it is, *"the place God made last and the Devil will take first"*. Not wishing to alarm you.

Past Morte Point, Rockham Bay has a small beach and a path up the cliffs. Bull Point lighthouse is a low building 54m above the water. The original light was completed in 1879 and functioned until September 1972, when the Keeper reported cracks appearing in the walls. Six days later, the cliffs collapsed or subsided up to 30m from the edge, taking much of the lighthouse complex with it! The damage took two years to rebuild and repair.

Lee Bay is a possible landing (see route 45) but the 5km to Ilfracombe pass some lovely cliffs. Look out for Brandy Cove (504 475) used by smugglers to land … well, you get it. Paddling past the fourteenth-century St Nicholas Chapel into sheltered Ilfracombe Harbour makes a pleasant finish.

VARIATIONS

Both Morte Point and Baggy Point are worth exploring in isolation.

© Bull Point lighthouse

Tide and weather

The tide stream flows NE and SW between Hartland Point and Bull Point, but weaker tide streams are found inshore within Barnstaple Bay. The beaches within the bay pick up any groundswell.

Rough water can be encountered with wind against the ebb outside the estuary. Overfalls form off Baggy Point. At Morte Point, the flood stream flows north, whilst the ebb stream goes west, turning south further offshore. Particularly large tide races extend between Bull Point and Morte Point on the ebb stream, with generally smaller races forming off Morte Point on the flood stream.

Additional information

North Morte Farm Campsite (459 455) in Mortehoe, tel. 01271 870381, www.northmortefarm. co.uk is accessible from Rockham Bay. Little Roadway Farm (472 425) is the quietest Woolacombe site, tel. 01271 870313, up a steep hill from the beach.

Lundy from the north

Lundy Island

No. 45 | Grade C | 80 km | OS Sheet 180

Tidal Ports	Milford Haven and Dover
Start	△ Lee Bay (479 466)
Finish	○ Lee Bay (479 466), via Lundy Landing Beach (144 438)
HW/LW	HW Lundy occurs 5 hours and 30 minutes before HW Dover.
Tidal times	At Lee Bay, the west going (ebb) stream starts 25 minutes before HW Milford Haven. The east going (flood) stream starts 5 hours and 40 minutes after HW Milford Haven. Around Lundy, the WSW going stream starts 30 minutes before HW Milford Haven. The ENE going stream starts 5 hours and 30 minutes after HW Milford Haven. Lundy sits in the path of these streams and the current splits around it, beginning 3 to 4 miles away.
Max Rate Sp	Between Lee Bay and Lundy, the rates reach up to 4 knots. Inshore around Lundy, the rates reach 1 knot, however the races at the north and south points reach 5 knots.
Coastguard	Swansea, tel. 01792 366534, VHF weather 0150 UT

Introduction

On a hot day, you won't see it from Woolacombe. As the air cools towards evening, suddenly it is there. It fills the horizon and appears improbably huge. It is 5km long and 142m high. It is an

© Lundy downtime

enormous block of granite, with lighthouses guarding the northern and southern extremities and a disused third towering 180m above the sea. This is Lundy Island.

Description

THE CROSSING

Lundy is 30km west of Morte Point and 18km north of Hartland Point. The crossing requires no heroic ability or risk-taking, just good planning and common sense.

Lundy can be reached from Lee Bay or Hartland Quay. Starting from Lee Bay (also consider Ilfracombe) the full distance is around 30km. This, the longer of the two crossings, is easier to plan and execute. Lee Bay has a small car park, but launching is awkward until about 30 minutes after HW. With a launch window within an hour of local HW, the tide stream will do much of the work for you. You will be slingshot at speeds of 2-4 knots before you dip a paddle in the water! The stream drags you south of your destination, so plan the appropriate bearing to compensate. Depending upon the tides and the group pace, 3-5 hours is normal for the crossing. A GPS with your destination pre-programmed won't get you there but may offer reassurance, in the initial hours when you can't yet see the island, that Lundy really is out there!

You will encounter the strongest tides and possibly the most demanding conditions in the tide races (and associated eddies) near the start and finish. The race leading past Bull Point is prolonged with big rolling waves. On Lundy, your target is The Landing Beach, overlooked by the South Light lighthouse. It is sheltered from westerly and southerly wind and swell on the south-east of the island, with a jetty and small sea wall. The final leg to Lundy's Landing Beach can be testing, as the tide attempts to drag you south of Rat Island.

Eventually the time will come when you have to return to the mainland. This is simple. Reverse the tides, times and bearings from your outward passage. What could go wrong?

LUNDY

After landing, carry your boats and gear high above the shoreline. The 7m tide range sometimes even covers the road and has caught out more than one group. A road winds up to the village and campsite high above, a hard slog carrying camping gear!

Landing is difficult for most of the 15km paddle around Lundy. The west coast is exposed to Atlantic swell. The 'Hen and Chickens' tide race forms around the northern tip of Lundy, whilst, named less ambiguously, 'The Race' guards the southern edge. If paddling clockwise, consider launching from The Landing Beach at slack water as the WSW stream finishes. This eases the paddling around the South West Point, although some uphill paddling may be required through the inshore rocks for the first kilometre of the west coast. You then pick up the north flowing stream and it is worth staying close inshore to avoid being swept past these magnificent surroundings too quickly! The cliffs are composed of steeply inclined smooth granite, renowned amongst climbers.

The first landmark is Battery Point. You will spot the well-preserved ruins of the Fog Signal Station from which cannons were fired before the North and South Lights were completed. Directly opposite is Dead Cow Point, pierced through by an inviting looking tunnel. Jenny's Cove follows, where the largest seabird populations are found, as well as Lundy's largest sea cave (there are at least 36 others).

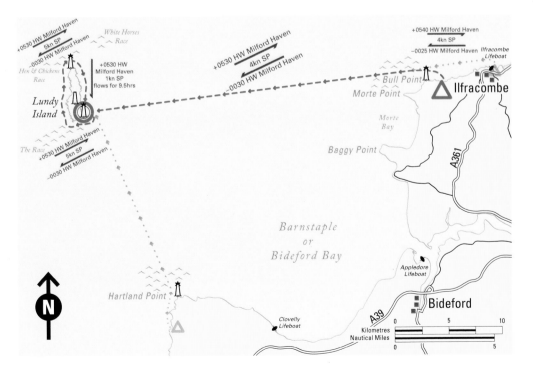

Last landmark of the west coast is the Devil's Slide, a 120m smooth ramp soaring from the sea … the seal launch from Hell? The tide accelerates towards North West Point and the Hen and Chickens race will look intimidating if there is any swell. Conveniently, it is often possible to avoid the race by sneaking inshore of the rocks below the North Light. Even better, tunnels honeycomb the granite beneath the lighthouse and these can provide an exhilarating passage right under Lundy's north tip.

The paddle south along the east coast is comparatively anti-climatic, but there are points of interest. Just after rounding the North Light, worn steps reach down to the water, a difficult landing place. Gannet's Rock which follows speaks for itself. As you return towards The Landing Beach, you will notice the remains of industrial workings from the short-lived Lundy Granite Company that operated in the 1860s.

Tide and weather

Look for several forecast days of high pressure and low wind, with little or no groundswell (check surf forecasts). Winds from the east make landing and launching on Lundy awkward. Carry equipment, food and supplies for an extended stay; the weather can turn on you!

Lundy blocks the Bristol Channel's ENE/WNW stream. During the ENE stream, along the north three quarters of the west coast currents flow north, whilst currents along the south quarter of the west coast gradually shift from south-east to north through the ENE stream. On Lundy's east coast, the current flows south for 9 hours and 30 minutes, beginning 5 hours and 30 minutes after HW Milford Haven. The currents reach only 1 knot at springs, however the races at the north and south tips can reach 5 knots. It is sometimes possible to avoid these races by paddling inshore.

Lundy's tide races work constantly. The Hen and Chickens extends north of the island. The Race extends south-west of Shutter Point on the ebb, and east of Rat Island on the flood. The White Horses forms over Stanley Bank, about 4km ENE of North East Point. It is of *exceptional violence* (*Admiralty Pilot*) on the flood.

VARIATIONS

The shorter crossing, from Hartland Quay (222 248) via Hartland Point, is trickier. From serrated Hartland Point and its lighthouse, the tide flows strongly across your path. A carefully planned ferry glide is needed to ensure that you don't wind up in Ireland!

Additional information

Lundy is managed by the Landmark Trust for the owners, the National Trust. Unscheduled arrivals are frowned upon. Camping on Lundy needs to be pre-booked with the Lundy Shore Office, tel. 01271 863636. There is a limit of around 40 spaces, due to the finite supply of fresh water. See www.lundyisland.co.uk.

Despite having twelve permanent residents, Lundy has a small shop and Post Office, a church and possibly the best pub in the UK, the Marisco Tavern. Lundy even has its own beer, 'Lundy Experience'. Inside the Marisco, record your visit in the 'Sea Kayaking Book'. This tatty tome dates back to the Eighties, with names that you may recognise.

Lundy West Coast

Lundy Island

Enjoy sunset atop the Old Light, Britain's highest lighthouse. Work began on this in 1819. Cloud regularly obscured the light, 180m above sea level. The North Light and South Light replaced it in 1896.

Lundy's Wildlife

As Lundy's waters are England's only statutory Marine Nature Reserve, with fishing and diving restrictions, the seas literally teem with life. Consider taking a snorkel. Lundy's grey seal population feasts on this oceanic banquet. Dolphins, porpoise and basking sharks are commonly encountered.

Lundy is South West England's largest seabird breeding colony and a stopping off point for innumerable migratory species. Guillemots, razorbills, gannets and Manx shearwaters abound. 'Lundy' derives from Old Norse, *Puffin*. Puffins have unfortunately taken a battering from non-indigenous rats, but can still be seen.

On top, look for Soay sheep, Lundy ponies, Sika deer and the endemic Lundy cabbage, which is more exciting than it sounds.

MV Oldenburg

The MV *Oldenburg* belongs to Lundy and makes regular crossings from Bideford or Ilfracombe between April and October. The crew have been known to strap sea kayaks to the deck for the voyage out, or for the return trip if the weather has unexpectedly turned foul. This only happens at the discretion and good will of the Captain and Island Manager, and obviously involves a significant charge.

© Elwill Bay

West Exmoor ▣▣▣▣▣

No. 46 | Grade B | 22 km | OS Sheet 180

Tidal Ports	Milford Haven and Dover
Start	△ Ilfracombe (524 478)
Finish	◯ Lynmouth (722 497)
HW/LW	HW Ilfracombe and Combe Martin are 5 hours and 25 minutes before HW Dover. HW Lynmouth is 5 hours and 15 minutes before HW Dover.
Tidal times	At Ilfracombe, the E going (flood) stream begins 5 hours and 40 minutes after HW Milford Haven. The W going (ebb) stream begins 25 minutes before HW Milford Haven.
Max Rate Sp	Rates reach 1.5 knots on the flood and 2 knots on the ebb. Off headlands such as Highveer Point they can reach 4 knots.
Coastguard	Swansea, tel. 01792 366534, VHF weather 0150 UT

Introduction

The moorland hills of Exmoor National Park meet the Bristol Channel rudely and abruptly, plunging over 300 metres to sea level. The height is lost through steeply wooded slopes topping the highest cliffs on mainland Britain. This makes for a spectacular coastal trip, with the added challenge of the Bristol Channel's strong tides.

46

Description

Ilfracombe Harbour has plenty of parking, but it might not feel that way in the summer months. The harbour dries out in low water, but it is possible to launch onto the sandy beach outside the harbour wall. Another possibility is to launch 1km east at Hele Bay (536 479).

Outside the harbour, the tide stream is soon picked up at Rillage Point, conveying you past the narrow inlet of Watermouth. This pretty bay is the first of several idyllic beaches dotting both sides of Combe Martin Bay. Combe Martin (576 473) is another possible launch point and excitedly boasts the longest village main street in Britain.

Exmoor National Park starts just outside Combe Martin. It will need no introduction for suddenly hills rise precipitously from the sea to over 300m, an impressive sight extending to the horizon. The hill backing Combe Martin Bay itself is Little Hangman, followed to the east by Great Hangman. The gruesome names are thought to be derived from the Celtic *An Maen* (Hill of Stone). The latter hill has the distinction of generating the highest sea cliff on mainland Britain (250m). This immense craggy wall faces the dark cleft of Great Hangman Gut.

The coast that follows continues to awe, the cliffs intersected by deep chasms and the occasional waterfall. At low water, a rocky landing is possible in many places to explore this complex and wild landscape. You won't meet many walkers! The highlights come after paddling between the Mare and Colt, a pair of pyramidal rocks guarding the entrance to Elwill Bay. The next 2km pass slowly, as you explore huge rocks, tunnels and caves. The narrow inlet that will just demand that you reach for your camera is North Cleave Gut (636 486).

Landing for a leg stretch at Heddon's Mouth (655 497) is highly recommended. The pebble beach is obscured by cliffs until the last moment, but the valley's uniqueness is even more startling. The bubbling Heddon River barely finds space to flow in this v-shaped 'cleave'. German U-Boat veterans have claimed that they would land by night to re-supply fresh water. Note the scree slopes on both sides, and the restored lime kiln beside the beach. Consider making a beeline for the Hunter's Inn, 1.5km up the footpath.

Back on the water, Highveer Point kicks up a tidal race that carries you to the Cow and Calf cliffs. These crowded cliffs support nationally important breeding populations of approximately 400-500 guillemots and razorbills and 250 kittiwakes. At the eastern end is a natural arch called Wringapeak. Local lore claims that for centuries the dangerous 'Gurt Fish of Wringapeak' has lurked beneath, awaiting swimmers to feast upon.

Woody Bay is a delightful haven, the name giving the game away. There is another lime kiln close to the beach. Lee Bay follows, home of the Lee Abbey religious community. As with Woody Bay, emergency road access is possible. The remaining 3km to Lynmouth offer no such escape, with a final stretch of cliffs. These rise to the Valley of Rocks, which once possibly carried the flows of the Lyn Rivers. The valley is peppered with strange rock formations, including granite tors towering above the cliffs.

Landing or launching at Lynmouth needs forethought. The town was famously devastated in 1952 after nine inches of rain fell in a single night and the East and West Lyn massively flooded. This and previous floods created a large delta of boulders stretching out into the Bristol Channel. This reef makes landing awkward at LW and can generate surf. Arrival is easiest at HW when you can paddle up the East Lyn River into the harbour, avoiding surf by following the channel marker posts. A long carry is unavoidable at low water; land just west of the river mouth or on the beach east of the reef.

VARIATIONS

It would be very silly not to paddle East Exmoor's coast (route 47) too, perhaps as part of an overnight trip.

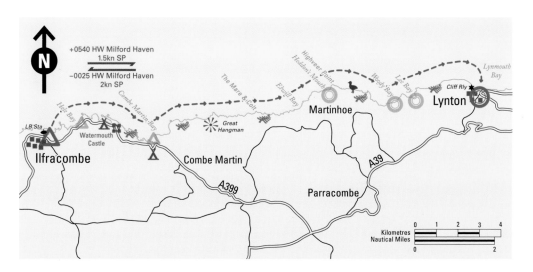

© Elwill Bay caves

Tide and weather

During the E going (flood) stream, you may encounter a W going eddy current along the shore.

The Bristol Channel's huge tidal range must be factored into planning landing and launching.

Additional information

Two campsites are accessible from the water; Newberry Farm Touring (574 470) in Combe Martin (01271 882334 www.newberryvalleypark.co.uk) and Little Meadow Camping Site (554 479) in Watermouth Cove, tel. 01271 866862, www.littlemeadow.co.uk.

© Below Selworthy Beacon

East Exmoor ☷☷◩◔

No. 47 | Grade B | 27km | OS Sheets 180, 181

Tidal Ports	Bristol and Dover
Start	△ Lynmouth (722 497)
Finish	◯ Minehead (971 471)
HW/LW	HW Lynmouth is 5 hours and 15 minutes before HW Dover.
	HW Minehead is 4 hours and 50 minutes before HW Dover.
Tidal times	Off Foreland Point, the E going (flood) stream begins 30 minutes before HW Avonmouth. The W going (ebb) stream begins 5 hours and 30 minutes after HW Avonmouth.
Max Rate Sp	Rates reach 1.5 knots on the flood and 2 knots on the ebb. Off Foreland Point, rates reach 4 knots on the flood, and 4.6 knots on the ebb.
Coastguard	Swansea, tel. 01792 366534, VHF weather 0150 UT

Introduction

This splendid trip traverses lovely wooded hills, with pretty Porlock Bay interjecting. An exposed headland and big tide race at the start deserve respect; otherwise this is a surprisingly straight-forward paddle, with landing possible much of the time.

© Start of the south-west coast path, Minehead

Description

47

East Exmoor

The eastern half of Exmoor's coast differs in character from the west. Although there is still an impressive 300m drop from moor to sea, there are fewer cliffs and instead, steep wooded slopes descend to bouldery beaches.

Launching and landing at Lynmouth can be awkward around LW (see route 46 for details). The easiest option might be to trolley or carry kayaks down the beach and concrete groyne in front of the harbour.

Foreland Point is 3.5km away, jutting into the Bristol Channel with imposing cliffs facing Lynmouth. Although the headland is 300m high, Lynmouth Foreland lighthouse reaches only 67m above the water to avoid low cloud. Foreland creates a large tide race. Awkward eddies form behind the headland, so hitting the Point close to slack water will make inshore passage easier. The tower structure offshore of Foreland Point is an experimental tide-powered generator.

The following 5km are full of surprises. The hanging valley of Coddow Combe terminates with the first of many tumbling streams. In all seriousness, consider making this trip after rainfall! Hidden behind Desolation Point is a strong contender for southern England's prettiest waterfall (712 500). About 1.5km further, plates of rock strata form the natural arch of Giant's Rib. The cliffs recede, and henceforth steep woodland is the order of the day. Glenthorne House is practically the only evidence of other humans between Foreland and Porlock. You will envy whoever lives there, with their personal beach and waterfalls! Glenthorne also signifies the county boundary between Somerset and Devon. Another 1.5km further at Embelle Wood Beach, a steep track is briefly visible. This might offer an emergency exit, although this is part of a very private estate.

Porlock Bay is a convenient stopping point. A 4km long steep pebble barrier sweeps across the bay. In October 1996, Hurricane Lily partly breached it, forming marshy Decoy Lagoon behind. The first opening reached is however the harbour of Porlock Weir. This picturesque village was a busy working port dating back to the Middle Ages. In 1931, the *Democrat* made the final delivery of coal from South Wales. The deep water harbour subsequently silted up and only small vessels can now enter. Paddlers should be able to enter for up to three hours either side of HW, if surf inhibits a beach landing. Beside the harbour, there is a small museum outlining Porlock Weir's maritime heritage, well worth a visit.

Hurlstone Point guards Porlock Bay's east end, with the bulk of Selworthy Beacon looming large behind. The Point is faced by smooth rock slabs and the 'tower' above is actually a ruined Coastguard station. Just past the point is Selworthy Sand, a sandbank exposed at low tide. Otherwise, it is possible to paddle close inshore all the way to Minehead. The steep slopes recede and the green fields in front of Greenaleigh Farm give notice that Minehead is just around the corner. Land just before, or within, the harbour.

VARIATIONS

Porlock Weir (865 480) is the obvious place to shorten this trip, and allows the tide race at Foreland Point to be bypassed.

Lynmouth is a good place from which to attempt the open crossing to Wales, should this be your sort of thing. Launch at low water and paddle north, riding the flood stream up the Bristol Channel to Nash Point (916 681) or thereabouts, a crossing of 27 km.

Tide and weather

Major tide races extend around Foreland Point, and are best avoided in windy conditions when the waves break heavily. Smaller tide races form off Hurlstone Point and Minehead Bluff.

Additional information

Sparkhayes Farm Campsite (886 469) is 1km inland in Porlock, tel. 01643 862470, www.porlock. co.uk/camping).

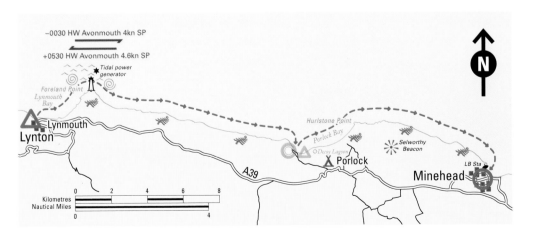

East Exmoor

© Selworthy Beacon

The Louisa

Whilst paddling between Lynmouth and Porlock Weir, look up at the steep hills and ponder the story of the *Louisa*. On 12 January 1899, the Lynmouth lifeboat crew were summoned to go to the aid of the 1,900 ton *Forrest Hall*, foundering offshore. The crew were barred from launching their lifeboat *Louisa* by monstrous waves in Lynmouth Bay. Coxswain Jack Crocombe proposed transporting the *Louisa* 13 miles overland to Porlock. Overnight, they dragged the 10 ton lifeboat through the storm up a 1 in 4 gradient to the 300m contour and then across Exmoor, whilst locals worked to widen corners, demolish walls and fell trees in their path. This superhuman endeavour involved 20 horses (four of which died) and 100 men. After ten hours, the *Louisa* arrived in Porlock. The cold and exhausted lifeboatmen crew rowed out through the surf, succeeding in rescuing all 18 of the *Forrest Hall's* crew. The story of the *Louisa* is perhaps the RNLI's proudest memory.

Bridgewater Bay ◼◼◼◼◼

No. 48 | **Grade C** | **50km** | **OS Sheets 181, 182**

Tidal Ports	Dover and Avonmouth
Start	△ Minehead (970 472)
Finish	○ Clevedon (402 719)
HW/LW	HW Minehead and Watchet is 4 hours and 50 minutes before HW Dover.
	HW Burnham-on-Sea is 4 hours and 30 minutes before HW Dover.
	HW Weston-Super-Mare is 4 hours and 35 minutes before HW Dover.
Tidal times	Offshore of Hinckley Point, the ENE going (flood) stream begins 5 hours and 55 minutes after HW Avonmouth. The WSW going (ebb) stream begins 15 minutes after HW Avonmouth.
Max Rate Sp	Offshore of Hinckley Point, tide rates reach 3 knots.
	Rates off Brean Down exceed this. Inshore flows in Bridgewater Bay, Weston Bay and Sand Bay are not strong, due to the shallow water.
Coastguard	Swansea, tel. 01792 366534, VHF weather 0150 UT

Bridgewater Bay

Introduction

The coast between Minehead and Clevedon is not a sea kayaker's paradise. For the entire distance, the tide recedes too far to make launching or landing practical outside HW, exposing sucking mud flats and soft sandbanks. Hence, this trip is described from the perspective of paddling through, rather than exploring. All that said, the exposed crossing is a worthwhile challenge in itself, and the headlands in the second half of the trip are interesting and attractive.

Description

The very large range between the high water and low water marks begins at Minehead. Arriving at the seafront, you'll be dismayed to see mud and stones stretching into the distance, but don't lose heart. Follow the seafront west past the 'giant hand' statue (marking the start of the South West Coast Path) and just past Minehead harbour. The beach beyond is your launch point (970 472), viable as it shelves steeply into deep water.

All to be done now is to set a bearing for Brean Down, 33km away! This committing shortcut across Bridgewater Bay will take you up to 9km offshore, but this distance is meaningless in terms of exposure as even close inshore, landing is always either difficult or impossible away from HW, and usually dangerous. Burnham-on-Sea is fronted by *8km* of mud flats. A further consideration is that you are passing north of Lilstock Naval Bombing Range, check first with the Coastguard to find if it is in use. The positive factor is that the tide will make the distance fall away quickly.

Brean Down is an unmistakeable target, a 100m high Mendip limestone ridge pointing out to Steep Holm Island. A fierce tide race forms off the tip below Brean Fort.

Weston Bay is a possible place to finish. A public slipway in Weston-Super-Mare (314 619) is usable for around 1 hour either side of HW. If landing in bustling Weston doesn't appeal, another possibility is to follow Brean Down up to the mouth of the River Axe at Uphill (310 582), where there are slipways for small boats.

The north limit of Weston Bay is marked by Birnbeck Island. This unusual islet is connected to the mainland by a crumbling 300m pier and was a popular holiday attraction as recently as the 1990s. The decrepit state of the pier forced closure of the island to the public, with only the lifeboat crew now permitted to cross the pier and access their station. Birnbeck is a ghostly sight today, the shuttered and abandoned buildings frequented only by sea birds.

Landing is possible at HW on the south side of Sand Bay, where there is a free car park (328 633). If you are continuing the full distance to Clevedon, the only remaining landmark is Sand Point. Like Brean Down, this headland forms a tide race and is worthy of exploration. There are landing beaches on the north side at Middle Hope and Swallow Cliffs, both accessible close to HW. Don't venture far inshore past Middle Hope (335 664), as St Thomas' Head is a firing range. There is a buoyed firing area, and a warning light is displayed on the Head when firing is taking place. This unusual location is used as the sand flats allow retrieval of test rockets.

The direct route between Sand Point and Clevedon is barred by more sand flats, but a diversion shouldn't be necessary close to HW. This final 10km will recall the first half of the trip, with a

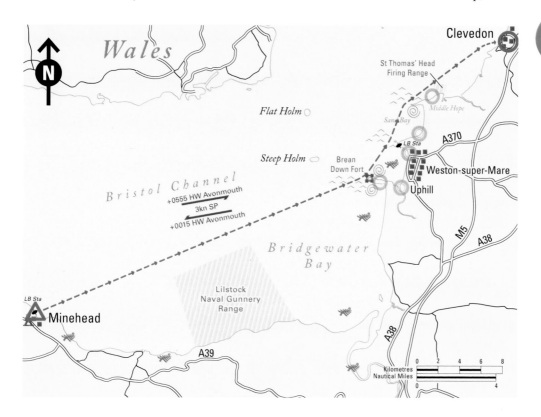

distant glimpse of two grounded ships forming the only diversion in a featureless sandscape. Clevedon Pier (402 719) with its convenient slipway is however a pleasant place to finish this mammoth journey.

A trip to specifically explore Brean Down, Birnbeck Island and Sand Point would be worthwhile, however limited by the need to land and launch at HW. One possible solution could be a spot of overnight camping.

Tide and weather

It is feasible to complete this whole trip in one push due to the strong tide flow, perhaps with a short break at Brean Down. Good weather is essential, given the degree of exposure involved.

As noted, Brean Down and Sand Point both form tide races, whilst confused tides are encountered at Birnbeck Island with the water beneath the pier often flowing counter to that off the island.

Semi-submerged fishing stakes are found on all of the tidal flats along this trip.

Additional information

Minehead & Exmoor Camping and Caravan Park (952 458) is 2km inland, tel. 01643 703074.

Brean Fort

Brean Fort is a complex of nineteenth-century and WWII emplacements ringing the tip of Brean Down. From the water you see the outlying searchlight station, with a pair of inclined rails pointing to sea. These launched experimental WWII weapons, including a bouncing bomb that bounced off and detonated early.

A bigger explosion occurred in 1900, when a soldier arrived from Steep Holm. He missed his island friends, venting his disaffection by firing his rifle down a shaft into three tons of gunpowder. The resulting blast woke everyone on Steep Holm.

It is possible to land at rocky Sprat Beach on the north side of Brean Down to explore. Rock hewn steps lead up to the fort.

Steep Holm & Flat Holm

No. 49 | **Grade C** | **27km** | **OS Sheet 182**

Tidal Ports	Bristol and Dover
Start	△ Sand Bay (328 633)
Finish	◎ Sand Bay (328 633)
HW/LW	HW Weston-Super-Mare is 4 hours and 35 minutes before HW Dover.
Tidal times	Between Flat Holm and Steep Holm, the E going (flood) stream begins 6 hours and 10 minutes before HW Avonmouth. The W going (ebb) stream begins 15 minutes after HW Avonmouth.
Max Rate Sp	Rates in Weston Bay and Sand Bay are not strong. Between Brean Down and Steep Holm rates reach 3.2 knots on the flood, and 3 knots on the ebb. Between Flat Holm and Steep Holm they reach 3 knots going E and 4 knots going W.
Coastguard	Swansea, tel. 01792 366534, VHF weather 0150 UT

Introduction

This is a superb expedition, taking in two unique but rather different islands. The name Holm stems from the Viking word for 'river island' and it's appropriate; the Bristol Channel behaves much like an immense river, making crossing to the islands a serious undertaking. You are never a great distance offshore, but watching the twinkling lights of Weston-Super-Mare and Cardiff from either island at dusk, you could be forgiven for feeling that those towns are on a separate planet.

Description

THE CROSSING

Landing or launching from the English shores of the Bristol Channel, high tide is everything. Low tide exposes vast expanses of sucking mud, avoid at all costs! A public slipway in Weston (314 619) works for around one hour either side of HW, but Sand Bay is much quieter, with free parking (328 633). As the names imply, it is impossible to mistake the islands. Steep Holm is the hulking loaf of rock, whilst Flat Holm is the flat(ter) island with the lighthouse. Both are around 10km from Sand Bay.

This trip outlines visiting Steep Holm en route to a stay on Flat Holm, variations are of course possible. You will wish to plan precisely to adjust for springs or neaps, but one possible approach is to 'drop' onto Steep Holm. Launching an hour before HW allows you to paddle towards Flat Holm until HW, placing you almost 'upstream' of Steep Holm. The ebbing tide then drags you towards the latter island and you can fine-tune your course accordingly. You are aiming for Steep Holm's eastern side, where there is a tiny pebble beach (232 607) beside a ruined Inn. This beach expands as the tide falls and a convenient eddy appears, but initially you are faced with the prospect of clawing a landing in mid tide race! Large groups, beware. If you really do miss the beach, there is a possible rocky landing (231 605) on the south side, accessed by a precarious path.

STEEP HOLM

Steep Holm's limestone bulk is actually an outlier of Somerset's Mendip Hills. Since 1976 it has been owned by the Kenneth Allsopp Memorial Trust and administered as a nature reserve. Unless you have informed them that you are coming, you will find yourself faced by a locked gate above the beach.

Exploring Steep Holm is a must. From the beach, the path zigzags steeply to the summit plateau, 70m above. The path was actually an incline railway for hoisting supplies up. The island is solely inhabited by two wardens, but has seen various stages of occupation from twelfth-century monks to WWII soldiers. The summit plateau is overgrown, but paths lead through the undergrowth along the cliff edge. The first thing you'll notice is the gulls. Through July and August there are thousands in residence, and they are *loud*. Wear a hat, as they dive-bomb visitors' heads with guano or, worse, sharp claws. The cliffs are topped by impressive fortifications in various states of decay. Most were constructed in the 1860s as part of a defensive chain across the Bristol Channel. These emplacements became known as 'Palmerston Follies' because in hindsight, their commission by the then-Prime Minister proved unnecessary. Abandoned Victorian cannons literally litter the ground. Also surviving are WWII observation and searchlight posts, some of

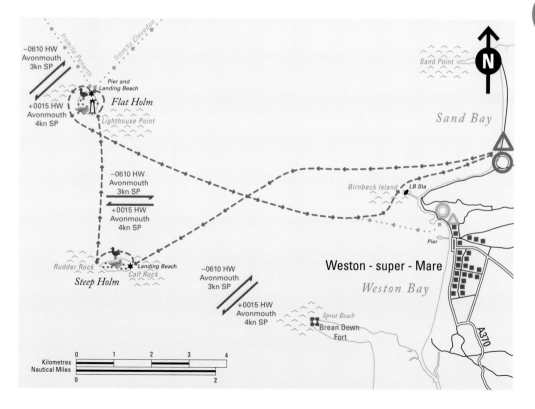

which, being located a long way down precarious guano-covered steps, are most safely viewed from the water!

The Victorian Barracks have been restored as an interpretation centre, and the wardens will supply tea. What more could one need?

The coast of Steep Holm does not need long to circumnavigate. Note that during the flood tide, strong flows run east along the south side. The north side can be more easily followed en route to Flat Holm, passing strange overhangs and hollowed-out galleries known as the 'Cormorant Cliffs'. The westernmost point is Rudder Rock, named as the parallel plates of rock resemble ... well, you get it.

It is 4km from Rudder Rock to Flat Holm. This crossing can most easily be made by taking advantage of the first hour of the flood tide to carry you up-channel. Tide races will be encountered close to both islands and the buoys between the islands are a reminder that large ships might also vie with you for space.

FLAT HOLM

Flat Holm has plenty of landing spots, best is the beach to the north-east (222 651) beside the remains of two jetties. This beach can disappear at HW springs and is allegedly awkward to reach during the ebb stream.

You are now in Wales, hopefully you remembered your passport! Above the landing beach is a giant compressed air foghorn, constructed in 1908. To the south-west, 200m along a track, is the farmhouse building, with bunkhouse and cooking facilities. Wardens will greet you and give a safety briefing (never mix alcohol and cliff top walks).

Unlike Steep Holm, Flat Holm has cleared fields and open spaces. Rabbits abound and there is even a wild tortoise (George), but again it is the gulls who dominate. They occupy every inch of ground and practically blot out the sky. A chalk board in the farmhouse currently indicates that there are 3743 pairs of black-backed gulls and 370 pairs of herring gulls, although it is unclear who counts them.

A walk around Flat Holm reveals more 'Palmerston Follies' like those on Steep Holm. The ruined buildings near to the Farmhouse were a Cholera isolation hospital. The lighthouse dates from 1819, its light marking the passage up the Bristol Channel from 50m above the water. Note the water catching surfaces beside it. It was from Flat Holm that in 1897 Marconi transmitted the first wireless signals over water, to Lavernock Point. The Morse code message was, *"Are you ready?"*

The return to Sand Bay is an 11km crossing, which of course needs to be completed close to HW. One possibility is to launch 2 hours before HW and head SW towards Brean Down for the first hour, before adjusting course accordingly to drop into Sand Bay.

VARIATIONS

The islands can also be reached by riding the ebb tide from Clevedon (see route 50).

The Welsh mainland is only 4.5km from Flat Holm and completing the crossing of the Bristol Channel is an appealing option, perhaps by utilising the flood tide to travel up-channel to Penarth.

Tide and weather

This trip is dependent upon settled weather. Even light winds against the tide flow make the crossings choppy and uncomfortable. Landings on the English shore need to be made at HW, to avoid 'shlopping' through deep mud. However, if HW is missed, rocky landings are possible on the north sides of both Brean Down and Sand Point. Neither have road access.

Tide races form either side of both Steep Holm and Flat Holm. Between the islands, the tidal stream does not follow the NE/SW trend of the Bristol Channel, but actually tends towards the SE (English) shore. However, north of Flat Holm, the current flows strongly NE/SW.

Inshore, significant tide races are found off Sand Point and Brean Down. Tide flows around Birnbeck Island are confused and unpredictable, often flowing in opposing directions on either side of the island.

Another hazard to be aware of is fishing stakes lurking in the shallow bays.

Additional information

Visits to Steep Holm are best prearranged by contacting Mrs Joan Rendell on 01934 632307. She will notify the resident warden of your visit. A landing fee will be charged on arrival. If you arrive to find a locked gate, the warden's phone number is written beside the gate. He might not be near his phone, though! Details from www.steepholm.freeserve.co.uk.

Visits to Flat Holm also require prior notification. The Flat Holm Project can be contacted on 029 2035 3917 or flatholmproject@cardiff.gov.uk. If you are planning to stay on the island,

© The Second Seven Crossing (route 50)

bunkhouse accommodation can be pre-booked by posting a cheque. Camping isn't normally permitted. More information from www.cardiff.gov.uk/flatholm.

 The Severn Bridge

The River Severn ⟳ ✕ ⫽ ⊏

No. 50 | Grade C | 42km | OS Sheets 172, 162

Tidal Ports	Avonmouth and Dover
Start	△ Clevedon (402 719)
Finish	◎ Sharpness (667019)
HW/LW	HW Portishead and Avonmouth is 4 hours and 5 minutes before HW Dover.
Tidal times	At the Second Severn Crossing, the NE going (flood) stream begins 4 hours and 30 minutes before HW Avonmouth. The SW going (ebb) stream begins 45 minutes after HW Avonmouth.
	At the Severn Bridge, the NE going (flood) stream begins 4 hours before HW Avonmouth. The SW going (ebb) stream begins 45 minutes after HW Avonmouth.
	At Sharpness, the NE going (flood) stream begins 2 hours before HW Avonmouth. The SW going (ebb) stream begins 1 hour after HW Avonmouth.
Max Rate Sp	At Portishead rates reach 4 knots on the flood and 5 knots on the ebb. At the Second Severn Crossing rates reach 8 knots (3 knots neaps). At the Severn Bridge, rates reach 6 knots and at Sharpness they reach 6 knots on the flood, and 5 knots on the ebb.
Coastguard	Swansea, tel. 01792 366534, VHF weather 0150 UT

© Clevedon Pier

Introduction

This final trip is characterised by motorway bridges, mud and power stations. An outwardly unappealing prospect, it is actually one of the South West's more challenging paddles. More surprisingly, it is an immensely enjoyable experience.

Description

Launch from the slipway beside Clevedon Pier. Whether or not you get excited about piers, Clevedon's will grab your attention. Opened in 1869, it is nearly 15 metres high and over 250 metres long, constructed using iron tracks from Brunel's failed 'Barlow' railway system. The unusually tall and slender design was intended to cope with the strong tidal flows.

You soon pick up the very strong tidal current that continues for the duration. The coast between the Victorian towns of Clevedon and Portishead is characterised by sandy beaches and low cliffs with green slopes behind. This modest backdrop is probably the day's scenic highlight.

Passing Battery Point's black and white metal lighthouse, you encounter the first of many tide races. If you stay inshore you'll hit an eddy, and the industrial expanses of Avonmouth aren't especially engaging anyway. The tide carries you offshore north towards the Second Severn Crossing, which as the name suggests was the second Severn Bridge to be built, opening in 1996. Its 5km width arcs across the horizon but it is quickly reached. The tide stream focuses into the Shoots channel, leading to the 456m wide central span, the Shoots Bridge. With pillars curving into the distance on both sides and the bridge's shadows flitting across you, you won't need to be a civil engineer to feel awed.

The original 1966 Severn Bridge is 6km away, across a pool where large boils and eddies confuse the route. The River Wye joins from the north, don't confuse the Wye and Severn Bridges! Upstream of the Severn Bridge, the Hen and Chickens tide race works on both the ebb and flood.

The remaining 16km to Sharpness are, frankly, anti-climatic with only two power stations to hold your attention. The good news is that it is over quickly, the tide maintaining its strength right past Sharpness Docks. Sharpness handles sizeable ships and it is sobering to watch them struggling with the flow! The lock gates open from 2 hours 30 minutes before to 30 minutes after HW, but paddlers are advised to land *outside* well before reaching the lock entrance. This entrance is potentially dangerous as the tide flows through the walls. There are various landing/launching spots at HW, the most convenient being 200 metres south of the lock picnic spot, just past the houses (667 019).

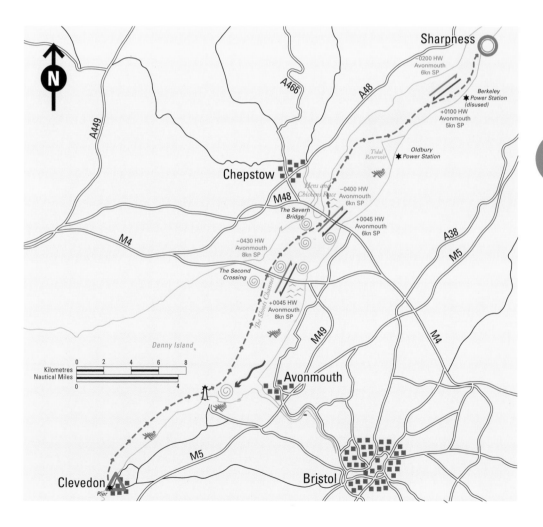

A challenge for your planning skills would be to paddle down the Avon and up the Wye.

South West completists could paddle 45km upstream to Gloucester Docks. On 13.5m+ tides, they will have to contend with the famous Severn Bore, forming 3km past Sharpness.

Tide and weather

The tide is what this trip is all about. The tidal range at Avonmouth reaches 14.8m and is the World's second highest, after Canada's Bay of Fundy!

Spring tides are recommended. They crank up the tide races, but ensure that the solid shore at Sharpness will be accessible and speed paddlers through the distance.

Paddling the trip on the ebb tide from Sharpness allows you to launch exactly when the tide changes, with the mud banks covered. You have just over five hours to complete the trip before the tide turns. Paddling on the ebb is not recommended with wind from the south or west.

Launching from Clevedon for the flood tide gives around seven hours, although the tide flows are weaker. A disadvantage is that you must carefully time your trip to arrive at Sharpness around local HW (to land safely) and before the tide turns.

The most notable tide race forms along the reef under the eastern spans of The Second Crossing, best avoided. The only safe bet around the bridges is to follow the buoyed deep water channel and to stay clear of the bridge pillars and associated eddy lines.

Tidal flows vary in direction depending upon the state of the tide. Around HW, the water flows direct but as the water drops, it is diverted into channels around the banks and rocks. At the turn of the tide there is no slack water, just confused currents with tides flowing in different directions on either side of channels.

Low tide exposes large areas of mud, in the form of either flats or steep banks, all with the consistency of quicksand and impossible to cross. There are *no points of exit* outside HW springs. Taking a chart is recommended, to follow the buoyed channel and avoid the awful prospect of becoming stranded high and dry.

You'll also be jostling for space with shipping.

Three hours before HW Avonmouth on the east flowing flood, a west flowing eddy forms inshore between Battery Point (463 776) and the River Avon breakwater.

Additional information

www.gloucesterharbourtrustees.org.uk and www.bristolport.co.uk report shipping movements and include excellent navigational information.

Public campsites are hard to come by locally.

50

The River Severn

Appendix A – Her Majesty's Coastguard (CG)

In UK waters, HM Coastguard co-ordinates rescues and emergency services. They monitor VHF Channel 16 and you should use this channel to make initial contact; you will then be directed to a working channel. There are five HM Coastguard stations that fall within the scope of this book.

Coastguard stations make Maritime Safety Information (MSI) broadcasts, including weather forecasts and potential hazards in their area. The initial announcement will be made on Channel 16, directing listeners to another Channel. The times here are for Universal Time (UT). During the UK summer, add 1 hour for British Summer Time (BST).

HM Coastguard	Telephone	Weather announced on CH16 - UT
Solent	02392 552100	0130, 0430, 0730, 1030, 1330, 1630, 1930, 2230
Portland	01305 760439	0130, 0430, 0730, 1030, 1330, 1630, 1930, 2230
Brixham	01803 882704	0110, 0410, 0710, 1010, 1310, 1610, 1910, 2210
Falmouth	01326 317575	0110, 0410, 0710, 1010, 1310, 1610, 1910, 2210
Swansea	01792366534	0150, 0450, 0750, 1050, 1330, 1650, 1950, 2250

Appendix B – The Royal National Lifeboat Institution (RNLI)

The RNLI (www.rnli.org.uk) is a charity which saves lives at sea. Its lifeboats cover all UK coastal waters up to 50 miles offshore, manned by volunteer crews. Nearly 40 lifeboat stations cover the south west region. Many are open to the public, and paddlers are recommended to visit and familiarise themselves with the RNLI's equipment and operations. Furthermore, paddlers should strongly consider materially supporting the RNLI in their work.

Appendix C – The National Coastwatch Institution (NCI)

The NCI (www.nci.org.uk) is a charity dedicated to the safety of mariners in UK coastal waters. They have re-opened abandoned CG lookouts to maintain a visual watch. They monitor VHF Channel 16 and log all passing small craft. Any life-threatening activity will be directly reported to the CG; for many stations, this includes all paddling. They will report local weather conditions by telephone, on request. There are currently 20 NCI lookout stations within this book's region, with more planned.

Appendix D – Weather Information

The Met Office (www.met-office.gov.uk) was founded in 1854 to provide weather forecasts to mariners and it still initiates weather warnings and prepare forecasts for dissemination by the Coastguard and media. Although the internet has opened up a plethora of alternative weather information sources, paddlers in UK waters are recommended to use the Met Office's forecasts and reports first and foremost. These are obtainable via the internet, VHF (MSI broadcasts), BBC radio and telephone.

BBC Radio 4 (198 kHz LW, 774 kHz MW, 92.4-94.6 FM)

0048 (LW, MW, FM) – Shipping and inshore waters forecast, coastal station reports

0520 (LW, MW, FM) - Shipping and inshore waters forecast, coastal station reports

1201 (LW only) – Shipping forecast

1754 (LW, FM on Sat/Sun) – Shipping forecast

BBC Local Radio (Hourly forecasts and reports)

BBC Radio Solent (96.1 & 103.8 FM, 999 & 1359 AM)

BBC Radio Devon (103.4, 94.8 & 95.8 FM, 801, 855, 990 & 1458 AM)

BBC Radio Cornwall (103.9, 95.2 & 96.0 FM, 630 & 657 AM)

Telephone

If you have a WAP-enabled mobile phone (and reception), it is possible to access the Met Office's maritime forecasts on their website. Finding the correct page is a pain first time, so remember to bookmark the link.

Marinecall (www.marinecall.co.uk) also offer Met Office forecasts, via premium rate phonelines;

Marinecall inshore sailing areas	Telephone
Selsey Bill to Lyme Regis	09068 500 457
Lyme Regis to Hartland Point	09068 500 458
Hartland Point to St David's Head	09068 500 459

Marinecall also offer text message forecasts. Type MC plus the name of the location you require to 83141. A list of available locations can be found at their website.

Appendix E – Mean Tidal Ranges

Tidal Port	Mean Spring Range (m)	Mean Neap Range (m)
Portsmouth	3.9	1.9
Southampton	4.0	1.9
Poole Harbour	1.6	0.5
Portland	2.0	0.6
Dartmouth	4.3	1.8
Plymouth	4.7	2.2
Falmouth	4.6	2.2
Avonmouth	12.2	6.0

Appendix F - Pilots

Admiralty Sailing Directions: English Channel Pilot, UKHO 2008, ISBN 0707718619

Admiralty Sailing Directions: West Coasts of England and Wales Pilot, UKHO 2005, ISBN 0707718805

Isles of Scilly Pilot, Robin Brandon, Imray 1994, ISBN 0-85288-411-7

Lundy and Irish Sea Pilot, David Taylor, Imray 2001, ISBN 0-85288-448-6

Shell Channel Pilot, Tom Cunliffe, Imray 2006, ISBN 0-85288-894-5

Solent Cruising Companion, Derek Aslett, Nautical Data Ltd 2002, ISBN 190435811X

West Country Cruising Companion, Mark Fishwick, Nautical Data Limited 2004, ISBN 1-90435-825-X

Index of Place Names